Friends as Family

Friends as Family

Karen Lindsey

BEACON PRESS   BOSTON

Grateful acknowledgment is made to Family Synergy, P.O. Box 2668, Culver City, CA 90230 for permission to quote from their newsletter.

Beacon Press books are published under the auspices of the Unitarian Universalist Association, 25 Beacon Street, Boston, MA 02108

Published simultaneously in Canada by
Fitzhenry & Whiteside Limited, Toronto

Printed in the United States of America

(hardcover) 9 8 7 6 5 4 3 2 1

Library of Congress Cataloging in Publication Data

Lindsey, Karen, 1944–
    Friends as family.
    1. Family.   2. Interpersonal relations.
3. Friendship.   I. Title.
HQ734.L567   306.8   80-70360
ISBN 0-8070-3242-5   AACR2

FOR ALL MY FAMILIES:

for Mom, Pop, Keith, and Warren
    for John Paul
    for Jane, Ed, and Dale
    for Mark, Kathy, Lisa, Steve, Lynn, Steve, and all
        the "cousins"
        and for Ti and Gene

Acknowledgments

Like any book, this is in many ways a collaborative effort and would not have existed without the love, encouragement, and help of a number of people. I am grateful to Kathy Parker, Mark Blumberg, and Lisa Leghorn, especially, for all their emotional and practical help during the year I worked on this and to my agent, Sarah Jane Freymann, who has been a dear friend as well, and who has shown much patience and wisdom nurturing a sometimes overwrought author. Leah Fritz, Marge Piercy, Molly Lovelock, Pat Harrison, Anna Warrock, J Wattles, Elly Janesdaughter, Carolen Collins, Ellen Slavitz, Louise Thomas, Laura Nemeyer, and Carole Levin have provided support, humor, advice, and warmth at various times when I've needed it. Diane Mariechild, feminist psychic and good friend, helped me through a persistent writer's block by a series of guided-fantasy exercises. Karla Grinnell managed to wade through my appalling typing and even more appalling handwriting to type my manuscript in record time. Beverly Smith offered me important insights into chosen family among black people and among lesbians.

Several people gave me names of people to contact and research material to use: Tijuana Malberg, Anne-Marie Benfatto, Aimee Liu, Ruth Redesky, and Marilyn Truesdell were very helpful this way, as were many of the people I've already mentioned.

I'm also grateful to my parents, who told me many of the old family stories I'd forgotten — and who provided me with my first biological and nonbiological family.

Ms. magazine and *Sojourner* both published early articles which led to the idea for this book.

Leora Zietlin kindly allowed me to quote from an unpublished article of hers.

I'm grateful also to my two Beacon Press editors — MaryAnn Lash, who originally approached me with the idea for this book, and Joanne Wyckoff, who has struggled with me through agreements and disagreements and whose careful editing has helped give the book structure and coherence.

Finally and most importantly, I want to thank all the people who shared their wonderful stories with me. There is no way to avoid the cliché — this book really is theirs as much as it is mine.

Contents

Friends as Family

Introduction

T he traditional family isn't working. This should not come as a startling revelation to anyone who picks up this book: it may be the single fact on which every American, from the Moral Majority member through the radical feminist, agrees. Statistics abound: 50 percent of couples married since 1970 and 33 percent of those married since 1950 are divorced. One out of every six children under eighteen lives with only one parent. The number of children living in families headed by women more than doubled between 1954 and 1975.[1] The family no longer has room for aged parents. Increasing numbers of the elderly live alone or in nursing homes: only 11 percent live with their children or with other relatives.[2]

Even when the family stays together, it often does so under grim conditions. As many as 60 percent of all married women are beaten at least once by their husbands.[3] One in every hundred children is beaten, sexually molested, or severely neglected by parents.[4] And between 500,000 and one million elderly parents are abused each

1

year by the adult offspring they live with.[5] Whatever
the family in the United States is, it isn't "Father Knows
Best."

There are a lot of people who refuse to believe this,
who prefer to attribute both the problems within families
and the increasing breakup of families to the "new narcissism" or the evils of the "me generation." This theory,
promulgated by many conservatives and liberals, and
legitimized by intellectual pseudo-leftists like Christopher
Lasch, suggests (Lasch, at least, is shrewd enough never to
come out and say it) that if people would only stop
worrying about their own personal fulfillment and return
to the loving bosom of the patriarchal family, the world
would be a happy place. Such apologists for the family
tend to ignore the issue of intrafamily abuse, since it
paints a somewhat different portrait of "those basic
things we used to know."

Lasch is totally remarkable in this regard: in neither his
massively popular *The Culture of Narcissism* nor his earlier
and even more reactionary *Haven in a Heartless World*[6]
does he discuss wife abuse or child abuse. Indeed, to
perpetuate the myth of the new narcissism, he can't
afford to acknowledge family violence. The myth of the
new narcissism is more than a myth. It's also a lie. And
it's important to remember that, although we often
confuse the two, "myth" and "lie" are not by definition
synonyms. Myth, as the dictionary tells us, is "a traditional story of ostensible historical events that serves to
unfold part of the world view of a people or explain a
practice, belief or natural phenomenon." Or, as the introduction to *World Mythology* says, it is "the spon-
taneous defense of the human mind faced with an un-
intelligible or hostile world."[7]

Objective reality neither affirms nor negates a myth.
Athena and Zeus never existed; Jesus existed but little

is known about his life; George Washington, Florence Nightingale, and Bo Derek are real people about whom a great deal is known. But all exist mythically, apart from their objective existence or nonexistence.

What is true of mythical people is true of mythical concepts. Heaven and hell, the nuclear family, the Russian Revolution: all are myths, though clearly two are also historical facts. They are myths because, apart from whatever reality they have, the way in which we view them helps clarify, even shape, our vision of the world. It is in this sense that I speak of the myth of the family.

The myth of the new narcissism bases itself on the myth of the family. As Lasch and others conceptualize it, the theory of the new narcissism is that nobody cares about social causes any more, nobody cares about anybody else, and everyone is single-mindedly devoted to self-fulfillment. People of the '70s took the liberation ideologies of the '60s and individualized them, creating a selfish and decadent society concerned only with material or psychological gain. This was symbolized most strongly by the breakdown of the family. The agenda of the '80s is thus clear: return to the good old days, before the breakdown of the nuclear family.

According to this new myth, the world is now divided into *Cosmopolitan* or *Redbook:* You can have a life of sex clubs and high-powered careers or a life of Mommy staying home and cooking, Daddy going to work all day and spending the evening at home, and 2.4 happy and obedient kids. There is nothing else. The acceptance of these alternatives as the parameters of human experience leaves us little real choice. If we wish to retain our humanity — to be caring, nurturing people and, by the same token, cared-for and nurtured people — we must opt for the traditional family. Whatever evils we perceive in the nuclear family, the freedom to live without human relationships is ultimately no freedom, but hell. And so the acceptance of the myth as truth has the very real possibility of turning us — at least women — into collaborators in our own oppression.

The myth of the new narcissism is a perfect example of what Mary Daly calls "fales naming." False naming, Daly argues, creates a concept of reality which is a tool of oppression: it invents a definition of reality and forces us to live under the terms of that definition. Speaking specifically of the oppression of women, Daly writes: "Women have had the power of naming stolen from us. We have not been free to use our own power to name ourselves, the world, or god . . . women are now realizing that the universal imposing of names by men has been false because partial. That is, inadequate words have been taken as adequate."[8]

And so it is essential to our survival to name the lie, to look beyond the words to the reality they obscure. To do this, we must start with the base of the myth — the notion that there was once an ideally happy family which has only recently been destroyed by the forces of organized selfishness. Whether that ideal family is supposed to have occurred in the confines of the historically recent nuclear family, or in the older extended family, it exists as a vision of that which has been destroyed, that to which we must return. As Will Rogers said, things ain't the way they used to be, and maybe they never were.

When *was* the Golden Age of the happy family? Myth-makers vary on this question, but their most common image suggests it was sometime during the nineteenth century that the world was a Norman Rockwell painting. (Lasch, perhaps the shrewdest of the Golden Age mythologizers, never places it in any historical period, though he repeatedly implies that it did indeed exist.) Was it in 1869, when John Stuart Mill wrote *The Subjugation of Women*, decrying the fact that thousands of husbands routinely "indulge in the utmost habitual excesses of bodily violence towards the unhappy wife"?[9] Was it in 1878, when Frances Power Cobbe wrote of the area of Liverpool known as the "kicking district" because so many of its residents kicked their wives' faces with hobnailed boots?[10] Was it in 1890, when the *Encyclopaedia Brittanica* noted that the "modern crime of infanticide shows no symptoms of diminishing in the leading nations of Europe"?[11] Was it a little earlier — in the 1830s or '40s, when thousands of temperance societies sprang up throughout the United States in response to the growing number of abusive drunken men? "The drunken spouse could (and did) spend the family money as he chose, sell off his and his wife's property, apprentice their children, and assault wife and children alike."[12]

Perhaps, then, the nineteenth century is too late in history — perhaps the evils of industrialism had taken hold and destroyed the Golden Age. Perhaps we need to look back further to find our happy family — maybe to the Middle Ages, before the forces of industry had torn the family apart, when husband, wife, and children all worked the farm together in domestic harmony. The only problem is that during this period, "men were exhorted from the pulpit to beat their wives and their wives to kiss the rod that beat them. The deliberate teaching of domestic violence, combined with the doctrine that women and children by nature could have no human rights, had taken such hold by the late Middle Ages that men had come to treat their wives and children worse than their beasts."[13]

Well, there's always the Renaissance, bringing light to the primitive mentality bred by the Middle Ages. The Spanish scholar Vives, so influential in the court of England under Henry VIII and his first wife, Katharine of Aragón, is usually viewed as one of the more enlightened

intellects of the era: he was influential in spreading the
theory that girls, as well as boys, should be well educated.
He, like dozens of other scholars in the Tudor era, published tracts on childrearing and domestic harmony. Vives
wrote approvingly that he knew "many fathers to cut the
throats of their daughters, bretheren of their sisters, and
kinsmen of their kinswomen" when these unfortunate
women were discovered to be unchaste.[14] He explained
that his own mother had never "lightly laughed upon me,
she never cockered me . . . Therefore there was nobody
that I did more flee, or was more loath to come nigh, than
my mother, when I was a child." Showing affection,
or "cherishing," he said, "marreth sons, but it utterly
destroyeth daughters."[15]

It was perhaps fortunate for both daughters and sons
that they *didn't* feel too comfortable at home, since they
were likely to be betrothed at infancy and married off in
adolescence — often, in the case of upper-class offspring,
never to see their families again. Margaret Beaufort,
grandmother of Henry VIII, was married off at 12, gave
birth to Henry Tudor,[16] and never had another child
— probably as a result of early childbirth. Her granddaughter, Margaret of Scotland, was also forced to marry
at 12, and left her home to live with her husband, the King
of Scotland; her letters home are filled with misery and
homesickness.[17]

Wifebeating and childbeating were approved by most
of the tractwriters of the time, though often the husband
was advised to use physical abuse only as a last resort.
Needless to say many husbands *didn't* obey these pious
exhortations. On at least one occasion, the Duke of
Norfolk (Anne Boleyn's uncle) had his servants help
him beat his wife; they stopped only when blood began
pouring out of her mouth.[18]

The statistics on physical abuse in various historical
periods tell us something about family violence in the past.

But they don't tell us about the nonviolent forms of misery in people's lives. We can make assumptions about the viability of marriage and family life today because divorce is permissible: people who leave their families are presumably unhappy in them. But how do we know what human misery (as well as human happiness) existed among people who had no option but to live together? How many parents despised the children they had no choice but to raise? How many wives loathed their husbands; how many husbands hated their wives? How many people lived together in a helpless toleration that later ages would call contentment? Such records as we have are usually diaries and letters written by members of privileged classes — people who could read and write, people who had the luxury of privacy in which to record their thoughts.

The story of Anne Askew, the sixteenth-century Protestant martyr who wrote about her life and religion as she awaited execution, and whose maid was able to smuggle the document to the exiled Bishop Bale, provides a terse but poignant picture of miserable cohabitation between a brilliant young woman and a cloddish, conservative husband.[19] How many other Anne Askews were there whose stories were never told, even to their closest friends? We have the words of Lady Jane Grey, the doomed child who was to briefly become England's queen in the same era, complaining to the scholar Roger Ascham of her parents' abuses and coldness. How many such children never voiced their complaints, or voiced them to less-concerned listeners than hers?[20] We are told by Martin Luther, the leading light of the Protestant Reformation, that his parents were severe and abusive, and his childhood miserable.[21] We have a chilling vision of intrafamily hatred in the story of the 350 Lollard heretics discovered in Lincoln County in 1521. The reason so many were caught is that parents and children, husbands

and wives, eagerly informed against each other.[22] How
many people in how many eras would have left their
husbands, wives, and parents if there had been any possibility of their doing so?

There is another aspect of family which the proponents
of the Golden Age like to ignore: the family has always
been a very different reality for each of its members.
The father had absolute power over all the other members;
the mother had some power over her sons and very much
power over her daughters; the son was under his parents'
control, but knew that one day he would probably be
able to rule his own family and perhaps even the mother
who now ruled him; the daughter had no power and
could anticipate little. The family may well have been
— and may well still be — a "haven from the heartless
world" for many men. But for women and children,
it has always been the very *center* of the heartless world,
from which no haven existed. For man, the limits of the
family have been tacitly recognized, and legitimate or
quasi-legitimate institutions have been established to
supplement their needs. Men have always been permitted
mistresses, even if official morality has shaken its head;
women have rarely been able to get by with taking lovers.
The very existence of prostitution, which has always
coexisted with the family, offers implicit approval of
men's search for extrafamilial fulfillment. Both Saint
Augustine and Saint Thomas Aquinas recognized this,
when they likened prostitution to a sewer, ugly but
necessary to keep the palace functioning.[23] Monogamous
marriage, which the Golden Agers celebrate, has usually
meant only monogamous wifehood.

I'm not trying to suggest that families have always been
devoid of love, or caring, of the "cherishing" that Vives
found so destructive. There are records of happy families,
as there are records of unhappy ones. And in any event
the human need for communication, for sharing, for love

would certainly find a way to be satisfied in almost any situation. The very quality of shared experience, shared history can build strong bonds of love and affection among people. In a family, in a commune, in a prison, people can make deep and indissoluble connections with one another. But if it isn't recognized that the family, historically, *was* a prison, which people entered not by choice but by necessity, the real happiness as well as the real misery becomes mythologized into something quite distinct from the reality. The family becomes, in Daly's words, a creation of false naming.

The false naming that creates the myth of the happy traditional family has its corollary in the false naming that says life outside the family is miserable and empty, that people who choose childlessness have no real relationships with children or with the future, and that friends are never as fulfilling as family. In our culture, there is family, and there are friends. Sometimes friendship is deep, even heroic — especially, perhaps exclusively, among men. Damon and Pythias, Jonathan and David. But mostly, friendship is secondary: friends are who you pass pleasant time with, who you like but don't love, to whom you make minimal if any commitment. Above all, *friends are not family.* Blood is thicker than water. Your friends are always "other"; your family is who you are. Friends, in that most demeaning of phrases, are "just friends." And we have believed it; we have mystified it and mythologized it. We have taken the lie for the truth, and in doing so we have almost made it true.

But people are larger than the myths they try to live by. And the truth hidden by the myth is that people have always created larger families than the biological family — larger, and infinitely more diverse. It has been there for many of us, perhaps for most of us, and we have always said to ourselves, this is different, this is me and my life, this has nothing to do with the way things are.

Side by side with the language of our oppression, other phrases have evolved and been assimilated into our vocabulary without our understanding their importance: "She's been a second mother to me." "He's just like a brother." "You are the daughter I've never had." "We're all one big happy family." Why have we never suspected that these innocuous phrases contain as much revolutionary potential as anything Karl Marx or Emma Goldman or Mary Wollstonecraft ever said? Such phrases suggest that the family is something more than your husband or wife and the offspring of you and your spouse and the people who are related to you because somebody somewhere has the same blood parent, that someone totally outside the limits of that kinship definition can be your family. The family isn't what we've been taught it is. Thus we are not trapped between the Scylla and Charybdis that the lie of the new narcissism offers; we do not need to choose between living without human bondings, or with bondings not of our choice. We can create our own bondings, choose them as they meet our needs; we can define, with others we have chosen and who have chosen us, what the nature of our bondings will be.

I think that some of the power that marriage has had for us — at least for women, although possibly for men as well — lies in this concept of choice. In an era when half of all marriages end in divorce, when couples openly live together, when the taint of "illegitimacy" is fading, marriage still has a powerful hold on women. And the power isn't only over women of the mainstream. Radical and socialist feminists marry; women who have lived with their lovers marry; women who have lived with *many* lovers marry. Even women who eschew monogamy marry. Sometimes they marry to placate parents, sometimes to make life easier for the children they plan to have. But I suspect that often these are simply the surface explanations for far more fundamental, more mythic, reasons.

The mythic power of marriage is threefold. To begin
with, it offers a feeling of protection, of economic security.
Historically, this has been accurate. A woman without a
husband to protect her was at the mercy of her relatives
and of strangers. The only other economically viable
option was the convent, and even here a woman might
find herself the "poor relation" of nuns from more affluent or prestigious families. Even today in the United
States, women earn 59 percent of what men earn, and the
poor are largely made up of women and their children.[24]

The second, and related, mythic power of marriage
rests in its promise of permanence. The myth of true-
love-forever may be comparatively recent, but a few
centuries is long enough to embed a myth into a culture.
Further, the permanence of marriage predates romantic
love. A man might abuse his wife, he might take on mistresses, he might functionally desert her. But he — or his
kin, when he fails to meet his obligations — must support
her and their children, and abandonment of one's wife
carries strong social censure. Henry VIII's fame as an
historic ogre rests not on his dissolution of the monasteries
and consequent impoverishment of thousands of monks,
nuns, and the beggars who relied on them for charity,
not on his arbitrary executions of hundreds of "papists"
and "heretics," but on his open willingness to discard,
through divorce and execution, four wives. Especially
when a woman has children, she is given the right to
expect that her husband, whose bloodline she has preserved, will continue to provide for her needs.

The third myth, and the one that is the concern of this
book, is that of the spouse as chosen relative. It is true
that only in very recent history has a woman had any
actual choice in whom she marries, that it has historically
been assumed that a spouse will be chosen by the parents
of both men and women. But alongside this reality has
always existed the story of the woman who defies the

rule — who chooses, or attempts to choose, her mate. Cleopatra chose Marc Anthony, Dido chose Aeneas, and in so doing they destroyed both their empires and their lives.

This is a negative image of choice, and in any case most women don't have the options available to women who rule nations. But the stories of royalty have always provided the mythology of the lower classes, and at the very least these stories introduce the *concept* of choice into the selection of a mate. In recent centuries, the concept has significantly changed. The choice has been transmuted into a good one; it is worth losing everything to maintain the integrity of that choice, select one's true love and reject the choice of others, even when that choice seems more sensible. Indeed, in contemporary mythology, that choice often *guarantees* happiness — marry Mr. Right and your troubles are over.

But however the myth varies, its power rests in the fact that except in the atypical instance of adoption, your spouse is the only relative you are ever permitted to choose. You are born to your parents and, by extension, to their kin, and you raise the children you give birth to. The young, modern woman who chooses her mate has behind her a string of spiritual ancestors as long as Banquo's ghost, ancestors to whom, at least once, however briefly, the thought of choosing their own mates must have occurred. It is a thought so monumental that its very existence must have changed something in the mind of its thinker. Few women could have voiced this change, and even fewer could have acted on it. But we are the heirs of that change nonetheless.

Now an even greater concept has entered into our minds. We can choose most of our family. We can choose *all* of our family. In some ways, recognition of this possibility has begun to surface in popular culture. Recently, several magazines published articles about the need to create new, familial ways to celebrate holidays, and described festive scenes shared by former and current spouses, in-laws from both marriages, and offspring from the divorced parents' current and former marriages.

As far as it goes, this represents an important step in breaking through the oppressive definitions of family. For people who have shared history, who have loved each other and lived through major parts of each other's lives together, the concept of "family" should apply, in much the same way as it applies to parents and grown siblings who no longer live together or share the same interests but who are indelibly part of one another's lives.

But it isn't only spouses who share or have shared each other's lives, who have created a common past with each other. Friends, neighbors, coworkers have often lived through as many experiences together as husbands and wives — have created, perhaps unconsciously, equally strong bonds. And slowly these bonds too are seeping into popular mythology.

A good barometer of the change is television, which is probably the most potent force in mid-twentieth-century American mythmaking. In the '50s, the model of the family was clear-cut. Mommy, Daddy, and the kids. "Father Knows Best." "I Remember Mama." "Ozzie and Harriet." "Make Room for Daddy." "I Love Lucy." "Life of Riley." Even "Burns and Allen," miles ahead of the others in wit and sophistication, showed two nuclear families, and the Burns' had a son (though he never appeared till the later episodes). Only "My Little Margie," saccharine sweet as it was, dared to veer from the accepted family norm: Daddy was a widower who lived with his grown daughter.

In the '60s, things began to change. Divorce was a social reality, but a fantasy taboo, so TV compromised. The mortality rate among television spouses soared:

suddenly widows and widowers with kids were the norm.
"The Diahann Carroll Show." "The Doris Day Show."
"The Andy Griffith Show." "The Partridge Family."
And then the crème de la crème, "The Brady Bunch":
widow with cute large brood marries widower with cute
large brood, re-creating the two-parent family with a
vengeance. It was an interesting attempt to cover up by
half admitting what was happening to the family. Viewers
who were divorced or separated could identify with the
one-parent (or re-created two-parent) family, but could
not have the validity of their own experience confirmed.
Death is a tragedy, not a choice: the family still works
until something more cosmic than human need disrupts it.

By the '70s even that wasn't enough, and the workplace family began to achieve some recognition. It started
with "The Mary Tyler Moore Show." Mary Richards, the
character Moore played, had just broken off with her
boyfriend and had come to Minneapolis to seek a job.
Her coworkers and her best friend, Rhoda, became her
family. This was no accident: the characters on the show
talked about being a family. In one episode, Rhoda refused
a job in New York because it would separate her from
Mary. With little fanfare, "The Mary Tyler Moore Show"
tastefully broke a taboo.

Then there was "Mod Squad," the story of three stereo-
typically alienated kids who become cops, and in the
process also become each other's family. Corny as that
show was (and reactionary in its basic theme — three
dropouts become narcs), a caring and commitment among
the three came through as it never did in any other cop
show. The relationship, in fact, may have scared some of
its creators. A year or two ago, they aired a two-hour
special, "Return of the Mod Squad," in which the three,
now living separate lives, are reunited essentially to estab-
lish that the old "family" was an adolescent phase and
they have now outgrown each other.

But the model of on-the-job families continues — perhaps to reassure all the divorced people, the not-yet-married people, the not-in-romantic-relationship people, that they aren't totally alone. Good shows and bad, serious and silly, they are astoundingly numerous. The cops on "Barney Miller," the soldiers on "M*A*S*H," the radio personnel on "WKRP in Cincinnati." Even on as vacuous a show as "Love Boat," the workmates in more than one episode are described as a family. Last season, in fact, the "Love Boat" family was solidified by its adoption of a child — Captain Stuebing's illegitimate, ten-year-old daughter, Vicki. In the episode introducing Vicki's residence on board the ship, a social worker at first is reluctant to permit the girl to live in such an unstable environment, with no family but the captain. But she is soon persuaded that Vicki does indeed have a family on the ship. Vicki, she says, is "one lucky lady . . . You have not one parent but five, all of them loving, caring people."[25]

In "M*A*S*H," too, the family has been verbalized. At one point, fatherly Colonel Potter says, "The 4077 is not just a roster of people; it's my family. Not only that, but a loyal family." In another episode, Corporal Klinger, shattered by the news that his wife is divorcing him, comes to realize that "I may not have a family anymore in Toledo, but I sure have one here." In yet another, Margaret describes the unit as "like a family," and then corrects herself. "No," she says firmly, "it *is* a family." Sometimes the familial relationship among the characters is mirrored in the relationship of the actors. An interview with the cast of "M*A*S*H" brings up familial references. Gary Burghoff, who played the boyish Radar O'Reilly, told one writer that since the death of his own father, "I think of Harry [Morgan] as my new father."[26]

Some of TV's workplace families are more believable than others: the warmth of the "M*A*S*H" personnel comes through beautifully; the poke-in-the-ribs camaraderie

of the "Love Boat" crew evokes little feeling of connection or commitment. But, however successful each is,
TV has come to recognize, and institutionalize, the workplace family.

In 1978 a brief-lived show called "The Apple Family"
attempted a truly radical idea—the story of a group of
unrelated people who came together with the idea of
forming a consciously chosen family, not an office family
or a thrown-together family. The show didn't last. It
wasn't very good, and in any event lots of shows don't
last, so maybe that doesn't mean anything. On the other
hand, maybe it does. Maybe it means that television,
which influences so much of our thinking, can't afford to
tell us we can choose our own families. It is, after all, a very
dangerous message. It will be interesting to see the fate of a
fall 1981 program, "Love, Sidney," in which a gay man
lives with a heterosexual woman and her daughter, forming,
in the producer's words, a "surrogate family."[27]

In writing this book, I've had to make choices about
terminology. This is always sticky, since words inevitably
attempt to pin down human experience, and human experience always exists in countless variations. What do we
call the family as we know it? The nuclear family is only
a recent phenomenon, springing out of the older extended
family. "Family of origin" is inaccurate if it attempts
to include grandparents, aunts, uncles, and cousins whom
we may not even meet until we are five, ten, or thirty,
but who are still part of that concept called family.
"Biological family" comes closest, and I have chosen to
use it, but not without trepidation, since both marriage
and adoption are integral parts of it. I've chosen it because
it seems to me to encompass not the whole reality, but the
whole *myth*: blood is thicker than water. Much of the
power of the patriarchy rests on the concept of biological
kinship: a man needs a son to carry on his genes and his

name; hence woman is forced into marriage and monogamy. Marriage historically is the integration of two bloodlines, and it is this, not the more recent myth of romance, that is the central mythical commitment of marriage: "She is the mother of my children." The stepmother in the fairy tale *must* be wicked, because her natural alliance is to the children of her own body, not those of her husband's body. Adoption of children not of one's own bloodline is always an adaptation. When one can't have children of "one's own," one creates a substitute, in effect pretending that the child is blood kin. The reality has changed; the myth remains untouched. Hence, I am using "biological family" to encompass the myth in all its facets, since it is the myth rather than the fact of genetical inheritance that governs our lives.

The same problem of terminology arises when I find myself defining the kinds of contemporary nonbiological family. Definition, the creation of categories — these are useful and necessary, but they are also dangerous. They are useful if, like clothing, they can be worn when they're comfortable and can stretch to fit whatever they cover, allowing themselves to be discarded when they no longer fit properly. If they become straitjackets, restricting and confining, they are destructive; they have become false naming. True naming is a process of infinite growth, infinite flexibility. And so I have drawn up categories of nonbiological family. I think they are useful categories, helping to put into focus a reality we're been taught not to see. But they are loose categories. A given relationship may fall into one, or two, or three categories. There may be — there must be — other categories. I've chosen mine because they fit my experience and my observations.

The three kinds of nonbiological family I've seen are the "honorary relative" family — the family friend who is your "uncle" or "aunt" as you grow up; the workplace family; and, finally, the chosen family — the friends who, with no outside force throwing you together, you have consciously or unconsciously chosen to be your family. Part I looks at the first two categories; Part II explores the third. In both parts, people from vastly different backgrounds and lifestyles tell the stories of their non-biological families.

The chosen family isn't always an unmitigated good: I'm not attempting to erase "Father Knows Best" and replace it with an equally silly picture of happy little chosen families creating heaven on earth. Sometimes the chosen family mirrors the worst of biological families — the patriarchal power, the crippling dependency, the negation of the individual selves that can exist in a secure framework. Charles Manson was the leader of a chosen family; so was Jim Jones. Armies create families of men who are permitted and encouraged through their bonding to rape and kill. To expand definitions, to create choice, doesn't guarantee that the choices will be either wise or moral. But choice itself *is* good, and with it comes a greater potential for good than exists in its absence.

This book, then, is about that choice — how it's been exercised in the past, how it's being exercised in the present, and how we might expand its parameters in the future.

I.

Families without Names

*T*he notion that ours is a culture of narcissists bent
on destroying real human relationships is a false one,
but there is one kind of narcissism that we, as a generation,
can be accurately accused of. We tend to think of our
ancestors, immediate and remote, as hidebound and uni-
formly locked into tradition. We recognize the notorious
exceptions — George Sand and Chopin, Emma Goldman
— but we tend to assume that, in the main, people have
blindly followed custom like ineffectual if unhappy
lemmings. Like the teenager who thinks she's invented
sex, we act on the assumption that we and we alone are
willing to create new kinds of family.

This arrogance blocks from our view one of the con-
stants in human nature which is our birthright — a constant
that the doomsayers of the "new narcissism" also ignore.
People are wonderfully capable of creating what they
need out of what is available — often without giving it a
name. Like the lesbians who quietly lived together as

*respectable spinster-companions, many people have
retained the respectability of the traditional family structures while creating new structures within them. For the
most part, they have not thought of what they've done
as "alternative." But it has been. Throughout history
and into the present, people have been able to bond with
one another, to create familial relationships with people
who are not blood kin. They have done this in a number
of ways, but essentially these ways fall into two categories:
they have adopted honorary kin into the conventional
family — fictive "aunts" and "uncles" who are the close
friends of one or both parents. And they have formed
strong, familial friendships at the workplace — whether
that workplace has been an office, a factory, or a suburban
neighborhood in which women raise children together.*

*There are limitations to these familial relationships,
limitations which the consciously chosen family can
more easily transcend, since its members acknowledge
their deviance from the traditional family. Perhaps the
most pervasive limitation can occur between women and
men in the workplace. Margaret Adams, in* Single Blessedness, *her book on single people, calls this "the subtle but
persistent devaluation of the platonic, as opposed to the
erotic, basis for a heterosexual relationship."*[1] *Women
Adams interviewed said that professional relationships
with men they worked with were a source of emotional
gratification, but that they felt guilty and confused about
such relationships. One, working on literary research with
a male professor, felt that she was somehow being unfair
to the man's wife in sharing so important a part of his
life with him. "This type of relationship," notes Adams,
"is a social anomaly and as such is constantly liable to
be misinterpreted." Wives often feel threatened when their
husbands have close, nonsexual relationships with female
colleagues, even when there is no suspicion of sexual
infidelity involved. Thus relationships that have strong*

familial feelings are denied and negated — while, of course, real sexual infidelity continues to occur anyway, in and outside of the office environment.

This is less of a problem in honorary kinship situations, since honorary kinship usually involves large generational differences. Still, "sisterly" and "brotherly" friendship between adult women and men is rare, and with the emphasis on the sexual in today's culture, combined with man's traditional image of himself as an always-sexual being, it is difficult to achieve, and always suspect.

Yet such relationships have existed, and have enriched the lives of their participants. More commonly, however, familial relationships between members of the same sex have flourished in the workplace, and adult-child relationships have flourished among adults and the children of their close friends. Because these relationships have remained unnamed, and because they have not formed an open threat to the patriarchal family, they have been permitted to exist.

Hence the failure to name the traditional forms of the nonbiological family has at once allowed it to continue unchallenged and prevented it from growing to the extent that it might grow. It has functioned as a kind of unconscious and unacknowledged resistance, containing a potential power that it has rarely used.

If we are to claim that power, to begin consciously creating new forms of family, it is essential that we look at these nonbiological families of the past and present. For those of us who are trying to create new alternatives, it is crucial to acknowledge and to celebrate these created families — to take what they have given us and build it into something stronger.

1.

The Way We Were — Nonbiological Families of the Past

L eftists and liberals have criticized the nuclear family for being a prison. But often they have limited their criticisms to the present, and created an idealized picture of the traditional extended biological family and of the traditional community, in which villagers knew each other, took responsibility for each other's welfare, and were deeply involved in each other's lives. Yet in reality the community too was a prison, entrapping as much as it nurtured.

But if the family (and the community) has been a prison, there have always been some people who have managed to find their way out of the prison — or at least to expand its walls to better meet their genuine needs. Nonbiological family has for centuries coexisted with biological family, though it has rarely been named. And the absence of a naming is significant. When no one

23

declares that the emperor has no clothes, then the emperor is armored not only in his own power but in the ignorance he has forced on the people. History and biography, as a legion of feminist scholars and writers have shown us, are written from the biases of those with an investment in patriarchal institutions — at the very least, by those who so totally accept the definitions they have grown up with that they are unable to see the other realities in front of them. Thus, for the most part, we need to read between the lines of the stories told us by biographers and historians to find the pieces of information concealed in their works that reveal the images patriarchy chooses for us.

The research I've done on the past, like that I've done on the present, is in no way comprehensive: I have randomly chosen from my own spheres of interest and from the suggestions of friends examples of people who in the past created nonbiological family. What I've looked for is a range — I wanted to find whether in the past alternative family was an upper-class luxury, a lower-class necessity, or, as I suspected, a phenomenon found among a large range of individuals in differing social situations. I've limited the "past" here to only two centuries, and to the United States and England because to search much further would prove an unwieldy task for such a short survey. I hope that some scholar, or scholars, will pick up the subject, giving it the time and intensive study that it deserves.

The one form of alternative family that has been acknowledged by historians — possibly because it's too obvious to ignore — has been the utopian community of the nineteenth century. The community functioned *socially* as a family: it provided food, lodging, care in illnesses, and leisure entertainment for its members. But did it function *emotionally* as a family? Were close, satisfying, personal bonds formed between members, linking them to each other as individuals as well as to their community?

In one community, at least, such relationships were not only absent but strongly discouraged. John Duss grew up in the Harmony community, which existed, sometimes stormily — beginning in Pennsylvania, moving itself to Indiana, then returning to Pennsylvania — for nearly the whole of the nineteenth century. In his late middle age, Duss wrote an account of Harmony. The community, in the last few years of its existence, had been under his leadership. His tone is one of reverence for the community, its founder, and its ideals.

During his childhood, Duss writes, there were about fifty "families" in the society, each with about five or six members. These families were artificial constructs: membership was frequently and deliberately rearranged so that "selfishness and jealousy tend to disappear, yet the economic convenience and efficiency of the small family unit is preserved."[1] The family had been wholly redefined: no longer a "separate and basically selfish organization of parent and children" or otherwise emotionally connected individuals, it was simply "a house unit and intrinsic part of the larger society."[2]

Only twice does Duss tell us anything about his own relationships within the community. Once is to record the death of his friend Bennie. "Between Bennie and me there existed bonds of more than brotherhood," he writes. "Our relationship was that of a Jonathan and David."[3] Yet the claim rings hollow: in a fairly detailed autobiography, this is Duss's first and only reference to the doomed Bennie. Later, he tells us — in the tone of a mature man confessing the follies of his youth — that he had had a close friendship with a boy named Ira. Hurt when his friend snubbed him, the young Duss wrote a note expressing his pain and confusion. A classmate found the note, changed the "Ira" to "Ida," and circulated the paper among the teachers, who laughed at what they thought was Duss's infatuation for Ira's sister. Duss tells

this story to make a moral point. "The story is here told,"
he writes piously, "as a warning against partiality — which
is always an evil or an error."[4]

Yet in spite of the Harmonists' antipathy to "partiality,"
there is in the community's history a moving story of two
men who were not related by blood, yet were bonded
by the love and the competitiveness of a strong father-son
attachment. The story's principals were the two leading
lights of the community, George Rapp and the man he
adopted to carry on his work, Frederick Rapp. The adoption seems to have taken place for purely legal reasons:
George was to be in charge of the "external and financial
affairs" of the Harmonists. But it was clearly more. Duss,
so opposed to individual relationships, waxes ecstatic
about the early friendship of these two men. "A true
spirit of kinship and brotherhood shines throughout their
letters to each other," he writes. And indeed, the examples
that he cites suggest a deep and needy love between the
men. In 1910, George Rapp wrote to his son that he was
withdrawing as much as possible from his work "so that
we may longer enjoy each other's company. I can hardly
recollect when you went away — it seems such a long
time." His letters — and there were many — were signed
"thy loyal father and brother."[5] Over the years, however,
the two became estranged, in part because the elder Rapp
had trouble relinquishing his total power over the community. "The common adoration of Frederick began to
arouse feelings akin to jealousy in George Rapp,"[6] writes
Duss. For Duss to make such an observation, however
discreetly, in a book which venerates "Father Rapp"
and his ideology suggests that the jealousy must have
been very real and very ugly. The men went through
a series of quarrels and reconciliations, ending with
Frederick's death in 1834 of what, Duss implies, was a
broken heart. It was another member of the community,
rather than Frederick's "loyal father and brother," who

"pronounced the last words over his unmarked grave."[7] But what is most interesting about George and Frederick Rapp is that their relationship flourished, in all its complexity, even in an environment in which both saw such bondings as an evil.

The Oneida community, by contrast, did not stress the evil of individual relationships, and at least for the children provided a mechanism for warm, loving connections. Constance Noyes Robertson, whose grandfather was the community's founder and whose parents grew up, met, and married in the community, wrote a loving history of Oneida, composed largely of documents published in the community's periodicals.

The Oneida children lived in one wing of the huge New York State mansion occupied by the entire "family," and they were cared for by a corps of five women and one man. The biological parents regularly visited with their offspring and, as one of the articles explained, "the babies do not love their parents less, but they love some of the rest of us just as well."[8] While individual parents could raise their children in a nuclear unit if they preferred, most members came "to regard the whole Association as one family and all children as children of the family."[9]

How the outside world viewed this revolutionary notion of parenting is well illustrated by a charming anecdote that appeared in the October 22, 1866, *Circular*. A carriage "containing some fashionably dressed ladies" drove past the house, and the ladies stopped to talk to one of the children playing on the lawn. One of them asked the four-year-old where his parents were. "My Papa Noyes and Mama Miller are at Wallingford," the child told them. Asked his name, the child replied cheerfully: "My name is Temple Noyes Dunn Burt Ackley."[10]

The community provided a comfortable, homy atmosphere, in which people's favorite flowers, pictures, or bric-a-brac decorated the sitting room and family members spent evenings chatting, playing music or playing dominoes in groups of two and three, after the more formal evening meeting of the entire community.[11]

That Oneida respected the one-to-one familial relationships is evident too in their commitment to Complex Marriage, an ideal which permitted for nonmonogamous sexual relationships without succumbing to the doctrine of "free love" current at the time. An elaborate method of courtship was devised by which a man would approach a woman with whom he wished to share a sexual relationship through a third party, usually one of the female elders of the community.[12] It's an interesting concept, one that echoes today among people attempting to find means of creating sexual/romantic relationships that are neither straitjacketed by the institution of marriage nor doomed to the shallowness of conventional "swinging."

Yet neither Robertson's book nor that of Allan Estlake, a member who wrote an autobiographical memoir of the community at the turn of the century, gives any sense of deep, familial bonding among members. Estlake records that "all looked up to 'Father Noyes,' to whom in this parental relation no child's trouble was too trivial,"[13] and that Noyes's wife, Harriet, "who was known as Mother Noyes, was my dear confidante and councillor,"[14] but there are no stories of his own relations with his new "siblings," or of other close friendships in the community. Again, it seems that the deliberately created "family" lacked the individual emotional ties that families at their best can create.

Brook Farm, in Roxbury, Massachusetts, set out to be more of a community than a family, and chose its architecture in such a way as to "give the larger families a chance to place their members together in the natural family order." This community seems to have been more able to provide the emotional connections of family than did some of the other communities. Several unmarried adults, mostly men, were members, and one of them, John Thomas Codman, recalled fifty years later that because "there was lacking the family circle to draw around at night," the proposed new building was to be constructed so as "to place a family in each house and proportionally distribute the young men, when desirable to do so, among them."[15] Yet he describes himself as essentially a loner during his stay at the community, and records only one close friendship with another Brook Farm member.[16]

Marianne Dwight, another member, gives a stronger sense of familial bonding within the community, through her letters to her brother Frank and her closest friend, Anna Parsons. In one letter she tells Anna that she has been made foster mother to two of the community's children, Caspar and Willie Golderman, and that "the feeling of maternity has taken full possession of me."[17] The feeling appears to have fled as quickly as it arrived, however, as two months later she is telling Frank that "the Goldermans have gone, not to return. Don't you congratulate me on my release?"[18]

A more intense relationship with a member of her "family by adoption"[19] was her friendship with Fred Cabot and his fiancée, Mary Lincoln — though she expresses a fear that their marriage will lessen Fred's feelings for her: "I can't help feeling that, for a while at least he must belong less to *me* than he has done."[20] Her fears are well grounded: three weeks later Fred has so absented himself from the community that "he is as good as dead to us right now."[21]

In fact, the strongest note throughout the correspondence is Marianne's loneliness, her *lack* of family, her realization that only if Anna joins the community, as she has been hoping to do, will Marianne find the companionship she needs. Unlike John Codman, Marianne was not a loner, and the absence of warm, individual bonds made her experience at Brook Farm a lonely and isolated one.

One might conclude from all this that Christopher Lasch is right — that the effort to seek deep, committed, lasting personal relationships outside the traditional family structure is doomed. In fact, it suggests something quite different — that when the randomness of the family is replicated, without its shared history, a situation occurs that makes personal bondings extremely difficult. And when part of the structure's ideology insists that "partiality" in human relations is evil, as the Harmonists' did, the wonder is not that few personal relationships emerged but that *any* did. It is interesting in this context to look at a community that was similar in structure but radically different in purpose and ideology from any of the utopian communities — the "industrial community" of Lowell, Massachusetts, in which boardinghouses for unmarried female employees were built by mill owners to provide a safe and supervised environment to which parents could send their daughters without fear that they would be corrupted by city life. The young women employed by the Lawrence Mills had no choice but to live in these houses: they were not hired if they refused to do so.

Each house was supervised by a "housemother," usually a widow, who enforced a strict curfew and made sure that the girls were well chaperoned when they received male visitors. It was an institution at once oppressive and protective: working women were frequently exploited economically and sexually, with no one to turn to for protection or asylum. The housemother functioned as both policewoman and provider to her charges.

We know a little of how the mill workers felt about their enforced sorority through a publication they put out in the 1840s called *The Lowell Offering*. The articles are written usually as fictionalized accounts, often in the syrupy, sentimental style popular in the late nineteenth century, but they illustrate both the presence and the absence of familial relationships among the "mill girls."

One story tells of how the women functioned as kin for each other, much as in a Louisa May Alcott tale. The "girls" visit each other's rooms, squabble, moralize, and share each other's lives, growing closer as they realize what they can give each other. As a result of their various exchanges, familial relationships are established between two pairs of girls. On a walk with Isabel, Anne is moved to ask her friend to "be my sister":

> "Yes dear Anne; we will be sisters to each other. I think you told me that you have no sister."
> "I had none until now, and I have felt as if a part of my affections could not find a resting place, but were weighing down my heart with a burden that did not belong to it . . ."

In her newfound happiness, Ann realizes that another boarder, Alice, is lonely and dejected, and immediately begins to matchmake, effecting a friendship between Alice and Ellinora. Ellinora has been too flighty, Alice too grim, and when the former laughingly suggests "an exchange, offering a portion of her levity for as much of her gravity," Alice gratefully accepts, and, the narrator assures us, the exchange "seems actually to be taking place at this time. They are as intimate as sisters."[22] Sentimentalized though this account is, it is apparent that it is a disguised version of two actual friendships.

Another story, "The Affections Illustrated in Factory Life," shows the negative side of a tight, familial community. A newcomer, Hannah, moves into a boarding-house, but ranks are closed against her: only the gentle, kindly Ellen welcomes her into the fold. When Hannah begins receiving mysterious visits from a man (who, we later learn, is her brother), her roommates begin a slander campaign against her. Even the so-called mother,

Mrs. Matthews, turns on poor Hannah, who promptly falls into a Victorian decline, from which she is rescued by the efforts of faithful Ellen. The story ends: ". . . there was not one of the family but wished they had been as kind and forbearing with the gentle stranger as Ellen Campbell."[23]

Other stories, however, end less happily — there are many accounts of homesickness for a beloved family that has in no way been replaced by the boardinghouse sisterhood, and one grim essay tells of the suicide of a lonely mill girl. Like the utopian communities, the mill town was a structure modeled on the ideal of kinship but lacking the shared history of true kin, biological or nonbiological. But when friendships *did* form, they had the surroundings of int˙ ˙acy and domesticity to create families out of friends.

If mill workers had little control over their own lives and associations, slaves had none at all. Herbert Gutman's *The Black Family in Slavery and Freedom, 1750–1925* is a remarkable work, documenting a tradition of continuity among biological and marital kin in extraordinary circumstances: the book is a marvelous refutation of claims that the family structure of black Americans is weak or nonexistent. Unfortunately, Gutman doesn't recognize the significance of nonbiological family and provides little documentation of it. But what he does provide is fascinating.

There was among the slaves and the newly freed black people a tradition which one ex-slave contemptuously called "swap-dog kin."[24] The tradition was evident even on the slave ships: Africans were kidnapped, separated from their families, and thrown onto ships bound for a new and terrifying destiny. Children began calling adult shipmates "aunt" and "uncle," and adults regarded all the children on ship as their own. Gutman quotes sociologist Orlando Patterson: "So strong were the bonds between shipmates that sexual intercourse . . . was considered incestuous."[25] To Gutman, this indicates the importance of biological family: so strong are kin ties, he says, that when they are absent people find the closest substitute that they can. This is true enough, but it also suggests that the real need is less for bonds of blood and marriage than for bonds *themselves*. When the form of bonding that people are accustomed to is taken away, people create other bonds.

When the slaves had been on their plantations long enough to form their own marital and biological families, they attached great importance to blood ties and seem to have had less need for "fictive kin" — or at least, Gutman doesn't document any fictive kin in these situations. But conventional kinship units were a luxury permitted the slaves only at the convenience of their masters, and when a slave was sold to a distant plantation, contact with family-of-origin might be severed forever. The slaves were often able to replace those ties by creating substitute relatives on the new plantation. Gutman cites a few instances. One is a story from Solomon Northup, a slave on a Louisiana plantation, who lived in a cabin with an elderly slave named Abram. Abram treated Northup and the other young slaves "with a kind of parental feeling, always counseling us with remarkable gravity and deliberation."[26] Gutman also cites the biography of an ex-slave, the orphaned Allen Allensworth: "Aunt Phyllis showed him tender sympathy and remarked to Aunt Betty that it was a pity 'ter tek dat po' child fum his sick mama, and brung him on dis place . . .' This remark attached the boy to Aunt Phyllis and he loved her ever afterward . . . Aunt Phyllis was a big-hearted old soul, and she looked with commiseration on all who suffered affliction or distress."[27] The most interesting story Gutman recounts is that of Emanuel Elmore's father, whose first wife, Dorcas, learned that she was to be sold and fled the plantation, hiding in the woods. In her absence, a woman named Jenny moved in with Elmore's father and took care of the children, doing the job so well that Dorcas (whose reappearance is unfortunately unexplained) grew fond of Jenny: "Ma liked her and would not let anybody say anything against her . . ." Jenny went on raising the children until they grew up, and when she died, "We felt worse over her death than we did over Ma's, because she was so good to us."[28]

Gutman interprets the fact that slave children were taught to address all older slaves by kin titles as a partial effort to prepare them for the possibility that they would be sold away from their blood relatives — which would mean that the importance of creating nonbiological family was apparent to the slaves.[29] These patterns continued after emancipation. Newly freed slaves went to great lengths to locate lost relatives, but it often wasn't possible. Children who couldn't find their parents would be called "motherless children" by other ex-slaves, and both kin and nonkin took responsibility for them. A number of white relief workers took note of the tenderness with which these ex-slaves cared for such children, absorbing them into their own families.[30]

The accounts Gutman cites nearly all involve adult-child relationships — there appear to be no records of fictive kin connections among peers. Yet the love that slaves and ex-slaves felt for their natural siblings, which Gutman movingly documents, combined with their readiness to form fictive kin relationships between generations, suggests that there must have been some strong friendship attachments that served familial functions.[31] This is further attested to in the kind of fictive relations often found among contemporary black people in the United States — relationships which clearly follow in the tradition of the slave and ex-slave networks, and which do include intense, committed, and lifelong friendships.

But there is a side to fictive kinship under slavery that is less heartening — the use of kin terms by masters toward their slaves. A slave was often "Uncle" or "Aunt" (or, of course, "Mammy"), though the master was always "Mister." This was either to "use a nonreciprocal term of address that defined an essential status difference" between slave and master, says Gutman, or to show a master's personal attachment to a particular house slave.[32] But it's easy to see that the second, apparently benevolent, reason masked a more sinister reality — to bind the slave by kinship ties to the master rather than to other slaves. Whether or not many slaves ever really bought into this mythology, the image of the plantation as one big happy family ruled by a kindly patriarch and inhabited by happy "darkies" who were considered both adorably and permanently ignorant children and simultaneously revered "uncles" and "aunts" is a powerful one and must have served as a comforting rationale for slave owners who wanted to see themselves as nice people. One has only to see *Gone With the Wind*, with the ex-slaves loyally clinging to the home of the beloved master and angry at the freedom forced on them, to recognize the power and utility of this myth. Undoubtedly, there were times the pseudofamily structure served to quell latent rebelliousness in slaves, and the "Mammy" in particular must often have been torn between love and anger toward the child who was at once her helpless charge and her absolute master.

In addition to the nonbiological families which grew out of chosen or superimposed structures like the communes, the mill houses, or the plantations, others developed simply out of individuals' own lives and needs. Again, it's sometimes hard to trace these families, since they have been undefined and unrecognized by biographers. Yet they are often there, between the lines,

sometimes hinted at by familial similes such as "just
like a sister." They occurred among people with strong
biological family attachments as well as among those
who lacked family and needed to create it.

Charlotte Brontë and Jane Austen, for example, had
family relationships with people not connected by blood
or marriage. Both writers lived their lives with parents
and siblings to whom they had intense attachments; both
were very private women who seldom looked for any
sort of relationship beyond their family circles. Yet
each found a friend who became as dear to her as her
own sisters.

Jane Austen lived with her parents and her sister,
Cassandra, all her life. Among the sisters' close friends
were Mary and Martha Lloyd. Mary married Jane's brother,
becoming her sister-in-law, but it was Martha who became
her second sister. In 1804, after both Jane's father and
Martha's mother died, Jane and Cassandra invited their
friend to come and live with them. "It says much for the
reasonable nature of Jane and Cassandra's attachments
to each other that, singularly profound as it was, they
welcomed the idea of such a friend as Martha being included in their household," notes biographer Elizabeth
Jenkins.[33] It does indeed — but what Jenkins, with her
bias toward the biological family, fails to note is that
it also says much for the "singularly profound" attachment both women felt for Martha. Another biographer,
Jane Aiken Hodge, seems more aware of Martha's importance to the Austens: "From then on, to all intents
and purposes, Mrs. Austen had three daughters,"[34] she
observes, and later tells us that Jane, "Cassandra, and
their friend Martha were bound, for her lifetime, to old
Mrs. Austen."[35] Shortly before her death, Jane implicitly
acknowledged Martha's membership in her family when
she wrote to a friend about how well she was being treated
in her illness by Mrs. Austen and Martha: "if I live

to be an old woman, I must expect to wish I had died now; blessed in the tenderness of such a family."[36] Interestingly, eleven years after Jane's death, Martha became a literal member of the Austen family when she married Jane's brother Francis.[37]

Perhaps even more surprising than the relationship between the Austen sisters and Martha Lloyd is the intimacy of Charlotte Brontë and her friend Ellen Nussey — an intimacy that began in their schooldays and ended only with Charlotte's death twenty-five years later. "With Ellen," Louise Bernikow tells us, "she shared family life — thought of her as a fourth sister — daily domestic detail, relationship subtleties, asking for nurturance, for cradling."[38] Yet there is scarcely a woman or man in history more totally bound up in biological family than Charlotte was in hers.

It is even more remarkable that when we consider the difference between Ellen's personality and those of the Brontës. Ellen was thoroughly conventional — if there were any smoldering passions hidden behind her placid exterior, they don't appear in her correspondence with Charlotte's biographer Elizabeth Gaskell. But this was precisely what Charlotte needed, and what she could never get from her sisters or brother. In the brilliant and morbid little world that the Brontës inhabited — a world that spawned the tortured Heathcliff and the mad Mrs. Rochester — Ellen's normality may have been Charlotte's ballast. "Charlotte gave Ellen a great measure of her love," comments biographer Winifred Gérin. During the emotional and religious crisis which Charlotte often suffered, "she bared her soul to her, depending much on her for spiritual comfort."[39] In one very significant letter, Charlotte wrote: "In such moods as these, Ellen, it is my nature to seek repose in some calm, tranquil idea . . . and I have now summoned up your image to give me rest."[40] There is something reminiscent here of Louisa May Alcott's relationship with her sister Lizzie — the original of the gentle Beth in *Little Women*. Lizzie's calm resignation never became Louisa's temperament, but it provided a counter to Louisa's tempestuousness long after Lizzie's death. Charlotte didn't have a "Beth" in her biological family, but she had one in Ellen.

Throughout their lives, they made prolonged visits to each other's houses, sharing their joys and sorrows, occasionally matchmaking for each other. (Ellen tried to become Charlotte's "real" sister by setting her friend up with her brother, Henry. The effort was unsuccessful, though Charlotte did say that she was "strongly tempted" because if she married Henry, "his sister could live with me, and how happy I should be . . . .")[41] It was to Ellen that Charlotte turned for comfort when her brother, Branwell, and then her sister Emily died. Soon thereafter, Charlotte's other sister, Anne, became fatally ill with consumption: Ellen and Charlotte took Anne to the seashore so she could spend her last days by the sea she loved. Perhaps Anne, too, had come to see Ellen as a sister; perhaps she recognized that when she died, Charlotte would need her friend's presence to sustain her. In either event, Ellen's inclusion in the last few days of Anne's life speaks to a depth of intimacy rare for Charlotte Brontë.

The intimacy lasted for the rest of Charlotte's brief life. When Charlotte married, her husband evinced some jealousy over the friendship, but he could not come between them. As she had earlier written to her editor: "No new friend, however lofty and profound in intellect, could be to me what Ellen is."[42]

One of the few books I've come across that implicitly accepts, even celebrates, nonbiological family is Andrew Birkin's beautiful and compassionate *J. M. Barrie and the Lost Boys*. Birkin subtitles his book *The Love Story that Gave Birth to Peter Pan* — a recognition that love relationships aren't confined to either erotic lovers or

biological family. The book details the complex relationship between Barrie, the novelist, playwright, and author
of *Peter Pan,* and the five Llewelyn Davies boys who
inspired his most famous work. It's interesting to compare
Birkin's treatment of the relationship with that of another
recent Barrie biographer, Janet Dunbar. Birkin looks at it
on its own terms, seeing its beauties and its failures, and
describing both. Dunbar, though she clearly has an affection for her subject, can never get beyond Freudian
assumptions about a man who would attach himself so
deeply to someone else's offspring. Thus she attributes
Barrie's extreme grief at the sudden, tragic death of one of
the boys to his "having failed to achieve a normal home
life and children of his own," which caused him to be
"in the grip of deeply seated frustrations, perhaps the
strongest being frustrated fatherhood."[43] Since Michael
was not Barrie's offspring, either by blood or by legal
adoption, Dunbar can't see the obvious: Barrie had known
the boy since his birth, had spent as much time with him
in his childhood as any father (and many mothers), and
had raised him in his youth; he was, simply, shattered by
the death of someone he loved deeply.

It was, by any conventional light, a most extraordinary
relationship that Barrie formed with the Llewelyn Davies
boys and their parents — though Barrie himself never
seemed aware that it was at all unusual. He met the three
oldest — George, Peter, and Jack — in the park (the younger
two had not yet been born) while he was walking his dog;
they fell into conversation and soon met in the park
regularly. Barrie enchanted the children with his wonderful, imaginative stories. He knew their mother, Sylvia,
slightly; soon he and his wife were visiting the Llewelyn
Davies home regularly. It quickly became a given that
Barrie would meet the boys in the park every day, come
back with them, and stay with their parents until the
boys' bedtimes.

He wasn't on equally close terms with all of the Llewelyn Davies'. Arthur Llewelyn Davies, the boys' father, was ambivalent about this new addition to his family in the beginning, although later he grew fond enough of him to say: "We look on him as a brother." His early resentment of his new "brother" is scarcely to be wondered at. He was a kind and intelligent, fairly conventional upper-middle-class family man, who worked hard at his law practice and relished the time he had alone with his wife and children. Suddenly he found that time being shared with a distinctly unconventional, wholly charismatic little man who moved into the family circle with ease and alacrity, charming both the boys and their mother.

Dunbar seems puzzled by Barrie's relationship to Sylvia, probably because it doesn't fit into any obvious definition. He was too intimate for a friend, too romantic for a brother, too platonic for a lover. He called her by her middle name, Jocelyn, because nobody else did, and he wrote to her in terms of a courting lover. But his feelings were never sexual and probably not all that romantic, and he delighted in the complete devotion she felt for her husband. (It's worth noting that, apart from his early attachment to his mother, his two deepest relationships were with women who were totally in love with their husbands. Neither Sylvia nor Lady Cynthia Asquith after her ever took Barrie's loverlike language seriously. Both recognized it as a pleasant and flirtatious vehicle for a very real and very platonic love.)

On the surface Barrie and his wife, Mary, both became close to the Davieses, vacationing with them and spending much of their free time together. In reality, Barrie was much closer to Sylvia and the boys, possibly even to Arthur, than he was to his own wife. Their marriage had been a failure from the first, and Mary probably felt even more alienated from the new family arrangements than Arthur did. (They were divorced, amid public scandal, in 1909.) But Barrie was clearly part of the Davies family. In June 1900, when the fourth Davies boy, Michael, was born, Barrie regarded him with the beaming pride of a third parent.[44]

To the boys, Barrie was a magic hero: he devised all kinds of complex games with them, many around the pirate theme which he would later immortalize in *Peter Pan*. They adored him. When he was away from them, they wrote him letters. One, from Jack (who would later become disenchanted with the writer), expressed great longing to see Barrie and ended with a peremptory command which must have delighted the man: "P.S. I expect a letter."[45]

In 1904, the Davies' moved to the countryside, where their fifth and last son, Nicholas, was born. The move meant that Barrie must see less of his adopted family, but it didn't affect his commitment to them. Letters became more frequent now that visits were fewer. In one charming letter he told Peter that when he walked in Kensington Gardens with his dog, Luath, "I see a vision and I cry, Hurray, there's Peter, and then Luath barks joyously and we run to the vision and then it turns out not to be Peter but just another boy, and then I cry like a water cart." He signed this letter "Your loving godfather," although the boy had, in fact, never been christened. Years later Barrie did become godfather to one of the boys. When Nico, at the age of fourteen, was christened, he asked Barrie to be his godfather.[46] But it was just a formality. In Barrie's own eyes, and in those of Sylvia and the boys, he already *was* their godfather — indeed, as Peter later described him, he was their "guardian angel."[47]

Whatever the early relationship had been between Barrie and Arthur Llewelyn Davies, in 1906 the event occurred that turned Barrie into Arthur's staunch friend. Arthur learned he had terminal cancer. During the last year of his life, when he was in constant pain, no one in his family was more devoted than Barrie. He was, wrote Peter later, "an incalculable comfort to the doomed Arthur as well as to Sylvia in her anguish."[48] He visited Arthur daily at the nursing home, bringing him gifts, reading him the newspaper, running errands for him. He paid all of Arthur's medical bills. For the first time, his letters to Sylvia revealed a tenderness for her husband. From Ireland, where he had to go for the Dublin opening of *Peter Pan*, he wrote: "How I wish I could say to you that now I am going up to Arthur, it is the only thing I seem to want to do nowadays."[49] For a while, his life had revolved around Arthur's sons; now it revolved around Arthur. He was as broken by Arthur's death as Sylvia and the boys were.

He promised Arthur that he would look after his family after he died, and he kept his promise, taking on their financial support as matter-of-factly as he had taken on his role in their family. And he became especially close to two of the boys: George, the eldest, and young Michael. He hated spending time away from them. "I feel they are growing up without my looking on," he wrote Sylvia during one absence. "I grudge any blank day without them . . . all five know me, as nobody else does."[50]

They were soon to know him much better. Sylvia fell ill and died two years after her husband's death. Barrie—by now Uncle Jim, "clearly seen in the role of leading uncle, if not step-father," according to Peter[51]—took over the rearing of the boys, a task he shared rather grudgingly with their housekeeper, Mary Hodgson. That he saw himself as unquestionably their family is clear in a letter he wrote a friend several months after Sylvia's death: "I have in a sense a larger family than you now. Five boys whose father died four years ago, and now their mother last summer, and I look after them and it is my main reason for going on." He invited his friend to visit him, but "preferably not on a weekend as I am rather tied with the boys then."⁵²

His letters from this point on—and his correspondence was always voluminous—are as filled with the minutiae of his adored boys' lives as any doting mother's. Nicholas has learned to ride a pony; Michael has won a cricket competition at Eton; Peter has grown a beard. Jack is engaged: will his fiancée like Barrie? (It was a good question: there turned out to be much friction between Barrie and Jack's wife.)

His letters to George during World War I, when George was a soldier stationed overseas, are among the warmest and most moving he wrote. George, on his part, wrote "Uncle Jim" almost constantly. Shortly before the young man's death, Barrie wrote: "I don't have an iota of desire for you to get military glory . . . I have the one passionate desire that we all may be together again . . . There may be moments when the knowledge of all you are to me will make you a little more careful, and so I can't help going on saying these things . . ."⁵³

George died in battle. Peter, himself deeply mourning the loss of his brother, recognized the depths of Barrie's grief. Years later he wrote that Barrie had been "shaken to the core" by the death of Arthur, "prostrated, ravaged, and utterly undone when Sylvia pursued Arthur to the grave," and then faced the death of "George, whom he had loved with such a deep, strange, complicated increasing love" and who "would have been such a pillar for him to lean on in the difficult job of guiding the destinies of Sylvia & Arthur Llewelyn Davies's boys — 'my boys.' "⁵⁴

Barrie's relations with Peter and Jack had become strained, and the grief they shared over George's death didn't bring them together for long. Barrie seems to have suffered what many parents of soldiers suffered during the years following World War I: the experience of the war had embittered the young men, and the world they now lived in was not the world the generation before had inhabited. Barrie had trouble accepting the fact that his charming boys had become battle-scarred men. The fictional Peter had refused to grow up, but the real one had little choice: the battlefields of France were a far cry from Never-Never Land. With real grief, Barrie watched his boys grow away from him. He wrote to his friend Elizabeth Lucas: "It must be lovely to have Audrey developing under your eyes. So soon they fly away . . . but there are sudden moments when they are children again."[55]

Dunbar, however, exaggerates the depth of the boys' alienation, interpreting it in the light of her own prejudice against the unorthodox composition of the family Barrie and the Llewelyn Davies' formed. The clashes Barrie had with Jack and the deep ambivalence Peter felt toward his "Uncle Jim" sound little different from problems that often exist between parents and children. If Barrie's inability to cope with his boys' adulthood was neurotic, it is a neurosis shared by many, perhaps most, parents.

Comments made in later life by Nico, Jack, and Peter are quoted in Birkin's book, and they are interestingly varied. Jack's are wholly bitter toward the man he felt usurped his parents' place in his life; Nico's are completely loving. Peter's are ambivalent: there appears the confusion and resentment of a conventional man raised by an unconventional parent—with the memory of a far more conventional parent to compare him to. Peter loved Barrie but was clearly embarrassed by him—and by the fact that Peter was always, mistakenly, taken for the single model of Peter Pan. (It was actually all five boys who provided the inspiration for Peter Pan: Barrie would have been wiser and kinder to have given the eternal boy a completely original name.) Whatever alienation any of the boys felt toward Barrie, they continued to relate to him as a parent, visiting often and spending holidays with him for the rest of his life.

Barrie's relationship with the family he so loved was always stalked by tragedy, and in 1921 the hardest blow of all fell. The war was over, and Barrie felt relieved of the constant fear that Michael would be drafted and die in battle as George had. Then, in May 1921, Michael was drowned in a swimming accident that may have been suicide.[56] That death haunted Barrie the rest of his life.

One can't leave the subject of Barrie and his boys without discussing the notion of homosexuality that invariably connects with the subject. Barrie may or may not have been homosexual, but it's virtually certain that he had no consciously erotic designs on the boys. Nico, the only one of them still living when Birkin wrote his book, firmly denied the rumors;[57] neither the angry comments from Jack nor the ambivalent ones from Peter ever hint at sexual advances; and it's not likely that Sylvia Llewelyn Davies would have entrusted her sons to Barrie's care if she had any suspicion of sexual intentions on his part. In our post-Freudian, sexually obsessed age, it is difficult to view any relationship not covered by incest taboos without a suspicion of sexual motivation.

It is perhaps made more difficult in Barrie's case because his attitude toward the boys display such an obvious tenderness. He was less father than mother. As Dunbar frequently notes, he was possessive, but he was also extremely nurturant—qualities not necessarily mutually exclusive. Birkin sees this: he writes of Barrie's "motherhood" to the boys, and of his "maternal" feelings. Peter recognized it when he wrote that Barrie's feelings toward the boys had "a dash of the paternal, a lot of the maternal, and much, too, of the lover."[58] Barrie himself was aware of it: in one remarkable letter to George in the army, he wrote: "I shall have many anxious days and nights too, but I only fall in line with so many mothers."[59]

What "mother" means, of course, is "nurturer." In the mid-nineteenth and early twentieth centuries, nurturance always was seen as a feminine trait. A few writers with a touch of the visionary might proselytize about training men to be nurturers (Louisa May Alcott, with her strange mixture of sugar-and-spice conventionality and feminist militance, was one of them), but for the most part society, conventional and unconventional, hewed to the rule that God had assigned women exclusive possession of nurturing instincts. There was no word for what Barrie was to his boys—there still isn't. Until the concept of "family" is broadened to fit its reality, "maternal" is the closest we can come.

Barrie's nurturance wasn't confined to his boys. As they grew up he formed yet another remarkable relationship, similar to the one he had shared with Sylvia Llewelyn Davies. In 1918, Lady Cynthia Asquith became both Barrie's secretary and his second acquired family. Barrie, as one friend pointed out to Cynthia, needed a "Dulcinea" figure,[60] and Cynthia, like Sylvia, was perfect for the role. A society beauty with a warm heart, a strong intelligence, and expensive tastes that her inheritance and her husband's income couldn't quite support, she accepted Barrie's extraordinary job offer happily, and Barrie moved into her life as deftly as he had moved into Sylvia's. Like Sylvia, Cynthia was utterly devoted to her husband, a devotion that delighted Barrie.

The relationship paralleled that with the Llewelyn Davies' in yet another way: "Beb" Asquith was no happier to acquire a new family member than Arthur had been. He accepted it with as much grace as possible, because Barrie meant so much to Cynthia, but he always resented his wife's closeness with Barrie.

Cynthia soon became Barrie's hostess as well as his secretary, and the two spent long hours together. It was Cynthia and Beb who came to Barrie's side the night he heard the news of Michael's death, Cynthia who handled the funeral arrangements for Barrie, Cynthia who took him off to a seaside holiday to recover from the first shock of grief. In February 1922, he wrote her that it was "strange and terrible that I should go on getting any happiness out of life since Michael's death, but I owe it all to you."[61]

They became indispensable to each other, though their relationship didn't always run smoothly. She felt at times torn between Beb's and Barrie's demands on her: she didn't doubt the love of either of them, but she found it at times exhausting. Once she wrote in her diary that she felt "completely vampired" by Barrie's demands.[62] She and Barrie quarreled often, always making up soon afterward. When one was ill, the other became a constant and tender nurse. Barrie fretted whenever Cynthia showed signs of ill health. His letters show a solicitousness not warranted by mild illness, but any sickness in his new Dulcinea must have brought frightening reminders of Sylvia's last year.

Their relationship lasted for nineteen years, ending only with Barrie's death in 1937. In his will, he left a few small bequests to his nieces and nephews. The rest of his estate, however, he left to his true family—a large part to Nico, Peter, and Jack, and the largest to Lady Cynthia Asquith.

One of the most interesting familial relationships in nineteenth-century history is also one of that century's most important political alliances. Susan B. Anthony and Elizabeth Cady Stanton worked on the women's suffrage cause together for over fifty years. Writes Alice Rossi in *The Feminist Papers: From Adams to Beauvoir*, "From the spring of 1851, when they first met, until Elizabeth's death in 1902, they were in and out of each other's lives and households . . . Their friendship and shared commitment . . . were the solid, central anchor in both their lives."[63]

Those lives, however, were lived very differently.

Elizabeth was married, with seven children to care for. Susan was a spinster with little patience for marriage and motherhood. She was given to scolding her married friends. In 1856, she wrote to Elizabeth: "Those of you who have the talent to do honor to poor womanhood, have all given yourselves over to baby-making . . . it is a crime . . ."[64]

Susan may not have "made the babies, but she soon found herself helping to raise them. Periodically, when she and Stanton were working on some project together, she would pack her bag and move into the Stanton household. Elizabeth's husband was unsupportive of her feminist activities, was unlikely to assume any child care responsibilities, and in any event was away from town on frequent extended business trips. "Aunt Susan" became something of a coparent during her long visits — in fact, Elizabeth, writing to Susan, referred to the Stanton offspring as "our children."[65] This familial relationship with her friend's children lasted into their adulthood — after Susan had "retired" to her farm in Rochester, they often came and stayed for prolonged visits.

If Susan acted as a third parent to Elizabeth's children, she also functioned in many ways as a second spouse to Stanton herself. "The place their friendship held in their personal lives," notes Rossi, "is suggested by their terms of address and reference to each other. They were not in terms of 'sisterhood' but of 'marriage.'" She quotes Stanton: "So entirely one are we that . . . like husband and wife, each has the feeling that we must have no differences in public." She described their hearts as "eternally wedded together," and, when rumors began circulating that the famous partnership was dissolving, she wrote in playful horror to Susan: "Have you been getting a divorce . . . without notifying me? I shall not allow any such proceedings." Significantly, she added: "I consider that our relations are to last for life."[66]

They did. It was a "marriage" with much conflict,

but much more love, and its basis was the interweaving of a deep personal and political commitment. There were storms to weather, and they weathered them. For two women to whom the essence of life was political, political disagreements were never abstract. They quarreled bitterly over allying with the controversial suffragist and free-love advocate Victoria Woodhull and over Anthony's single-minded devotion to the cause of suffrage, which ruled out the possibility of creating a larger, multiissue movement. There was anger and pain; there were even public accusations of narrowmindedness and bigotry. Their friendship survived it all.

It is worthwhile to compare their relationship to that of a "real" family of suffragists, the Pankhursts in England. Like Anthony, Christabel Pankhurst and her mother, Emmeline, wanted to focus exclusively on the vote; like Stanton, Christabel's sister, Sylvia, wanted to embrace other issues. The disagreement was equally intense, equally bitter. But Emmeline and Christabel banished Sylvia from the Women's Social and Political Union, and from their lives. The political differences destroyed the family.[67]

The family of Anthony and Stanton was stronger. They worked together on writing the *History of Woman Suffrage;* they remained staunch friends after they no longer had common projects to work on. When Susan and her sister, Mary, moved into the spacious family farm in Rochester in 1891 (Susan's "retirement," during which she worked as hard as ever), Susan begged her now-widowed friend to move in with them. Though she decided against doing so, Elizabeth was a frequent visitor at the Rochester home for the remainder of her life.

The friendship of Stanton and Anthony was not unique. Political commitment often served as a catalyst for life-long kinship ties among women in the nineteenth and early twentieth centuries. Perhaps it did for men as well, but the roles women were cast in, and the characters they developed as a result, lent themselves more readily to fostering familial intimacy. Moving into a friend's home and taking over domestic chores and child care creates a level of intimacy few men were likely to achieve: it's a bit difficult to picture, say, Big Bill Haywood doing Joe Hill's ironing while the two built labor strategy together. For men, nurturance has historically been that which is provided by others. But women have always understood the importance of nurturing—and, being so often the nurturers in nonreciprocal relationships, have been able to value the nurturance they've received from each other. Creating family has always been "women's work." So we find variations of the Stanton-Anthony friendship throughout women's political history.

Blanche Weisen Cook, in an essay on the support networks of several political women, writes: "Networks of love and support are crucial to our ability as women to work in a hostile world . . . frequently the networks of love and support that enable politically and professionally active women to function independently and intensively consist largely of other women."[68]

One of the most interesting of the women Weisen Cook discusses is Lillian Wald, who, in 1867, founded the Henry Street Settlement, a neighborhood philanthropic center in New York City, and lived there for most of her life with a group of other women who "worked together on all projects," lived and vacationed together for over fifty years, and traveled to various countries around the world together.[69] Cook speculates, from the tone of many of the letters Wald's friends wrote to her, that Wald had sexual relationships with some of these women at different times in her life. She certainly had familial relationships with them; the nucleus of women stayed together and corresponded warmly throughout their lives.

Wald had other familial friends who didn't live in the settlement, but who were nonetheless involved in the settlement's work. Most were younger than Wald, and saw her as a mother figure. One habitually signed her letters "your daughter" or "your spoiled child."[70] Another called herself Wald's son: in one letter, she wrote that she was feeling depressed but that she'd feel better "if I just had my nicest mommy to snuggle up to and talk it out straight for her son."[71]

Wald herself had deliberately chosen a familial mode for her work. "I was conscious only of a passionate desire to have people . . . know each other that they might sympathize and understand the problems and difficulties of each other," she wrote, adding that she had been "engrossed in the edifice which was taking form and in which my friends and I might dwell together."[72] On the day she died, she told her nurse that she had been a happy woman, because so many people loved her and she loved so many people.[73]

But politics wasn't the only bonding force among women of this era. Often it was religion that turned friends into family; sometimes it was simply the fact of friendship itself. Nancy F. Cott and Carroll Smith-Rosenberg have both documented deeply emotional friendships between women of the eighteenth and nineteenth centuries.

The infamous Aaron Burr was married to a deeply religious woman, Esther, who considered her friend, Sara Prince, "nearer than any sister I have," in spite of the fact that both had several biological sisters. Sarah Osborn and her friend Susan Anthony built a devoted friendship out of the revival preaching of the 1740s Awakening movement: together they hoped to "join hand in hand, to promote the cause and interest of our infinitely worthy redeemer."[74] It's ironic to note that

women were able, in all sincerity, to use the worship of
a male god in a patriarchal religion to forge sisterly bonds
with one another.

Smith-Rosenberg—the author of the article "The
Female World of Love and Ritual: Relations between
Women in Nineteenth-Century America," published in
1975, which has become the basis for much of the study
of women's friendship networks since—went over countless diaries and letters of middle-class American women.
Over and over, one theme is reiterated: even when friends
are parted for years they are each other's chief emotional mainstay, and they regard their presence in each
other's lives as a constant. One of the most revealing
correspondences is that between Mary (Molly) Hallock
Foote and her friend Helena. They met in 1868 at Cooper
Union Institute School in New York, and they spent all
their time together during their school years, visiting
each other's families and their mutual friends, going to
museums and galleries, studying. Their friendship lasted
long past their school years, throughout the rest of their
lives. Like Elizabeth Cady Stanton, Molly saw her relationship with her friend not in terms of sisterhood but in
terms of marriage: she loved Helena "as wives do their
husbands, as *friends* who have taken each other for life."
When the women were in their late twenties, they decided
to live together, but Molly succumbed to pressure to
remain at home with her parents. Helena was angry, and
the decision drove a wedge between them strong enough
to alter the intensity of their friendship. Soon afterward,
both became involved with men, and they transferred their
romantic needs to their husbands. The friendship, however, remained a major part of their lives, retaining its
tenderness if not its passion. Twenty years after Helena's
marriage, Molly wrote to her friend: "It isn't because you
are good that I love you—but for the essence of you
which is like perfume."[75]

Wellcome

Burroughs Wellcome Co. is pleased to send you this pocket notebook for the many occasions during the coming years when you will wish to make notes. We hope it will prove useful to you.

Sincerely,

Freda Coe Jr.

F.A. Coe, Jr.
President

Burroughs Wellcome Co. is part of a unique international organization. There are no public stockholders. All distributable profits are channeled into research in medicine and allied fields.

In the United States, funds from The Wellcome Trust have established research professorships and aided research in such fields as circulatory dynamics, parasitology and pharmacology. On a global scale, support of medical research is equally diversified.

Thus, it is with pride that we say

RESEARCH IS
OUR ONLY
STOCKHOLDER.

In *Bonds of Womanhood: "Women's Sphere" in New England, 1780–1835,* Cott comments on the fact that the role women were forced into lent itself to a special bonding between them: "the identification of women with the heart . . . implied that they would find truly reciprocal relationships only with other women. They would find answering sensibilities only among their own sex." [76] Smith-Rosenberg notes that the framework this created was not only emotional, but logistical: "Women helped each other with domestic chores in times of sickness, sorrow, and trouble. Rural women developed a pattern of more extended visits that lasted weeks and sometimes months . . . When husbands traveled, wives routinely moved in with other women . . . Summer vacations were frequently organized to permit old friends to meet at water spas or share a country home." [77]

Women expected and received the same familial nurturance from their woman friends that they had gotten from their mothers. Smith-Rosenberg tells of Nelly Lewis, who learned that her daughter, away at school, was fatally ill. Though Nelly's husband was living, it was not to him but to her friend Elizabeth Bordley that Nelly turned. Elizabeth took care of Nelly's other children and helped Nelly care for the dying girl. Later she helped make the funeral arrangements, and thereafter periodically visited the girl's grave. Nelly grieved for years, and Elizabeth was her sole confidante. "Mr. L.," Nelly wrote to her friend, "knows nothing of this." [78] If "Mr. L." mourned his daughter's death, he did so alone: it was only with her friend that Nelly shared her sorrow.

Nelly and Elizabeth had met at boarding school, an environment that fostered familial connections among women. "Female academies," in fact, set out to form kinship bonds among their students. In one such academy, an organization was formed called "The Band of Sisters," in which girls planned to "live in perfect harmony and

friendship and no young lady belonging to the Society
is to speak unkindly to a Sister." In another such school,
students were advised to "consider yourselves as a little
band of sisters united for a time in one family."[79] Mean-
ingless kin imagery, of course, is not uncommon, but the
female academies appear to have taught their creed in
earnest, judging from the number of lifelong, committed
relationships that grew out of them.

And the commitments frequently lasted beyond a single
generation. Often, Smith-Rosenberg tells us, friends from
school days would send their daughters to the schools
they themselves had attended, hoping the girls would
become friends as their mothers had. Nelly and Elizabeth
were two who maintained this tradition, and "Elizabeth
virtually adopted the daughter of her school chum."
Nelly's daughter wrote Elizabeth letters that began
"Dearest Mama." A similar relationship developed between
Eleuthera DuPont and her mother's friend Elizabeth
Smith. To the girl, Mrs. Smith became "Mother," while
her own parent was "Mamma." In a letter to her sister,
Eleuthera said that "Mamma" made a visit to "Mother's"
house—an interesting twist on the two-parent family.
Among the students themselves, an older girl would often
take on the role of mother for a younger friend, and would
actually be called "Mother": sometimes the "mother-
daughter" relationship thus formed would last into adulthood and even through old age.[80]

Of all the people I've discussed in this chapter, only
the Utopians consciously attempted to create alternative
family structures—and they, ironically, appear to have
been the least successful. In attempting to eliminate
personal affinity from their new communities, they
stripped family of one of its most important qualities;
the baby was lost with the bathwater. Lillian Wald came
much closer to consciously creating a form of family

that nourished both freedom and continuity, commitment and individuality. But none of the others were conscious of doing anything revolutionary: not the wealthy and eccentric Barrie, not the slaves and ex-slaves taking what they could when everything had been taken from them, not the school chums who gave each other lifetimes of practical and emotional sustenance. They simply knew, instinctively and probably unconsciously, that the family structures allowed them were not enough. And so they created what they needed. They made their friends their families.

2.

Honorary Kin

I am sitting talking with John Paul. "Of course," he is saying in his rich and deceptively young voice— the voice of the actor he has been most of his life—"you were the love of Ti's life; you know that. The only person that I ever knew that he cared anything more about was his own niece, Jean. He used to talk about you constantly—when you were a baby, and when you were a young lady, as you were growing up. Ti would have been so proud of you for what you've done and what you're doing."

Ti died 16 years ago, when I was 20. He and John Paul had lived together since I was born, since before my parents met them. There was never a time when they weren't part of my life.

Of all my honorary aunts and uncles, John Paul is the only one left. Clair and Betty moved away and eventually lost touch with my parents. So did "Our John," and Aunt Eva, though we get news of Eva now and again from John Paul. Uncle Walter, Gene, and Ti all died.

Of these, the ones I was closest to were Gene, Ti, and John Paul. I miss Gene still, and especially I miss Ti. Ti was an alcoholic, even before John Paul met him; his drinking worsened with the years, and he became morose and bitter most of the time, but he was always good to me, and we grew closer as I grew up. He got me my first and longest-lasting job. It was always said in the family that his drinking would kill him, and it finally did.

I felt a little lost a few years ago when "Roots" was broadcast, and everyone was going back to the family tree. I couldn't honestly care who my great-great-grandparents were; I hardly knew my grandparents, and never felt any great need to know them better. I'd assumed my "roots" were only political ones, my heritage only in the suffrage movement and the other protest movements of this country. But now, as I talk with John Paul, listening while he tells me how he first met Ti and Eva and Walter, and how they then met my parents, I realize that I have personal roots as well.

"I have something for you." John Paul gets up slowly. He's a remarkably strong and hearty man for his age, but his age is 82, and I feel myself rebelling against that. Every time I see John Paul lately, I remind myself of all the people who live into their nineties. But that's not enough—I want John Paul for more than another ten years.

He comes back into the room with an 8" by 10" glossy photo—a publicity picture of Ti, taken in the mid-thirties when Ti was an aspiring actor. The face is thin, sullenly sexy, the face of a matinee idol. The Ti I knew had a red and puffy face, but I recognize this young man as my friend. "You can keep this," John Paul tells me, casually, but we both have tears in our eyes.

For all the years I've known John Paul, we've never talked this intimately before. It had never occurred to me before now to talk about our relationship. But I realized, starting to work on this book, that I didn't know how Ti and Paul had met my parents, or how much time in my early childhood I spent with them. A child's family is timeless; they are *there* — eternity begins with one's own existence. Was John Paul ever *not* in my life?

"I met Ti in 1937, in Cincinnati," John Paul tells me. "I was involved in a WPA theater project there. They put me onto writing the book for a musical." Ti was an actor in the play; so was Eva. My parents and Walter were in an acting school in Cincinnati; that's how John Paul, Ti, and Eva met them. Ti and John Paul moved to New York. Shortly afterward, my parents followed, living with Ti and John Paul in a small Manhattan apartment for several months, then returning to California. John Paul was at that time stage-managing the musical *Brigadoon,* and one of the earliest toys I remember owning is a stuffed Scotch terrier named Briggy, a gift from John Paul. I had Briggy for years.

Uncle Walter knew my parents in Cincinnati; when they moved permanently to New York (my mother very pregnant with her second child) they lived with him for several months before moving to Queens. He died when I was nine or ten; I have dim but affectionate memories of him. Once, during the 1952 presidential campaign, I told him he looked like Eisenhower. He laughed and gave me a quarter. I figured I'd latched onto a good thing, and told him he looked like Stevenson. He gave me 50¢.

Then one day my parents were crying and telling me Uncle Walter was dead. I remember thinking that this was a terrible thing, but not feeling anything; death was incomprehensible. And so I never really mourned Uncle Walter.

Pop got jobs modeling while he tried to get jobs acting, and he became friends with several other models. One of them, Gene, rented a room in our house for a time, when I was four or five. He was living with us when my youngest brother, Warren, was born. He eventually got an apartment of his own, but there was no question that he was still family. He spent most of his weekends with us after he moved out. (Many of my parents' friends stayed with us for days at a time. My brother Keith, in innocent curiosity, would always greet guests with a cheerful, "Hi! When are you leaving?")

Aunt Eva was about John Paul's age; we saw her less frequently, but I adored her. She was very, very theatrical, in the Tallulah Bankhead fashion, and she always told dirty jokes in a terribly grand manner. I thought she was the most elegant person I'd ever met.

But Clair was the most glamorous. She was in her twenties and very beautiful. She had an apartment in Manhattan with a roommate, and she was a Rockette. When I felt good about myself, I had dreams of being like Clair when I grew up. I knew I could never be beautiful or a dancer, but I thought I might be able to have an apartment in New York with a roommate, and that was all I really wanted in life. Queens is technically part of Long Island, though it hides the fact pretty well, and Clair and my parents had a joke about her visits. She'd tell her dancer friends she was spending the weekend with her friends who had a house on The Island. I never understood the joke. It was years before I realized that Long Island was considered classy and elegant, but even if I'd known that then it wouldn't have mattered. Clair lived in Manhattan: it was like an angel in heaven bragging to the other angels that she had friends on earth. Once my parents and I went to the city to visit Clair. The apartment she shared with two other dancers was small and cramped, and the closet barely had room for their toe shoes. But it was the most beautiful place I'd ever seen.

Then there was "Our John." When we moved out of the apartment in Queens, to a house a block away, Our John rented a room with us. He was "Our John" to differentiate him from my father's other friend John.

Like Eva, he was very theatrical—but in a Damon Runyon way. He smoked smelly cigars, and used Old Spice after shave lotion. He, too, told dirty jokes. His nickname, however, caused my mother considerable embarrassment one day when she and my brother Warren, who at this point was four or five, were standing on a street corner, waiting for the light to change, next to an elderly gentleman wearing Old Spice after shave. Warren sniffed, then beamed a smile up at the elderly gentleman. "You smell like Our John!" he cried in delight.

But Ti and John Paul and Gene were the core group— the closest, the best-loved uncles. I had my first Easter at Ti and John Paul's, when I was five. They thought it would be fun to see me hunt Easter eggs and squeal with delight each time I found one. They spent hours carefully hand-painting the eggs. On Easter Sunday, they hid the eggs before my parents and I arrived. Then, happily, they told me all about the colored eggs and how the Easter Bunny had painted them and left them for me. I wasn't very enthusiastic. "But I don't *like* hard-boiled eggs," I protested. "And anyway, why didn't the Easter Bunny leave them at my house?" John Paul reminds me of this story every time I see him. "It's a wonder you lived to see another Easter," he always chuckles.

Once a year or so, my grandparents would come to New York for a week or we'd get in the car and drive to Cincinnati where they and my aunts and uncles and cousins lived. I had a good time, usually, and I was glad to know that I had cousins, just like my friend Sylvia had. But although I liked my cousins and we got along perfectly well, it wasn't the same as it was with Sylvia and her cousins. There was no reason why it should have been. Sylvia's cousins were her family; mine weren't. Neither were my aunts and uncles and grandparents. My family was Ti and John Paul and Gene, Clair and Betty and Eva and Our John. And, as they gave a framework to our

lives, we provided one for theirs. We provided family
for them as much as they did for us.

Margaret Adams, in writing *Single Blessedness,* discovered many people like Ti and John Paul and Clair
and Gene. Particularly on holidays such people found
their friends a major emotional resource. They "tempo-
rarily abandoned their autonomous pattern of living
and . . . were usually invited to join a family with whom
they had a close and continuing quasi kinship relationship"
on holidays: "Those who relied on friends for this home-
based celebration tended to visit the same families
regularly each year, assimilating this annual recurrence
as a ritualistic feature of their own social pattern."[1]

Ti, John Paul, Clair, and Gene are what the sociologists
call "fictive kin." Fictive kin are in many ways the closest
to biological family of all the nonbiological family types.
They become absorbed into a preexisting definition of
family, becoming honorary aunts and uncles or, in some
cases, honorary cousins, even honorary siblings. The
sociologists rarely treat these relationships in depth.
Yet for many people, fictive kin are a major part of their
families as they are growing up.

Kay, a crisp, determined, late-middle-aged widow who
lives with a roommate in California, has a large network
of friends who have defined themselves as family. For her,
creating family has come naturally, an extension of her
childhood pattern. "This making of a family was sort of
customary when I was growing up," she tells me. Her
family were Irish immigrants, and they owned a house.
"I remember my mother used to sponsor Irish immigrants,
and there was one woman whom we called 'Auntie,' and
she lived with us for a while. And there was one man
and we called him 'Uncle.' I found out later that we
didn't have any blood ties with them. But we were sort
of like a central family there, in Yonkers, New York.
And people would come and stay with us transitionally

coming into the country. We always had at least one other
person living in the house. This one fellow, we called him
'Big Brother.' So we always had these odd relatives who
were coming in and out and that we kept in touch with
over the years and acted as family with.

"I remember during the Depression, there was a
family—my brother's friend's family—and there were
nine children in that family. The father was an engineer
of some kind and something happened, he was out of work
and they were out of money, and they had to move out
of their house. They came and asked my mother if she
would take the two boys who were my brother's close
friends—they were parceling everybody out all over the
neighborhood—and she said there was no use splitting
up the family, because we had a fairly large house with
several rooms in the attic. They stayed for several months,
and we were very close to them for a number of years
afterward." So integrated was this pattern into their
lives that when Kay's brother liked someone very much
he'd ask them to join the family. "He would say it quite
openly as a way of relating to people."

In cultures of poverty, fictive kin have often played an
important part in kinship networks, probably because
people need each other more in practical ways, which
then translate into emotional ties. Kay's experience in
an Irish community finds echoes in many black communities. In fact, from the reading and interviewing I've
done, it seems that among black communities the kinship categories are often far more flexible than in most
white cultures and subcultures. Particularly in the areas
where there is less physical mobility and people tend to
live most of their lives in or near the neighborhoods
they grew up in, the line between the honorary aunt
and uncle, the neighbor-as-kin, and the chosen family
becomes very nebulous. This is excellently documented

in Carol Stack's *All Our Kin: Strategies for Survival in a Black Community*. Stack, a white anthropologist, spent three years getting to know the residents of "The Flats," the poorest section of a black community in a small midwestern city. Her findings are fascinating. Taken with Herbert Gutman's study of the black family under slavery, they should finally dispel the myth that studies like the notorious Moynihan report — black children are raised solely by their mothers (a "black matriarchy") — have fostered. Stack's findings show a complex kinship network that includes women and men and that provides a number of both male and female parent-figures for growing children. Into this network friends are frequently absorbed.

One of the most interesting kinds of fictive kin relationships that Stack found was that which typically exists between a woman's child and her boyfriend. A boyfriend, especially if he is living with the woman, is expected to be a father to her children, and the biological father is expected to surrender many of his rights to the boyfriend (or to the mother's new husband). Stack quotes one woman who broke up with a boyfriend because he mistreated her children. A later boyfriend, Lee, "was something else. He was so nice to the kids that the babies cried when he left the house . . . After we was housekeeping for about six months, Lee said to the boys that they should call him their 'play daddy.' " Clover and Lee had broken up a year earlier, but Lee still visited her children to whom he remained the play daddy.[2]

Sometimes this relationship extends beyond the nuclear arrangement. A child may be close to an aunt's boyfriend or an uncle's girlfriend, and perceive the lover as an aunt or uncle, too. Ruby, one of the Flats residents Stack became close to, tells of "Uncle Arthur," who had been her Aunt Augusta's boyfriend when Ruby was a child. Ruby had lived with Aunt Augusta, Uncle Arthur, and her grandmother, and the tie remained strong. She also told of her Uncle Lazar, who had been involved with her mother's youngest sister. "My aunt has been married twice since, but Uncle Lazar just remained part of our family. He's been a part of our family ever since I can remember." He has also lived with the family. At the time Ruby was telling the story, he lived in the basement below Aunt Augusta's apartment, and Augusta, though not the aunt he'd been involved with, cooked for both him and her own boyfriend.[3]

So wholly integrated into the family life are these fictive relatives that often no one is quite sure how they came into the family. Stack asked a woman, Billy, what her Aunt Ola's original connection to her family was. "My mama once told me, but I hardly remember," Billy answered. "I think Ola was my mama's oldest sister's best friend and they went for cousins. When my mama's sister died, Ola took her two youngest children."[4]

Lydia, a black woman I interviewed, has a story similar to those recounted in Stack's book. Since she grew up in Roxbury, the major black ghetto in the Boston area, the integration of fictive kin into family networks was a natural, comfortable process. As she speaks, a sense of warmth, expansive energy, and a wonderful combination of self-irony and self-appreciation come through.

"Growing up, about six people lived in my house. My brother used to shine shoes in South Station. One day he brought home a kid who stayed with us for three and a half years until he joined the service and went away. He had run away from an orphanage in New Jersey and he was sleeping in South Station when Maurice found him and brought him home. And he stayed with us till he was a grown man. And then we had another little kid that somebody brought home named Donald, and he stayed about a year and a half. Okay? But that's only the big ones—the little ones are the ones that stayed two and three months at a time. See, any old day you'd get up and your mama would say, 'Liddy, Liddy, move over, Angie's getting in your bed.' So right away you're mad cause you know there's somebody else in Angie's bed. Any morning you might wake up and find a strange face looking at you across the breakfast table."

Often the ones who lived with Lydia's family for only a few months remained family members after they left, visiting frequently. "One guy only stayed four or five days, but he was always turning up about once or twice a month, bringing my mother flowers and chocolates and stuff. The time my mother died he was out of town and he didn't hear about her until two weeks after the funeral. There was a knock on my door and I opened it and he was standing outside my door with tears running down his face—'Oh, how could this happen to Ma when I wasn't here?' "

Lydia has never given birth to a child, but she has raised several for periods ranging from a few weeks to eight years. The one who stayed eight years was her godchild, Gail. "Gail's mother, Ruby, is my godmother," she tells me. "Gail's mother and my mother came over from The Islands on the same boat in 1916. So they've been friends for years, which is how Ruby got to be my godmother. So when Gail was 13 and picked up that phone and called me in New York and said, 'Aunt, come get me, please,' it never occurred to me that I shouldn't come to Boston and get her. And it never occurred to her mother that she shouldn't let her go with me. Do you understand what I'm saying? So now Gail's in California doing very well, financially and the rest of it, and she has her own business, the whole bit. And she's saying to me, 'When are you ready for Suzanne? [Gail's daughter].' And I said, 'What does John say?'—that's her husband. And John said, 'If you can do as well for Suzanne as

you did for Gail, she's in great shape.' And the beat goes
on.'' Ruby is Lydia's aunt; Lydia is Gail's aunt, and now
she's Suzanne's aunt. The beat goes on—and blood has
nothing to do with it.

The informal adoption of children is not, however,
confined to the poor. Like Lydia, Amanda grew up in a
house where new "brothers" and "sisters" were always
appearing. She came from a somewhat different background—a white upper-middle-class family which quickly
became a white lower-middle-class family when, early in
Amanda's childhood, her mother and stepfather were
divorced.

"When my stepfather left," she says, lighting a cigarette,
"Mom was left with this big house in Brooklyn, which had
been half remodeled. It hadn't been painted yet." So
her mother began to make arrangements with a few teenagers who were running away from home, or who had been
kicked out by their parents—they'd help put the house in
order in exchange for room and board. "My mother's
always been real friendly with people younger than she,
and whenever they were in trouble they knew that we had
a lot of space in our house." There was an apartment in
the basement; occasionally a youth would move into the
apartment. Mostly, however, "it was kind of communal."
They had a variety of personalities and problems, and they
stayed for different lengths of time—never more than
two at one time.

It wasn't always a positive experience, at least for Amanda
and her brother. Two of the boys later had nervous breakdowns and, coming from violent and unhappy family
backgrounds, made threats of physical violence against
Amanda's mother. Sometimes neighborhood gossip would
declare that Amanda's mother, a young-looking and
charming woman, was having affairs with the young men
living in the house: to Amanda and her brother, both in

their early teens, the rumors were painful. At times, too, her brother would feel in competition with the newer "family" members for his mother's love.

In other ways, however, the situation worked in his favor. In the late sixties, in a household otherwise composed of only a sister and a mother, both of whom were avidly feminist, it helped her brother to have a few other male family members around. For Amanda herself, dealing with her own inevitable problems with her mother, the presence of new siblings who saw her mother as an angel of mercy caused some frustrations. "Some of them had horrible childhoods, and they'd say, 'Your mother's so wonderful, my parents always beat me.' And I couldn't complain, my problems seemed smaller, so there was no place to go with them."

In spite of this, she feels good about her adopted family, and keeps in close contact with most of them. "The only friends I have that really approximate in closeness ties with my mother, father, brother, and stepmother," she muses, "are those people that I essentially made ties with when I was 11 and 12 and 13. It's a sense that these people will always be around, and will always be together."

One of the friends, Noela, who's now in her midthirties, has rented the downstairs apartment. "When I'm home, a lot of times we'll get up in the morning and go down to Noela's for coffee and sit around, and then Noela will sometimes come up for dinner."

Since Amanda has been working full time and since Noela has been living downstairs, the entrance of the new siblings has stopped. But the "family," with all its problems and rewards, has remained together. Amanda is convinced that it always will: "If I go home I don't always see all of them, but I usually see a good portion of them. I think we'll always basically be together, we'll always be friends, we'll always know what's happening in each other's lives."

Like Amanda, Russ has always had a variety of fictive relatives. A young Chinese American man, he is very conscious of his heritage. Born in the United States and raised here by adoptive Chinese parents, he speaks with a slight Chinese accent. Unlike Amanda, he expresses no mixed feelings about his honorary kin; he is wholly delighted with them. One of his honorary uncles Russ met only recently, yet he has considered the man his uncle throughout his life. "Forty years ago," Russ tells me, "he and my father were childhood friends. His name is Eddie, and he lives in Florida now. Last year I went down to visit him for the first time. We consider him our uncle. We call him 'Shuedoe,' which means, like, 'friend of the family.' They always said, 'Your uncle down in Florida . . .' So I decided I wanted to go to Florida, get a tan, and at the same time get to know my uncle down there.

"It was kind of strange at first, because he spoke just Chinese, Cantonese, and I didn't speak Cantonese very well. At first we didn't get along well, because of the language barrier. But after a while I would just sit down and he would tell me stories about China. He'd come to America when he was 16; he still has a wife and child in Canton who he still sends money to from his social security check, but he's never seen his wife since he was 16. He told me thousands of stories about China. I really miss him a lot, just from being with him those two weeks." To Russ, born in the United States, his uncle became a repository of his Chinese heritage.

"In Chinese culture," Russ explains, "if a person is good and they form good relationships with you or your family, they become part of your family even though they're not blood. Chinese people, because they're a minority in this country, have a tremendous unity. Chinese people have a strong family structure, but they also encompass people who have grown up with the family *as* family." An example in Russ's family is the woman he calls Bronxi-Pau, who was his grandmother's girlhood friend and whom Russ has known all his life. Indeed she is another grandmother, as her title reveals: "Pau" means grandmother, and the "Bronxi" is because she lives in the Bronx. "Every Christmas we'd go over to Bronxi-Pau's and have a party. And we were all one huge family; there was no other way of looking at it. There were also some Jewish Americans who'd married into Bronxi-Pau's family, and we consider them family too—there was no hangup about them being white or anything. We even called each other cousins. I look on them as being family, not just friends. If something happened to them I would really feel the loss. It's something that lasts. Maybe I don't see them all the time, but there's a feeling there."

Usually, it is the parents who bring the honorary relative into the family, and the children grow up with them. With one of Russ's family groups, however, the situation exists in reverse: Russ brought his friend into the family. "He's 22 years old, a year older than I am. We've been friends for ten years. We grew up together in New Jersey—we met in a Chinese organization. And since we've been friends, our families have become very close with one another. They come over at Christmas—Thanksgiving I'm going to visit his mother. We kind of joined our families together. Everyone went to his wedding. He really is a cousin, almost a brother to me. And now his wife is part of the family too—she's almost like a sister. It's incredible."

Russ sometimes uses kinship titles toward his honorary relatives and sometimes not. This is often the case: in my own experience, I never called any of those closest to me "Uncle" or "Aunt"; nor did my brothers. Conversely, as Raymond Firth, Jane Hubert, and Anthony Forge point out in *Families and Their Relatives,* a study of kinship relationships in a group of London families, the use of kinship titles doesn't always mean a real feeling of family exists. This is especially true in the case of children calling their parents' friends aunt or uncle: Christian names are deemed inappropriate for children to use toward adults, and the formality of "Mr." or "Miss" seems inappropriate as well. The authors report, "While the anthropologist may think that the use of the kin term implies that these people are thought of in some way as being kin . . . the parents deny this vigorously. Relatives and friends are different, and the use of the same words for each does not bring them together."[5]

Undoubtedly this is often true, but one has to wonder how much the denial is based on a concept of what the parent perceived *ought* to be, some guilty feeling that one *shouldn't* allow friends into the sacred category of kin. One story is especially interesting in this regard. A man whose mother died was brought up by her close friend. "I was very fond of her and called her 'Aunt' and treated her as badly as any son treats his mother . . . she was unique in my life . . . the center, the hub, the home . . . and I would feel that, as with my mother, I'd turn to her." But he did not think of her as a relative,[6] and it appears that both the "Aunt" and her biological family made a point of keeping their nonkinship clear. Yet his description is one of kinship in all but blood and name, and it is reasonable to assume that in a society that didn't make a fetish of those aspects of kinship, he might well have seen her as his true family.

Firth does, in fact, mention other cases in which familial friendship is recognized: "In several cases, a close friend was described by some of our informants as 'almost one of the family'; 'part of the family'; 'almost as close as a sister'; 'like a sister'; or called by a kinship term such as

'Auntie.' Or an informant said that 'a close friend becomes a relative,' meaning that 'one takes responsibilities for them as for relatives' . . . It is important to note that the friends were not equated with kin just because actual kin were lacking; most of the people concerned had brothers or sisters of their own."[7]

One such individual who is "almost one of the family" is Helen, a woman I met through a mutual friend. Her story is an unusual one, but in a culture that creates little room for nonparents to have important relationships with children, it is a heartening one. The "maiden aunt" of the past may be gone, but Helen has become a modern variant of that traditional figure. What is most interesting is that her relationship began not with the parents of the children, but with the children themselves. It was only after years of friendship with the children that she grew close to their parents.

If the folks who produce the soap operas ever decide to create a counterculture version of "General Hospital," they should consult Helen. Her story covers two communes full of people and is replete with the kind of incestuous marriage, divorce, and remarriage so dear to the hearts of daytime serial writers. Five minutes into her story, I had to interrupt her dizzying array of names. "If they make this into a movie, there won't be an unemployed actor in Hollywood," I tell her. She grins. "Yeah, sometimes it confuses even me."

Boiled down to its barest essentials, her story begins like this. She did some baby-sitting for a cousin who lived on a commune in the late sixties, and this gradually expanded to include regular child care for all the children on the commune. By the time her cousin had vanished from the scene, she had firmly established relationships with three of the children: Caryn and David, who were brother and sister, and Alec. Child care gave way to simple social visits with the children.

"Actually," she says, "I'd gotten to know David even before I started doing child care there. I ran into him and some other members of the household at a demo in Washington—against the war, for the Panthers, whatever we were demonstrating about in those days. There was a whole group of us, and there were just too many people for David, so when we went to dinner he came up to me and said, 'I want to sit with you; will you sit with me?' " It was a hard invitation to refuse from an earnest five-year-old, and Helen found herself growing very fond of her new dinner companion.

Eventually Caryn and David's parents broke up; so did Alec's. Caryn and David's father became involved with, and later married, Alec's mother. The newlyweds, Sarah and Danny, moved into a house, and the three children lived half time there and half time with their other parents.

Helen continued to baby-sit sometimes and to visit with the children in both households. Caryn, who was two, was having special difficulty dealing with the changes in her life. "She needed a lot of reassurance, more than either of her parents could give her. So she turned a lot to me. In a way, I was a constant for her—my place in the structure of her life was the one thing that hadn't changed. I still came in from the outside and spent a lot of time with her and the boys. Caryn and I developed a very, very special relationship at that time."

She was also very close to David and Alec, and especially enjoyed the time she spent with the children at Sarah and Danny's home. "After Sarah and Danny were married, it was really nice. Alec was also staying at their house part of the time, so it was the way I got to be with all three kids together."

Sometimes, Danny and Sarah would invite Helen to stay for dinner after she'd spent an afternoon with the children. But all of them understood that her friendship was with the children, not the adults. "None of us had any

sense that anything was going to develop out of this with
the adults. They were friendly and I was friendly. They
always very much respected my relationship with the
children—they thought it was lovely. I'd just go over to
the house a couple of times a week and play with the
kids, and very casually get to know the adults. It was
about five years before I got to the point where I thought
of myself as having a relationship with Danny and Sarah,
and it happened very much through my relationship with
the children."

Over the years, the relationship has gone through
the kinds of changes one associates with traditional
families. The children, now in their early teens, have felt
less need for adult companionship, and Helen has developed friendships and relationships apart from the
family that have consumed much of her time. Perhaps this
is the true test of friends as family: do you remain part of
each other's lives when you grow in different directions,
forming new interests and new relationships? Helen and
her family have. "I still spend my birthday and Christmas
and Chanukah and all that with them," she says. "I take
the kids to dinner and the movies, and I go to baseball
games with Alec—he loves the Red Sox.

"It's very much a family relationship—I don't know
when I started thinking about it like that, I guess maybe
five years ago . . . I've talked about it with the adults;
it's just seemed accepted. There are so many ways it's
more family than friends. There are certain kinds of conversations we don't have, there are certain ways we don't
push each other or raise issues that with close friends you
do, or questions about choices you make in your life.
It's very much like family in this kind of acceptance of
you regardless of what you do—whatever isn't comfortable
you just don't talk about. It's strange to think of being
in a relationship with contemporaries like that: I always
had that type of relationship with my parents. There's

also that close emotional sense of feeling like you can count on people. I have at different points stayed with them when things were going on in my life and I didn't want to stay alone . . . There's a way in which they'll always be a part of my life, even if I or they moved to California."

Helen has found a serendipitous extra in her honorary family in terms of biological family relationship. She does not plan to have children "of her own" (though she admits to an occasional fantasy of finding a permanent romantic relationship), and she is aware that this is a loss to her mother. "My mother doesn't have any grand-children, and would adore one," she says. Her mother has met Caryn, Alec, and David, and Helen talks with her about them often — "when Caryn learned to read, when Alec skipped a grade." This has created a kind of grand-motherly feeling in Helen's mother. "She was absolutely thrilled once when she spoke to Caryn on the phone, and Caryn, who was three or four at the time, called her 'Grandma.' My mother has adored her ever since."

People have sometimes expressed confusion about Helen's relationship with the children — often it's assumed that she's their mother, or at least their aunt. "I remember one time taking Alec out for breakfast at the Pancake House, and you know how those seats are sometimes very close to other people? There was this couple in their fifties sitting in the booth right next to us who were tuning in to our conversation, and at one point leaned over and said, 'Are you his mother?' and I said, 'No.' And they said, 'Are you his aunt?' and I said 'No.' So they said, 'Well, what are you?' I said, 'I'm his friend.' And Alec said, 'Yeah, she's my friend!' And they said, 'What do you mean, you're his friend?' I said, 'Well, I'm his friend, that's what I mean.' It took them a long time to believe that, that there was actually no blood relationship. And their next comment was, 'But you treat him just like a person!' I've had a number of conversations with people like that, when I've been with any of the three kids or any combination of them. I don't know if there's something in the way we relate to each other that makes it seem different from a baby-sitter or a family friend — a closeness that traditionally people don't expect from a friend of the family. David once got very indignant when someone practically insisted that I was his mother, and he said, 'No! She's my *friend*'—very protective of that relationship."

The problem perhaps has to do with the fact that these familial friendships don't have names—a fact that children seem well able to cope with, but outside adults don't understand. Nothing could illustrate the naturalness of the relationship between Helen and her young friends better than Caryn's bedtime chant. After her parents' divorce, Caryn was living with the mother and another single mother with a daughter. The mother was Anna; the daughter Louise. "Caryn was having such a hard time; there were all these insecurities about who people were in her life. To get herself to fall asleep, she'd go over everybody in the world and what their relationship was to her. She'd go to sleep every night saying, 'My mommy, my daddy, my Anna — no, Louise's Anna — my Helen, my . . .' And it didn't seem strange to her that she didn't have a name for what her relationship was to me. 'My mommy, my daddy, my Helen . . .' "

Caryn, at her young age, had not wholly absorbed the rules of the adult world. She knew, because her own experience had taught her, that "my Helen" was an authentic part of her family. Whether or not honorary kin are called "Aunt" or "Uncle" or "Cousin," they are genuine kin. They are the adults we grow up with, the people who frame our history. We may outgrow them, or grow in very different directions; we may find less and less in common as we grow older. But this happens in the biological family as well: many conflicts between parents and grown siblings come from precisely this kind of growth. But just as parents and siblings remain, for better or worse, our family, so do our honorary kin. They are an innate part of who and what we are.

3.

Workplace Families

At 16, I was homely, awkward, and horribly insecure. I went to a repressive and wholly alienating Catholic girls' school; at the end of the school day I ran home, got out of my uniform, and buried myself in a novel until bedtime. Books were my escape; the only glamour I saw was in the visits of Clair, our dancer friend, and she was part of a world I could never hope to share. I was thoroughly unhappy and lived in daydreams of some far-off future. There was little in the present that wasn't miserable for me.

Then Ti, the family friend with whom I had been closest in recent months, stunned me with a casual suggestion. He'd been working as a proofreader at *Newsweek* magazine for several years; sometimes they hired people for part-time work on weekends, and I was bright and a good English student. Why didn't I apply for a part-time job?

I was terrified, and horribly shy, but I eventually agreed to go for an interview. The night before, I was so nervous I cut a three-inch strip out of my leg, shaving. (My brother, watching me plaster Band-Aids on the streaming cut, was incensed: "You're using 3 Band-Aids!" he yelled.)

I got the job, working only "on call" until a regular spot opened up for me. At *Newsweek,* I entered the kind of environment I'd always dreamed of. The readers were a world in themselves, having little to do with the rest of the magazine. Most of them worked only part-time, chiefly Friday nights and Saturdays. This enabled them to do what they really cared about, and what they really cared about was a variety of artistic and intellectual pursuits. They were actors, writers, artists—old-fashioned bohemians, some cynical, some idealistic, all involved in worlds beyond the confines of the universe as defined by Mary Louis Academy for Catholic Young Ladies. And I was one of them. I was no longer the little girl listening in awe to Clair's tales of theater life; I was with people who regarded me as a slightly younger peer, people who didn't think I was crazy for not wanting to get married and have kids, people who were living the way I dreamed of living.

Like many teenagers, I kept a diary, and for the months following that first summer at *Newsweek,* it ran one long, monotonous, and impassioned theme. "It's Monday, I hate school, it's a week till I'll be at *Newsweek.*" "It's Wednesday, only 3 more days till *Newsweek.*" "It's Friday, school's over for 2 days and tomorrow is *Newsweek.*" "What a wonderful day; they're so wonderful, and I won't see them for another week." Other girls fell passionately in love with their boyfriends; I fell passionately in love with the readers' room.

Later, of course, I realized that the readers weren't perfect—there were neuroses, pettiness, a fair array of human failings. But what they gave me in my first few years there was something I could have gotten nowhere else. For the first time, I understood that what I wanted, who I was, weren't outlandish; there were real people living that way.

What they gave me in the last few years I worked there was even more important. I had moved into my own apartment, gotten involved in the antiwar movement and the sexual revolution, become a young—a very young—adult. When I graduated from college I became one of the four full-timers at *Newsweek*.

The others were all 15 or 20 years older than I was, and had been there when I first came to *Newsweek*. Ed was a quiet, shy man, handicapped since birth; he was in charge of scheduling readers (a hectic and time-consuming job, since readers were always in and out of town, in and out of performances or gallery openings) and as such the closest to "boss" in our little egalitarian haven. (The real boss, the first in a complex chain of hierarchy, was the chief Teletype setter in the room next to us.) Jane, a former actress, was a dignified, almost prim, spinster, whose sense of propriety was matched by her sense of humor and of tolerance. Dale too was a theater person, wandering in and out of directing and acting jobs; he was a practical joker and, though he was 20 years my senior, I called him my "kid brother." The office was a natural family, with Ed as the tolerant father, Jane the mother who had to sometimes curtail the over-exuberant kids, Dale and myself the occasionally trying youngsters.

The nature of the job lent itself to a growing warmth. We were separated by space and by interests from the rest of the magazine. The demands of the job were such that, when the work was coming in, which it sometimes did in mad rushes, especially on weekends, we were expected to work hard, but when it wasn't coming in we were under no constraints to "look busy." We read, wrote, and made phone calls during the lulls, but also we

talked to each other. Never with any obvious intimacy —
we rarely confided in each other or discussed personal
problems or emotional issues in our lives. What we shared
was homy, domestic detail. The school life of Dale's
son and what his wife had cooked for them; the opera
or play that Jane had gone to; the political rally I'd been
at; the call from Ed's parents in Pennsylvania — these
were asked after and thoroughly discussed. It made no
difference that the relatives in question were people the
rest of us had only slight or nonexistent acquaintance
with, that no one but Jane liked opera, that the others
disagreed with my radical politics. Our lives outside the
office were utterly different, but we brought them to the
office, sharing them with each other and ritualizing the
sharing. Other little rituals evolved. At one point, im-
mersed in English novels, I decided that we had to have
"tea" at 4:00. And so at 4:00 we had tea. Ed didn't
drink tea, and Dale was often eating his lunch at 4:00.
It didn't matter. Four o'clock was tea time because we
declared it so.

Tuesday morning was TV discussion time. Ed and I
always bought our *TV Guide*s in the little shop downstairs on Tuesday morning, and, since this was the beginning of our workweek, we had a weekend's worth of
TV to catch up on. Plots were dissected, performances
rated with great elaboration. When Jane switched job
shifts from Saturday afternoon to Saturday night, we had
to discuss Saturday-night TV without her. This was especially noticeable after "The Mary Tyler Moore Show" came
on and Dale, Ed, and I became great enthusiasts. Into our
office family moved the office family of Mary, Murray,
Lou, and Ted. Then, having analyzed past TV shows,
we'd settle in to read the current week's *TV Guide* and
comment on the shows we planned to watch during the
upcoming week.

Another of our rituals was the Logan *Daily News*,

the paper from Dale's home town which he brought in to us each week. It was full of wonderfully improbable names and parochial events: reports of the war in Vietnam were given only slightly more attention than the news that the Figgens boys had brought in rakes and hoes and cleaned up the old cemetery. We laughed at Logan, but lovingly; it became the surrogate home town of all of us.

And, though we rarely discussed one another's personal problems, we were acutely aware of them. If someone was depressed, an air of support and concern surrounded that person, unspoken but unquestionably real.

Sometimes, of course, we got on each other's nerves; sometimes we hurt each other's feelings. These times, too, we never talked about. But for the most part, we simply hung out together, chatted, enjoyed each other's company with an easy and casual acceptance.

When I left New York and moved to Boston ten years ago, the hardest part was leaving *Newsweek*. I needed a change; I needed to be away from Manhattan and my life there; I knew I was doing the right thing. I also knew I'd never have another job like my job at *Newsweek*, never have another family in which I was so loved and accepted, never spend every day in so comfortable and familial an environment. I was right.

Now when I go back to New York to visit family and friends, I make at least one visit to the readers' room. Ed, Jane, and Dale are still there. We chat for a while, fill each other in on news, tell each other all the old *Newsweek* gossip from a decade ago. Dale and I play little practical jokes on each other. They work, and I sit with them, reading a book, looking over the Logan *Daily News*. I'm always grateful to be home again, with my family, always aware that one day they'll retire or leave *Newsweek*, that the "home" won't be there to go back to. I wonder, at those times, if we'll still see each other when that happens. I hope, of course, that we do, and I think it's likely that we will, at least once a year or so. But if, for any reason, we don't, nothing is changed. If "family" has any meaning, it is that people have become woven into the fabric of your being—that they matter deeply, that they are a part of you. Separation is saddening, but it doesn't change that. Ed, Jane, Dale are my family. They always will be.

Ed, Jane, Dale, and I were a fine example of the workplace family. We spent long hours together every day for a period of years. We spent more time with each other than any of us — even Dale with his wife and son — spent with anyone else. Though in our case the bonding was one of "labor," in others the bonding is that of "management" — and sometimes, rarely, it can be a combination of both.

An interesting "management" family that I came across is one composed of two young women who, at first sight, seem unlikely candidates for the image. Claudia and Sally met six years ago, when they were in their mid-twenties and working together in a bookstore in a New England college town. Claudia was single and lived alone; Sally, the wife of an architect, had one daughter. They weren't happy with their working conditions, and complained to each other. "One day we turned to each other and basically said, we can do this on our own," says Claudia. They decided to take out a loan and open their own store.

"Getting to know each other better was a matter of necessity," explains Sally. She is the quieter of the two, an introspective and somewhat shy woman whose quiet friendliness contrasts with Claudia's exuberant gregariousness. "We spent so much time plotting about how to get money, how we'd work it out. Neither of us had ever done anything like this before, and we were pretty young, both in our mid-twenties." They took out a loan, bought a small store, and spent long hours over lunch and dinner working out the details of starting a business. Inevitably they talked about their personal lives as well.

It soon seemed natural for Claudia to be invited to Sally's house to discuss the business, natural for her to stay overnight or for a weekend. She got to know Paul, Sally's husband, and Flora, their daughter.

"They'd work late a lot in the beginning," Paul says, "and often I'd take Flora into town and meet them for dinner. And I'd come to the bookstore and help out when I had time—doing some rewiring, some construction for them. I always considered myself part of the business." Claudia laughs, "We used to call him the fifth Beatle."

None of them are sure when they began to think of themselves as a family. "It just sort of happened," Claudia says. "When you're working with someone that closely, that constantly, it's real hard to have secrets. You just tend to talk about yourselves, to share things. After a while Sally and I just got to the point where we couldn't remember that we hadn't always known each other."

"I'd start to say things to Claudia like, 'Remember when my cousin got married and . . . Oh, you weren't there,' " says Sally.

Claudia continues, "And I began to think of Sally in the same context that I thought of my oldest closest friends. You can't remember a time without the person, because you've essentially given her all of those important things in your life, verbally, instead of by her being there. By sharing all that stuff, you're essentially filling in that history that you wouldn't have had because you didn't grow up together or go to college together. But you've filled in the history so you understand all their references and know who all the people are."

"It's like marrying somebody from out of town," Sally adds. "You've got to catch up on each other's backgrounds. And it really *was* like a marriage in the beginning—we didn't have anybody working for us, and after a while we were working full time and it was just us, doing everything."

"And we started just naturally socializing," adds Claudia. "I lived in a crummy apartment, and Paul and Sally wanted to be with Flora in their house, so generally I'd come to the house. I still spend a lot of time here at the house. Paul will be puttering around the house, doing carpentry, Flora will be playing, Sally and I will be reading books."

Soon, Claudia began going to family functions with Sally and Paul—spending Christmas with them, going to graduations and weddings. Her own nuclear family lived far away. "It seems a natural thing to invite her to go to my family with us, and to other places," says Paul. Claudia and Flora often do things together themselves, but none of them see this as her doing child care: she doesn't do it to give them time away from Flora, but to spend time *with* Flora herself. "Sometimes," Claudia tells me, "I think I want to have a child of my own. And maybe I will. But being involved with Flora makes it less urgent. I often function as a relative, go to school recitals, things like that. My relationship with her, like my relationship with her parents, is something I see going on for all of our lives."

Flora, a serious, thoughtful ten-year-old, has no questions about Claudia's role in her life. "Claudia is like an aunt because I love her so much," she tells me. "She plays with me and she's important to me. I think I see her more than most of my aunts, because they live so far away. But I see my uncle a lot—he lives here. I feel closer to Claudia. I've known her since I was three." Flora understands that "family" is history and love. She has trouble understanding why I question her about Claudia, although she answers my questions politely. To her, her relationship with Claudia is obvious, a given. They are family.

As Claudia and Sally's business began to grow, it entered into what Claudia calls "the golden era." They began hiring people to work for them, and they hired people they were close to—Sally's brother, Claudia's boyfriend, a close friend both had worked with in their previous job. "Everyone who worked in the store was related by past history, intensity, in some combination or another. We spent time together outside of the store; we thought of each other in familial terms; and even used those words. It seemed like everything was always going to be perfect and tight and everyone was always going to be there for everyone else. I realize now that the situation had the seeds of its own destruction, by virtue of the fact that there had been past relationships and an ongoing lover relationship that were very touch and go to begin with, without adding the tension that was involved in a work situation. But at the time we all lived our work inside and outside the store and thought it was going to go on like that forever—the same kind of thing you have when families are particularly close," recalls Claudia.

Unfortunately, it didn't go on forever. Claudia and her boyfriend began having personal problems, which affected their office relationship, and as a result affected the office environment as a whole. When they broke up he left, and they hired someone new. His replacement worked out well, but it was the first "nonfamily" person they'd hired, and it changed the office atmosphere. As the business grew, they hired several more people. Sally's brother had long since left to go back to graduate school. And with their friend Toni, who had been with them since the beginning, they realized that a subtle shift had taken place: she began to see herself as less of a friend and more of an employee. They, on the other hand, were beginning to feel a slight strain with regard to Toni: they felt less free to criticize her work, to make employer demands on her, than they did with other employees. "It's still a friendly atmosphere, but it's different now, it's more business," Claudia says. "Partly that's just because it's logistically ridiculous—there's so many people working there, and the level of commitment is so different for Sally and me than for the others. We *own* the business—of course our investment in it is very different."

If "the golden era" has vanished, however, Claudia and Sally still remain a family—indeed the transition from "family business" to a more orthodox business has intensified their closeness. "We *had* to stay close," says Sally. "We *are* the business. Our commitment is the same; we're in the same position."

"Sally and I tend to function as a mutual support group, and when we lost the rest of the 'family,' we drew closer together," Claudia explains.

They don't, however, see the business as the only force binding them together. "The relationship may have been built and nurtured in work circumstances," Claudia says, "but I'd like to think that even if Sally and I weren't working together it would still be very important for us to be in touch. Sally is not just my business partner. These people on one level are my best friends, on another level my family. To lose my relationship with them would be cutting off a large part of what makes my life worthwhile."

Claudia and Sally may well find that their family relationship lasts long after they stop working together. My relationship with my workplace family has lasted; Kathy, my upstairs neighbor, has managed to keep hers as well.

Kathy, who is part of my own chosen family, does bookkeeping for a battered-women's shelter. Before that, she worked for several years as a typewriter repair woman. This job was, and is, considered to be in a man's field, and she felt isolated in the beginning. She became friends with another woman, also named Kathie, while they were training, though they ended up working out of different offices. They began a friendship that has grown out of their training together, one that has become strongly familial.

When she started working out of an office with male coworkers, it took a while to get close to anyone. When she did, however, she found that the barriers gave way to a warm and deep bonding. "The work was divided up so that you were in a group with about eight people, and you'd see those people most at work. We'd meet for coffee every morning and then call each other through the day if we needed parts, to see if the other person had the parts we needed. Sometimes we'd meet clandestinely during the day and talk about work. There was John, he said he'd never want to work for a woman and I got mad at that, but we were friends anyway—he respected *me*. I became friends with his wife too. They live in another part of town, so I don't see them so much now that I've left the office. But we go to each other's houses for dinner, and I'm going to the baby's christening next week.

"Then there's another friend, Dave—we'd go out for coffee a lot, and I worked his territory for a while. A lot of socializing went on at the bar after work. Because people live so far from each other, you get so spread out geographically that it would take a couple of hours to go to one person's house. When I want to see the people there, I just have to stop at the bar around 5:30 or so. They're the reason I was upset about leaving the job— I still miss them. I realize how much when I go back and visit them." She is happier with the work in her new job, but misses the people from the old. "The women here are nice, but so far I haven't felt that sense of family. And I miss that."

If Kathy found her family as a woman in a man's world, Mike found his as a man in a man's world, possibly the ultimate man's world—the army. In many ways, army friendships symbolize the worst of male bonding: soldiers are men linked by violence, whose loyalty to each other is inseparable from their training as killers. The mythology of the soldier-comrades has been glorified for centuries, celebrated in patriarchal literature and folk wisdom. Theirs is a relationship that mythologically transcends the love of a man for his wife or even his children, and for good reason: it reinforces his power over them, and gives him a peer whom he can love without contempt.

At the same time, the army buddies are often bonded together as "sons" against the authoritarian "fathers" who so completely run their lives. In the process of being trained to be more effective oppressors, soldiers are always being thoroughly oppressed themselves, and to the extent that, consciously or unconsciously, they realize this, their bonding can take on a more positive form.

Mike was in the army between 1964 and 1966, and he remembers his army family vividly. "Yes, it's a family atmosphere—it's the oppression more than anything that creates it. The more oppression there is the more people band together and serve all kinds of basic purposes for each other—the outgoing purposes of just going out together and doing things. They also serve the purposes of keeping people off one another's back . . . in basic training, everybody's in this big room, 30 or 40 people in bunkbeds, and you can't help but be in league with people, 18 and 24 hours a day. You come to know them very well; you either really like them or really dislike them. It's the only good thing I think the service really does. You can't go anyplace to get away from these people; you're forced to be there. It becomes a real family, it's the only family you've got, it's the only one you can trust. I think you develop as much love as you do for family, maybe more, because you have to rely more on each other. There has to be a good deal of emotional support. At times there has to be financial support—'Well, I've got $200 this month and you've only got $10; don't worry about it, next month . . .' and you'd never worry about it, it was never 'lent,' just 'spent.' Whoever had the most spent the most."

Did he feel as close to his army buddies as to his biological family? "It's closer. I get along very well with my mother, I love her, but there has never been any real closeness."

Mike and his friends were never in battle, and the major dynamic of their camaraderie was clearly a defensive grouping against their superiors. "We were stationed in Germany; five or six of us were radio operators, working for a man who had an IQ of 80 something. He was very dictatorial—it was the only way he could maintain his authority. And *his* boss, the top sergeant, was the same. So Wayne and Jerry and I and Chancy had great difficulty working with him. They decided that what they were going to do was to control us by making us pay attention to the minutiae that the army forces on you—the shined brass, the polished shoes, the wastebaskets absolutely clean—all that type of idiocy that you expect in basic training but not afterward. As a consequence, since we refused to do these things any more than we thought army regulations required, they'd pull a pass for a week, or two days, and we wouldn't go on pass, it was six months before we went on pass."

Since they weren't given passes to get away from camp, Mike and his buddies spent all their free time together sitting at a table in the enlisted men's club, plotting revenge on their "superiors." Their sense of themselves as a family, bonded against the senseless authoritarianism of their commanding officers, intensified.

Mike got out of the army two weeks after his friend Wayne did: the first thing he did when he got off the plane in New York was to call Wayne, who lived in a town outside of Boston, and tell him he was coming to Boston. "So Wayne drove 42 miles to the airport to meet my plane, and we drove back to his home and the next day he took me to Hingham, where I live, 65 miles away." They kept in close touch over the next few years, although their lives moved in different directions. Mike married, had a child, divorced.

"When I was getting divorced I went to Wayne and said, 'Look, I don't have any money.' I knew he was looking for something to do, and I knew he wasn't happy living with his family. He'd just sold an apartment building he owned, so he said, 'Look, I'll put up the money, you and I will buy a house and work on it, two or three years down the road we'll refinance it; I'll take my money back out, you'll take whatever you've put in it by that time.' And that's pretty much what we did. We bought this huge, monstrous, ten-room house, moved into it, and for two years we knocked down walls and rebuilt the thing. We converted it into two four-room apartments, one for each of us, with an office we rented to someone else. How do you remodel a ten-room house?" Mike asks rhetorically. "You have a glass of wine and plan it and the next day you do some work. Living together, it's like a family, because it's, 'What do you think's important?' 'Well, I think we ought to do this.' 'I think we ought to do that.' We'd scream and holler and argue—he couldn't do much work this time because he had to go somewhere, or I would do something, or one of us would say, 'You're not doing your share.' The same types of fights that any relationship has.

"But if we hadn't been in the service together, it wouldn't have been the same, we wouldn't have been as close. We operated on trust. The house was purchased in his name completely, and I was never mentioned anywhere. Theoretically, if he had died or something, I'd have difficulty proving that I owned anything. A year ago, we did refinance the house and changed the papers so that I owned one half of the house."

They still live in the house, with Wayne on one floor and Mike on the other. They spend a lot of time together. "When we're both home, we sit down and drink and talk about virtually everything. Even when we're not together, it's nice to know he's there—like if you knew you needed something you knew your parents were there whether you see them or not."

Like Mike and Wayne, Martha also worked for the government. But it was not there that she found her workplace family—indeed, the nature of her job made bondings impossible, and she took an early retirement to escape it and find a more congenial atmosphere. Her government job had been with a security agency, and she had been ordered to be circumspect about the kinds of people she made friends with; among others, people born outside the United States were to be avoided.

"I took an early retirement just to get away from that security; then I worked for the telephone company for three years to finish out my social security requirements so that I could get both the government retirement and social security. In 1974, I moved to California. People warned me that I might have difficulty making friends, that I wouldn't have any family there," she says in a soft voice, tinged with a trace of southern accent. She had only one sister living in Maryland at the time, and in any case she felt ready for a change.

Before moving, she had been on the board of a magazine for older people called *Prime Time*. In New York, at a board meeting, she met another board member, the president and cofounder of a California-based organization called the Alliance for Displaced Homemakers. "Then when I decided to move to California from Maryland I wrote to Tish and asked her where a good place to locate out there would be, and she gave me some very good advice and invited me to a little action they were having over in San Francisco on behalf of older women, which took place three days after I arrived. I took part in it and ever since I've been working with her on various things."

The chief thing she began working on was the Alliance for Displaced Homemakers. Later, when Tish and her friend Laurie started a new organization, the Older Woman's League Educational Fund, Martha began doing regular volunteer work for them. "They have their office in their home; it's a big old two-story house. The offices are downstairs and their bedrooms are upstairs, so it's really nice—you can go into the kitchen and make a cup of tea, go out and sit on the patio and watch the squirrels." She has come to regard Tish, Laurie, and Margaret, the office manager, as her family. "They're the friends I have the most contact with—they'd definitely come through in an emergency, and I wouldn't hesitate to call them. I'd also do the same for them. When they're away I feed their cats, look after their house, that kind of thing. When I had to have an emergency operation in January 1980, they took care of my cat, visited me in the hospital, brought me home, and in general did the things a family usually does."

Martha has other friends she considers part of her "extended family," and she is close to her sisters, but she considers Tish and Laurie her closest family members. She knows that they regard her similarly. "Tish had a birthday the other day and she got a telegram of congratulations. When she opened it one of us said, 'It might be from your stepson.' But she said, 'No, you're my family now.'

"In some ways I feel a lot freer with the family I have that's not a biological family. I can say anything to them and they won't be shocked or outraged or disapproving, whereas my biological family . . . growing up in South Carolina, we were all conservative until I somehow got radicalized along the way, so for that reason I don't feel free to express my opinions among them, as I do among the people that I've chosen as friends.

"I think the commitment level is pretty similar with my biological and nonbiological family. But my brother and sisters have families of their own that their first commitments are to, and I'd feel a little better asking for help from Tish or Laurie than from somebody from my biological family who wouldn't have the time or money to help someone outside their immediate family."

Although she lived with a man for several years, Martha has never married. "I'm kind of a loner in a way, and the fact that I have so many close friends now is surprising to me, really . . . I think I'm the type that really enjoys living alone. I love to read and watch TV; when I want to do something I go out. Maybe some people regret not having children, but I don't. And I have my cat; I don't think I could live without my cat."

Most of the people she's close to are also unmarried. "Margaret is married—she was a displaced homemaker, but she remarried two years ago. I've met her husband, but we're not really friends. Aside from that, I'm not friendly with any couples. Very often it seems to me that married couples kind of have each other for companions and don't socialize with other people too much. Or maybe they socialize with one other couple or two other couples. Then when the husband, which is usually the case, dies, or leaves, the woman is kind of left without friends. I think the husband is usually the one who wants fewer contacts with outside people. A lot of them seem threatened if their wives have a lot of friends outside the marriage."

She feels this has a destructive effect on older women who are single, especially those who have been married and suddenly find themselves widowed or divorced. "A single woman is usually not welcome with couples, and she hesitates to barge into other people's groups. We get a lot of letters from women in that position, and they invariably want to meet a man who is unattached and has all the right qualifications. They don't realize that there are an awful lot of women their own ages who would be very good company if they would just seek them out. But they're looking for that ideal man to replace the one they lost."

Working as she does with the problems of older women, she is acutely aware of the economic and psychological hardships the elderly face. But she feels that some of the latter are brought on by the people themselves. "I've been corresponding for a few years with one woman who wrote to us because she was very depressed. She's one of the older people that expect to get all their satisfaction from their children. And that's just not possible; it's so hard on the children. I think if older people would reach out to other older people—not necessarily exclusively—but people of all ages that aren't related to them by blood, it would be easier on their families and the families would think a lot more of them too. This woman is driving her children crazy. I guess because I didn't have any children I was forced to reach out to other people. My aunt was like this woman—she tried to get all her satisfaction from her two sons, and, eventually, from being so isolated, her mind began to go, and she would be calling them in the middle of the night and saying that somebody was looking at her home and people were after her, and they ended up putting her in a nursing home, and she's been there for ten years now . . . it's really sad; she just allowed herself to become isolated from everybody but her family, and her family wasn't enough . . . So many older people, older women especially, live in isolation, and would be much happier reaching out to other people, whether of their own age or not. I'm not too good with younger people, especially children, but some of the older people love children, and they'd enjoy volunteering in a foster grandparent program. But so many of them just sit at home and wait for somebody to come and give them some emotional satisfaction. And you've got to get out and do it on your own, you can't just expect people to come to you."

Martha doesn't "sit home and wait for somebody to come." She has made close friends in a bird-watching group she belongs to, and in her bridge club. But mostly she has her office friends, Tish, Laurie, and Margaret. She spends every Thanksgiving with them, and they take care of each other in emergencies. For Martha, that's enough. She has her family and her solitude — and, after years of working in a restricting, alienating government job, she is delighted that her family is made up of coworkers.

Martha was able to move from a job she found isolating and dehumanizing into a retirement profession that provided her with warmth and emotional security. Such a step requires a certain amount of financial stability and, perhaps even more important, mobility. Many workers have neither. Coal mining is a job that has changed very little over the years, and the familial relationships among miners described by Norman Dennis, Fernando Henriques, and Clifford Slaughter in Coal Is Our Lives is probably not atypical of coal towns throughout the western world today.

In Ashton, the English coal-mining town where the authors did their study, the miners form familial relationships with each other that are at once life-preserving and destructive to others. In some ways, their lives are like the lives of soldiers, without the glamour and conquest. They face danger daily, and together: bonding is a necessary survival method. The miners often "stick together . . . for years on end, sometimes for a score of years and even a working lifetime." Some of them work in teams, and often the entire team will manage to stay together for years, although their jobs come in on a piecemeal basis. "The strongest and most permanent alliances are between pairs of men, though sometimes three men will stick together for long periods." This creates a familial relationship between the "mates," and "solidarity . . . is a very strongly developed characteristic of social relations in mining."[1] They spend their free time together in the "clubs" in town, which function as their home. Their wives and children are rarely seen; socializing is done among mates.

The wives of the coal miners also have their jobs. They are, of course, housewives. Housewives—or "homemakers," as we now prefer to call them, upgrading the name while keeping the job unpaid and performed 24 hours a day—are traditionally isolated, and in the coal towns which glorify male solidarity, childraising is assumed to be a woman's job alone. In the town of Ashton described in *Coal Is Our Lives*, "housewives boast of their attention to the needs of their husbands, and of how they have never been late with a meal, never confronted a returning worker with a cold meal, never had to ask his help in household duties."[2]

Since husbands and wives share few interests and husbands are rarely home in any event, the families seldom entertain friends in their home or go out together.[3] Men tend not to share stories of their work with their wives, and women do not go out of the household to socialize: "No 'self-respecting' young woman will go into a public house unaccompanied by her husband or if unmarried by her fiance."[4] As a result, women's entire social and emotional sustenance comes from relatives who live nearby, or from neighbors with whom they develop familial ties. "Every day a woman will receive a visit from one or another of the neighbors, or she will make such a visit herself. The usual practice, in fact, is for a group of three or four to gather over cups of tea and 'have five' [i.e., five minutes, which can be stretched indefinitely]." The women will gossip cozily about their families and neighbors, and share reminiscences. "These customs of visiting and 'callin'' with kinfolk and neighbors are the limits of social contact for Ashton wives."[5] Many of the neighbors are old childhood friends, and it is significant that the book lumps "kinfolks" and neighbors together. Clearly, for the Ashton women, their neighbors serve the functions we associate with family far more than the men to whom they are legally bonded but from whom emotional support is rare and unexpected. The book doesn't discuss whether or not these women consciously perceive each other as family; it's probable that they don't. But it's clear that the neighbors function for each other exactly as their parents and siblings do; these are the kin with whom they share intimacy, warmth, and companionship.

Coal Is Our Lives doesn't much dwell on the childraising aspects of these women's lives — indeed, a quick reading might make the women sound as though they were living lives of leisure. However, since most of the Ashton miners and their wives had children, and since none had the money to hire domestic help, reading between the lines makes it clear that most of the socializing described in the book must have taken place with children in tow. The women who were chatting and gossiping with each other were also changing diapers, supervising play, and doing all the myriad chores involved in child care.

Certainly no other job involves so many people of so many different races, classes, and lifestyles as the job of childrearing. It would be difficult to imagine a lifestyle more different from the women of Ashton than that of Eileen, a middle-class, elegant, and close-to-affluent woman who lives in a fashionable suburb outside

Philadelphia. Yet her job for many years was the same job as theirs—that of raising children—and her workplace family, like theirs, was formed by neighbors.

Eileen is my friend Kathy's mother. She is a slim, blond woman in her mid-forties, the kind of woman who inspires remarks like, "This is your mother? She looks like your older sister!" She doesn't look old enough to have two kids in their mid-twenties. Her speech, her gestures, her movements are all wonderfully graceful; it's impossible to imagine Eileen ever being less than elegant.

Her house, Kathy told me, is like a little museum; be prepared to be enchanted. Arriving there, I *am* enchanted. The house is large, and Eileen has filled it, tastefully, with antiques, good prints and some original artwork (she herself paints well and there are a few of her paintings, attractively framed, around the house), and bargains that she has seen and liked and bought over the years. Her affluence came late: her father was an Irish state policeman in Maryland, her first husband a salesman with a middle-class income. One gets the sense around Eileen not of boastfulness about her lifestyle, but of a certain, and charming, savoring of it.

She sits curled up on her white couch, sipping her after-dinner wine, contemplating her workplace and biological families. "Family that are neighbors," she says thoughtfully, "are less judgmental than biological family, because they don't have all the background information on you that your own family does. When you were two years old and four years old you kept a terribly messy room and how can you expect your children when you're raising them to be any better than you were . . . that kind of thing. But when you have neighbors as family they're in the same circumstances, generally speaking, raising children. And people are more receptive, they're ready to tell you more intimate things about their children

that you can share with them. They're going through the
same things with their children.

"I've often thought that your family, that you spend
perhaps 20 years in a life growing up with, spending every
single minute, day in and day out with—even sharing
a bathtub with the other guys—you reach a point and
get married, and you spend the next 20 years with your
own people, your husband and kids, and you grow away.
Your parents are still there, but the siblings you spent
just 20 years totally intimate with, you grow up and you
have absolutely nothing in common, and they're gone,
except for ceremonial occasions. You don't discuss anything but the best of what's happening in your life, unless
there is a real emergency. You'd never share day to day
trials and tribulations with them."

For Eileen, a few close neighbors became her family
shortly after her marriage. As a young mother raising
children, she quickly found herself allied with Myra,
a neighbor whose children were about the same age. A
striking difference between Eileen's story and that of the
Ashton wives—even more striking than the difference
in class and affluence—is that although childrearing
was still clearly woman's work, there was much more
shared socializing between husband and wife, and the
result was that in both of Eileen's marriages her husbands
figured in her workplace family.

Still, childrearing was the central bond with both of
the "families" Eileen formed. The first of these families
was Myra and Herb. Though the initial relationship was
the close friendship between Herb and Eileen's husband,
Eileen and Myra quickly became bonded through their
childrearing. "We raised our kids together. When they were
little we saved our sanity by letting them play together.
We'd dress them up on a hot summer afternoon, completely
clothed with little shoes and socks, and they'd turn the

sprinkler on. They thought they were fooling us. We gave them three hours — it took them 45 minutes to sneak up, half an hour for them to get soaking wet, and the rest of the time they were afraid to come into the house because they were soaking wet and thought we'd be mad. And all the time we were sitting in the house watching them out the window, sitting and talking and drinking iced tea or iced coffee . . . that's the first thing we say to each other, even now, even when we only talk every three or four months — how are the kids? Where are they? To the point that Kathy, who's 24, last year ran into Tom, Myra's son, in a record shop in Boston. They hadn't seen each other since his bar mitzvah, when they were 13. He recognized her right away, and they got together — they're like cousins.

"Their youngest son, Tim, he's my baby. He wasn't in on the great camaraderie of the kids, since he was so much younger, but he was always my baby. One day we were driving in the car, all of us, and Tim suddenly asked Myra, 'What is Eileen, is she my aunt? Is she your sister? Is she *my* sister? Well, she must be *some* relative!' He was about four — it was a child's view of what was going on. We said, 'Well, we're just like sisters; I'm just like your aunt, because we're such good friends.'

"That was the first of my 'family,' and they still are. We don't call each other every day or every week or anything like that, but there's a remaining friendship we've had all these years. She lives in a different city, but I still talk with her three or four times a year. I go to visit my family's house, then I go to visit her. She often comes to visit me — she says that she'll go to any place I live at least one time; she gets to 'see the world' that way."

Eileen and her first husband divorced 15 years ago, and the divorce caused a breach between her and her friends. "I think Herb felt a little threatened, my being single." She laughs, a little ruefully, but without rancor. "So for about three years I talked with Myra from time to time but it really wasn't comfortable, because Herb thought I was a threat of some sort, probably because I was leading a marvelously romantic life—taking care of two kids, living on no money, and working every day from three till midnight."

She began dating Jack, her current husband, three years after her divorce, and at that point reestablished contact with Herb and Myra. "They were my dearest friends, and I wanted them to like Jack. I called them, and Jack and I started going out with Herb and Myra. And then we were back together. When they had their tenth anniversary they were in Washington. They called to ask if we'd help them celebrate their anniversary, so we drove from Baltimore. We got married that weekend, because Myra said, 'If you get married now we can always celebrate our anniversaries together.' "

As it turned out, however, Jack and Eileen celebrate their anniversaries alone. A few years after their wedding, Myra and Herb got divorced. Eileen has seen Herb only a few times in the 15 years that have elapsed, but still views him as family. "I have a healthy feeling that if I was in a bind, or if anybody in my family was in a bind, and thought to go to Herb, he wouldn't hesitate for one minute, he'd give any support he could."

With Myra, the tie has remained much stronger. "Even before the divorce, and after, Myra has come to visit us wherever we've lived. Before they were divorced, they brought the whole family to Minnesota, where we lived at the time, for Christmas. They brought their kids and made decorations, though they were Jewish and didn't celebrate Christmas themselves. And we went to their house for Seders. Myra's mother is Irish and her father is Jewish, and she was used to having Christmas celebrations till she married Herb, who was Jewish. And we used to have all these conversations about how she could have a Christmas tree but she'd have to hide it in the closet,

and then her mother-in-law would open the closet door
and find it. So they'd celebrate with us. Even when we
moved to Minnesota—that's a pretty far trip to bring your
whole family. In fact, our own families never came to
visit us."

In the meantime, Eileen and Jack acquired another
neighbor family. "After we got married we moved to
Annapolis, and met Nancy, who lived down the street.
It's hard to explain the feelings between Nancy and me,
except that we go back 17 years and after all these years
we're absolutely comfortable. And the kids meet, the kids
are wandering around all over, and they're running into
each other on trains . . . I was there last summer, and
Nancy said, 'Where's Chip?' And I said, 'He's in Santa
Fe now,' and her son Jimmy said, 'No, he's not; I saw him
on a train.' Jimmy knew where Chip was when I didn't."

Jack and Hub, Nancy's husband, aren't as close as
Nancy and Eileen, but Eileen still sees them as each
other's family. "They feel very comfortable with each
other. Neither of them would dash out and do anything
terribly friendly together, like Nancy and I do. There's
never been any deep intimacy between them—but they've
always felt comfortable with each other. And that's how
it is in families, isn't it? Not everybody feels intimate
with everybody else. Jack and Nancy aren't close at all.
Nancy and I are very close. We spent much more time
together than Jack and Hub did, or Jack and Nancy, or
Hub and me. Nancy and I both worked at schools, we
were both doing the same kind of things, and we both
got home from work earlier than Jack or Hub. We were
both dealing with the kids; we probably saw each other
daily.

"Last summer, I hadn't seen Nancy for three years,
and she called me in Philadelphia and said, 'Do you want
to come up to Martha's Vineyard with me?' and it seemed
perfectly natural for me to say sure and go up there.

She had two houses; she and Hub were staying in one house, and her kids, only they're all grown up now, were staying in the other. And the kids came in to dinner and to spend time with us casually, and Kathy came down from Boston for a few days, and they all came around when they felt like it, just like a family."

Whether the workplace is a big-city publishing office, an army camp, or a suburban home, it can create a family in its midst. When people spend daily time together, sharing a common chore, and when that time expands to many months or even years, bondings can take place that are deep and loving. They can be as nourishing and enriching as any biological bonding—and they can last long after the job itself is finished.

II.

Friends as Family

T he honorary aunt or uncle becomes absorbed into the nuclear family structure; the workplace family duplicates the traditional family in that it consists of a group of people who live together for the major part of the day and whose relationship is defined by that context. When the chosen family is living together communally, it also reflects in some way the structures of the traditional family. Perhaps this is why it has been the most acceptable, or at least the most recognizable, form of chosen family.

But when the chosen family consists of people who do not live together, or people who function as a family with some mixture of living together and not living together, we reach a new dimension of the nonbiological family. And, because of the very lack of a predefined structure, we also reach a dazzling array of forms. The genuinely chosen family is in relationship to the other forms of family as free verse is to formal verse. It isn't that it's formless—playing tennis without a net, as Robert

*Frost said—but that it is constantly creating its own form:
to switch metaphors, the chosen family is a custom-made,
not off-the-rack, structure. As such, it is the most revolutionary, and hence most demanding, form of family.*

*It is also the one that lends itself most easily to misuse,
to inauthentic definition. Advertisers know this, hence the
rash of commercials assuring us that such and such a bank,
or such and such a maker of cold remedies, etc., is a
"family." But beyond those glib and exploitative dis-
tortions, there is a reality, and a very exciting one. People
create their own families through friendships, and these
families are as real as those created through marriage
and childbirth, although they are usually not validated
by social or legal institutions.*

*Often they exist unconsciously, not even naming
themselves family. In* Single Blessedness, *Margaret Adams
observes that, among those she interviewed, "bonds of
reciprocity were in fact in operation but were not perceived as such because of the nonentity status of singleness
in today's society and its nebulous social role."[1] Many of
the people I interviewed for this book didn't think of
themselves as "family" until I spoke with them. I myself
didn't think of my friendships in terms of family until
one day in 1978, when my friend Kathy's boyfriend
told us he was spending Easter with his family, and Kathy
grinned at me and responded, "Me too." We had been
planning to spend the day together playing Scrabble, not
out of any sentiment for the holiday but because it was
a holiday we* didn't *care about, and we were treating it
like any other weekend day. Still, when Kathy said that,
it both moved me and struck me with the realization
of how true it was—in our two-year friendship, we* had
become family to each other.

*Sometimes, however, people do set out to create family.
Often this happens with people who are past 30, un-*

*married and childless, who are coming to terms with living
as single people in a coupled society. Not surprisingly,
some of the people I talked with who were consciously
forming families were lesbians or gay men, who felt that
their sexual preference not only precluded their living
in a traditional family structure in which they were the
spouse/parents, but also weakened, and in some cases
severed, their ties with parents and siblings.*

*For single people, the pressures are twofold. As
Margaret Adams notes, we do not have "clearly defined
and institutionally recognized ties that would give [us]
a claim on other people in exchange for [our] own
acknowledged reciprocal availability to provide support."
We are also made to feel "isolated or redundant."[2] Single
people—especially single women—are trapped in a
mythology created by a patriarchal, biological family-
centered society. We are either, on the one hand, soulless
singles, collecting impersonal orgasms and ruthlessly
climbing our way to the top of some high-powered
profession, or we are frustrated and neurotic old maids
whom life has passed by. Robert Brain, in his sometimes
insightful* Friends and Lovers, *laments "the hideous life
of the single person in a single room,"[3] presupposing that
such a person has no meaningful bondings with others,
that the price of "independence" is invariably isolation.
Michael Novak, in a 1976 article in* Harper's, *takes this
division one step further: there are two kinds of people,
he tells us, "individual people" and "family people,"
and never the twain shall meet. According to Novak,
people who choose to be childless do so in order to remain
children themselves—getting married and having children
are the only ways to become adults.[4]*

*It's a fascinating argument, containing the seeds of its
own contradiction. For if the only way to become adult is
to submit ourselves to an outside social force, then we*

*have not become adult at all: we have simply substituted
the family structure for Daddy. Novak is partially right:
our society does encourage us to remain children—not
by its discarding of the biological family, but by its
adherence to it as the only possible kinship structure.
Adults, by definition, are people capable of making
decisions, making choices. They are able to weigh, to
evaluate, to explore all avenues of possibility before
electing one avenue. They are governed by neither
their own whims nor outside authority in making such
decisions. The rationale of parenthood is, after all, that
a child on her or his own will act on whim and, hence,
until she or he has matured, must be governed by authority. The good parent teaches the child to learn the skills
of decision-making, thus leading the child into adulthood.
Without choice, and the skills to exercise choice wisely,
we are perpetual children, simply moving from one form
of childhood into another.*

*When there is no choice, there is no adulthood. Novak,
Christopher Lasch, and other apologists for the traditional
family have at bottom a cynical view of human nature: we
cannot mature, we cannot make intelligent choices, we
cannot do anything on our own other than gratify
momentary whims. Therefore, we must submit to the
prestructured discipline of the traditional family.*

*Many single people, however, do not remain infantile,
despite the urgings of consumerism: many of us have a
vision of human relationships beyond being swinging
singles. Unlike married couples, we do not have a mythology to tell us that we've found our one true "other"
and hence have no need to seek beyond the very limited
boundaries of that relationship. We do not see friends
as simply casual people to pass the time with when we're
not with our spouses or children. For us, except with our
parents and siblings, family is never simply a given state*

of coexistence—it's an ongoing choice. We take responsibility for creating our family, we work to maintain the relationships we value most, and we regard the breakup of a deep friendship as comparable in seriousness to a divorce. And we do this in the context of a world that defines us as Novak does—that sees all friendship as peripheral, that defines platonic friendship between man and woman as suspect at best and impossible at worst,[5] and that places married and unmarried people in antagonistic, or at best incompatible, roles.

Not all married couples, of course, buy into these definitions and limitations. Many recognize that their immediate biological family need not comprise the parameters of their relationships. They have chosen families, which include both married and unmarried friends. Such people are acting as adults: they are taking what is workable for them from the traditional biological structure and adding to it what is workable outside that structure.

So deep, however, is our cultural commitment to biological family that even some of those who espouse creating alternatives do so with a curious reluctance. Ellen Willis, the Village Voice *columnist who is one of the most lucid and original thinkers writing today, wrote a brilliant analysis of the patriarchal family and its hold on us. At one point, she says that she has made familial bonds with close friends, but that they aren't really as meaningful as the bond with her biological family: "The difference has to do with home being the place where when you have to go there they have to take you in—and also being (as the less-quoted next line of the poem has it) something you haven't to deserve. I have friends who would take me in, but on some level I think I have to deserve them."[6] This is a courageous and painfully honest observation, but I find it a somewhat surprising one, in light of the experiences of many of the people I talked with. Most loved their families but talked of having to justify themselves to their parents, to explain their life-styles, to pay for the love they received by accepting hostility toward the lives they lived. By contrast, they felt that their friends gave with no strings attached: a friend might disapprove of what you do, might even tell you so or quarrel with you over it, but will rarely demand that you be different than you are as a condition of being loved or accepted. Family—parents especially—are always faced with the difference between the daughter or son of their dreams and the person you have become, and the adult offspring is always dealing with the anger, disappointment, and expectations of the parent.*

Jane Howard, in Families, *is much more positive than Willis about chosen family, yet she too implicitly sees it as second best. "If our relatives are not, do not wish to be, or for whatever reasons cannot be our friends," she writes, "then by some complex alchemy we must transform our friends into our relatives. If blood and roots don't do the job, then we must look to water and branches."[7] "If the real thing isn't handy," she adds, "then maybe the ritual or the pseudo can fill the gap."[8] But often people don't turn to friends simply because biological family hasn't "done the job." For many of the people I spoke with, their biological families had done the job quite well—so well, in fact, that they wanted to continue and expand the process by including friends. Often these were people who had grown up with honorary aunts and uncles and saw the mingling of biological and nonbiological kin as natural and fulfilling, who knew that Aunt Mary who was Mommy's friend was no less a part of the family than Aunt Joan who was Daddy's sister. And the fact that so many couples and parents are also part of chosen families sug-gests that it is not merely the absence of biological family that creates a need or desire for alternatives. Often, to be sure, people do choose family because their biological*

*families have been unsatisfying or nonexistent; it should be
a source of reassurance for them to know that they are not
necessarily settling for second best, that what they have
is something sought after and shared by happy couples
and loving siblings.*

*What are the criteria for chosen kin? Again, like free
verse, they vary from person to person—from creator to
creator. In some cases, even people one hasn't actually
met can function as family. Barbara Smith and Beverly
Smith wrote an article in the magazine* Conditions, *focusing on the correspondence of a group of black
feminists scattered throughout the country. The authors
comment that "there is a sense in the letters that the
writers are family. We got this impression because of the
many inquiries about and references to other letter writers
in individual letters, the loving concern they express,
as well as their commonality of experience and vision."⁹
Most of the correspondents are college-educated, and most
are lesbians. As such, they form a small group of women,
often totally isolated from anyone like themselves, faced
with racism, sexism, homophobia, and, worst of all, the
interaction of all three—they are isolated by the sexism
and homophobia of many black men and women, and by
the racism of many white feminists. Interestingly, in a
time when the art of letter writing is almost nonexistent,
these women may well be the inheritors, or re-creators,
of a tradition historically white and middle- or upper-
class—the friendship sustained by long-term and highly
intimate correspondence.*

*Among most of the people I spoke with, however,
family-friends have known each other for some time.
There were two major criteria that were expressed over
and over again. The first—and, for most of the people I
interviewed, the most important—is that the friend is
someone accessible in emergencies. "If I got arrested I*

could call them up and they'd bring me a lawyer," says
Kathy. "In an emergency they'd be there without question," says Barb. "Anyone I consider family, I'd always
give them money if they needed it, no questions asked."
"You might bring it down to who I know would come to
my funeral," says Jane. Jane Howard writes: "It means
you can ask me to supervise your children for the night
you will be in the hospital, and that however inconvenient
this might be for me, I shall manage it. It means I can
phone you on what for me is a dreary, wretched Sunday
afternoon and for you the eve of a deadline, knowing
you will tell me to come right over, if only to watch you
type."[10]   One of the women interviewed in All Our Kin
told Carol Stack: "When I have a friend and I need something, I don't ask, they just automatically tell me that
they are going to give it to me . . . And that's the way
friends should be." Such friends are considered kin; two
women friends who care for each other's needs in this way
are said to be "going for sisters."[11]

The second criteria—for me, but not for most of the
people I spoke with, the more important of the two—is
history. Friends become family when you've not only
known each other for some time, but have been involved
in important parts of each other's lives. "The best chosen
clans," says Jane Howard, ". . . endure by accumulating
a history solid enough to suggest a future."[12]

A man interviewed by Margaret Adams says that "the
friends he has made in his adult life . . . are the most
important reference points for reinforcing his identity
of today, and his sense of personal continuity is sustained
by the fact that many of these later-made contacts extend
over considerable geographical distances and spans of
time but can be effortlessly renewed even after long gaps
in meeting."[13]

To me, this sense of continuity, of history, solidifies kinship more deeply even than the sense of availability in emergency. We grow and change; we move from town to town; we become involved in new enterprises. One of the most positive things the biological family gives us is a sense of stability in the midst of this change—a stability that, at its best, encourages change and growth, since we are not threatened with utter rootlessness if we dare to grow in different directions from those we love. The sense of a deep and permanent connection with people who have grown in different directions is essential for maintaining continuity: I exist in this moment and this place, but I am part of my own past and part of my own future, part of others' pasts and others' futures. We are thus bonded to those we grew up with—parents, siblings, relatives, and honorary relatives who were regular parts of our childhood lives. As we grow older, we create other histories: just as my parents and brothers have shared a time in my life on a level no one else has, so have a few key friends shared times that my parents and brothers, and other friends, have not. Such friends become a part of the fabric of one's existence: as the cliché goes, they are "in one's blood." It is lovely when one continues to share interests and enthusiasms with such friends, or with one's parents and siblings, and it allows the relationship to grow and deepen, but it is not essential to the continuation of the bonding. At some point the bonding becomes permanent— the absence, even the death of the other person doesn't eliminate it.

Love, commitment, continuity—these create deep and indelible bondings. Whatever the structure they exist in, they are the material of which kinship is made.

4.

Living Together

C hoosing one's kin isn't always a conscious process. For myself, as for many of the people I spoke with, it has been a very *unconscious* process — one knows and is close to someone for a number of years, and only gradually comes to realize that the relationship has become familial.

One of the most frequent ways that this can happen is when people live together. It is, after all, the fact of having lived together that creates the most authentic and deeply felt connections among members of biological families: there is a shared history that can transcend, or at least mitigate, personality differences and the distance created by later, unshared history. The same thing can happen in nonbiological families. People live together and over time become part of one another's lives. Unknowingly, they create a condition in which they are permanently connected.

Bob, Phil, and Larry are three men who have shared a house in Boston for ten years. Their living situation started out as a large collective, and has gone through several evolutions since then. What has remained a constant has been the three men themselves. What makes their relationship remarkable is that one of them, Larry, is a quadriplegic, injured in an accident the year before he moved to Boston.

They are friendly, open men, but, as the woman who suggested I contact them warned me, they had trouble understanding why I was interested in interviewing them. They see nothing unusual about the way they live. Nonetheless, they were more than willing to talk with me and, despite the fact that they were in the midst of renovating the house, invited me to dinner.

Their personalities are interesting, and complementary. Larry seems the least shy—used to handling with skill and humor the ill-disguised awkwardness of people not wholly at ease with the handicapped. Bob is gentle, almost diffident, with a slight New York accent and a wonderful, quiet sense of humor. Phil is handsome, strikingly so; he is open and pleasant, but there is an air of reserve about him that is noticeably different from the personalities of his friends. Like many people who have known each other well for a long time, they finish sentences for each other. Often, comments that start off addressed to me end up addressed to each other.

Originally, Bob and another friend, Andy, lived in New York; Phil was in the Boston area. Independently, they'd been thinking about collective living. "I was in my early twenties," says Phil, "and I was going through a lot of things that were forcing me to evaluate everything. It seemed like—not like the nuclear family wasn't good, but it was better to live with other people."

"Andy and I were working in Armenian activities in New York," says Bob. "We were doing a lot of different things, and there'd be a group of us going out somewhere working on something intensely and then going home to our separate homes. We always used to say that it'd be

nicer if we didn't have to say good night and then not
see each other for a few days, not have that separation."
The communal ideal never materialized while they were in
New York. Andy then moved to Boston to work with
conscientious objectors. A year later, Bob, too, moved to
Boston to work with Andy.

There they met Phil, who also worked with conscientious objectors, and they got to talking about living styles.
Phil remembers, "I said that I saw a closer relationship
with people as being more desirable. So Andy said, 'Gee,
so do Bob and I.'" As the talk became more serious,
Andy told him about his friend, Larry, who was living in
Florida, only recently out of the hospital, permanently
handicapped, and dealing with what he wanted to do with
his life. "When I got out of the hospital, I didn't want to
spend the rest of my life down in Florida with my
parents," he says. And Phil adds, "Andy said, 'Larry's
handicapped; what do you think about bringing him up?'
and we all said sure. None of us had seen this house
when we bought it. Somebody just said, 'Go check out
this house.' And Andy went and bought it—with Larry's
money."

Larry laughs. "I got a letter in Florida, saying 'Come on
up and bring up $12,000,' or something like that. I had my
sister, who's an architect, check it out. She said, 'It's a
sow's ear. It's a good house, but you'll never make a silk
purse out of it.'"

Sow's ear notwithstanding, they took the house. Along
with Andy, Larry, Bob, and Phil, there were two others in
the new collective. Of them all, only Bob had any reservations about caring for a handicapped man. "I was
reluctant to get involved in the nursing aspect of taking
care of Larry till I got to know him. It took me a while
to get used to it. Then eventually I became the person
who did it semiprofessionally. I'm getting some compen-
sation for taking care of him morning and night. But

there are times when I'm not here Phil will do it. It's
a matter of course for me now."

"It works in reverse, too," Phil points out. "I think
Larry in a sense takes care of us."

The commune went through a lot of stages, with different people moving in and out over the years. They
show me, a little ruefully, a series of "family photos"
taken every year for five years: the nucleus of Bob, Phil,
and Larry remains the same; the other faces change.

Phil recalls, "Andy had the perspective that 'this is
the way I want to live. We should all live together. I
never want to live with just one woman; I'll never do
that.' And he was the first one. He fell head over heels
in—he wouldn't call it love, but some kind of relationship.
He wouldn't say, 'I'm in love,' but he'd say, 'Boy, do I
feel strongly about Jan!' He was in seventh heaven for a
while." Andy eventually married Jan, and the two lived
in the collective for a while, but after the birth of their
first child, they found it too crowded, and moved into
a house nearby.

The collective never became as cohesive as Phil, Larry,
and Bob planned. "The relationships just didn't blossom
as they were supposed to," Phil says sadly. Eventually,
the household became just the three of them, and it has
remained that way for several years.

They have all stayed close to Jan and Andy, however,
and in many ways Larry has a more familial relationship
with the couple than with his two housemates. "Larry
spends a lot of time there getting his meals and going
to work with Andy in the morning," explains Bob, "and
the attachment between Jan, Andy, and Larry is closer."
Several months ago, Larry and Andy saw a large house
for sale in Jamaica Plain, and considered buying it
together. Then the owner decided not to sell. Larry
vaguely envisioned all of them moving in together, but

felt that he would still move in with Jan and Andy even if the others didn't.

Of the three, Phil seems least comfortable with the concept of their relationship as familial; he talks much more in terms of community, and one senses that he is more affected than the others by the failure of the collective. Interestingly, both Larry and Bob talk of other nonbiological families they have experienced. Phil doesn't. "I'm an only child, but I had a lot of aunts and uncles," says Bob. "I have a family tree that looks like a hedge. There were so many people I called 'Aunt' and 'Uncle,' and they weren't. They were either relatives that were too far removed to be related, or they were just friends." It's been only recently that he's learned which of his aunts and uncles were actually relatives.

Larry is very close with his older sister, Mary. He's also close with friends he sees as his family. "Your family's like another group of friends, and friends are like another group of family." He shrugs. "I have some friends that I went to college with—he was my roommate and she was his wife, who we met at a college mixer—and I can go any time to New York and stay at their house. Even though I only see them once or twice a year, we're really close."

None of them are certain if they'll remain living together for the rest of their lives. "Every once in a while your career goals or professional goals or political goals become a little fuzzy, or . . . Am I going to stay here forever, or would I like to live in New York for a year or two, see what that mad scene is like?" says Phil. Bob adds: "If a relationship evolves between one of us and another partner, that partner's going to be a factor in what happens in the relationship between us, in terms of our living situation. If there's enough room here, if it's compatible with that person, if that person wanted to live here . . ." He doesn't finish the sentence, but it's obvious that if the person *didn't* want to live there, there'd be a good chance that the couple would live someplace else. And, of course, Larry's already considered moving in with Andy and Jan.

Yet the fact that they are working so hard on renovating the house suggests that they plan to stay together for a while. And all three are certain that they have a permanent bond. "There are people in the world I have close ties with," says Bob. "I don't have to be living with them, but they're good relationships, intimate relationships, not in a romantic sense but in the sense of ongoing, lifetime commitments. And that would happen with the three of us, even if we weren't living together."

Among Bob's friends are two women, June and Rachel. June and Rachel also have a familial relationship, but theirs began when the two were college roommates. Now in their early thirties, they met in graduate school in Boston in the late 1960s, and quickly became friends. Indeed, their relationship is in many ways the classical "best friendship" that I've always dreamed of. June was raised Methodist in a small town in Pennsylvania; she is vivacious and wholesomely pretty. Rachel is Jewish, with a heavy Brooklyn accent and strong features. It's impossible, listening to them recount their history at June's apartment, not to think of Mary Tyler Moore and Rhoda. Like Bob, Larry, and Phil, they interrupt each other, finishing each other's sentences, clearly talking as much to each other as to me. Sentences that begin "she was" invariably end "you were."

June and Rachel met at a teaching fellows' meeting in a professor's apartment. There were doughnuts and coffee afterward, and both stayed because they "thought that would make a very fine lunch — neither of us had much money. So we struck up a conversation," June continues, "and she was saying that she didn't have living arrangements yet, she was staying with a friend. And I was just renting a room in an apartment that an older woman had. And Rachel said something like, 'Well, I have to be very careful about taking a roommate, because I'm taking my masters' exams at the end of this year and I really want to study very hard.' And I said, 'Oh yes, me too; I'm very serious about graduate school.' And so you said, 'You really have to be careful about who you room with because I don't smoke pot and stuff like that.' And I said, 'Oh well, I don't either.' And so we're sitting there and sitting there and you said to me . . .''

"I said," Rachel cuts in, " 'this morning I saw an apartment for $135, two bedrooms,' and I said, 'Do you want to live together?' and she said, 'Yeah.' So we went to the landlord and made the arrangements, and we walked up to the apartment, which was a dive. Unbelievable.'' Nonetheless, they took it, and they moved in the next night — 24 hours after they had met. "There was one dirty mattress to sleep on — so that Friday night we were sleeping together on a dirty mattress on the floor of this completely empty place. That year, from September 1969 to February 1971 . . . I have never spent so much time with the same person, and I never *want* to spend so much time with the same person, because we were totally inseparable. I remember once saying to June, 'You know, there's a good exhibit at the Boston Museum of Fine Arts,' and her saying, 'Well, maybe one time next week.' You know that it never occurred to me to go by myself? I also remember saying to June, 'I need some clothing, I want to go to Jordan's or Filene's.' And June saying to me, 'Okay, maybe in two weeks we can go.' It never occurred to me that I would go buy clothing by myself. I've never been as close to another person, and I never again will be — and I am legally wed. I don't spend as much time with my husband as I did with June at that time."

"We were very excited about being in graduate school," June says. "We were there to study, very seriously looking for the 'community of scholars.' But there was something more that was happening between us. I really did come in as the little midwestern girl — I'd won the American Legion Citizenship Award for work twice, and I'd read Barry Goldwater's *Conscience of a Conservative* and thought it was the greatest thing that ever happened. And then I ran into this socialist New York Jew, and other socialist Jews like Howard Zinn, and the war was on, and I went through this tremendous change of consciousness and Rachel sort of filled in the gaps in my consciousness. What was going on with me wasn't just reading what was going on in the newspapers or watching it on television; Rachel was right there filling in the gaps."

Their little apartment became a home for them, a place in which they shared food, money, and intense political conversation. "We had one hot plate and we had a pan and we ate all our meals, tuna fish and soup meals, out of one pan together," recalls June.

"I remember very clearly feeling, 'We have a home together,'" says Rachel. "I remember painting the kitchen orange like it was yesterday. It was the fantasy of some day you'll meet somebody and you'll have a home together. We bought a tablecloth that matched the wall — it was very schmaltzy. At the time none of this was fitting into the traditional structure, because neither of us was married, going with anybody, or, to be perfectly honest with you, interested in that kind of relationship."

What they *were* interested in was the approach to sociology they'd just discovered — the C. Wright Mills idea of the Sociological Imagination. "It was a time when the country was turned upside-down," says June. "We were in academia, which we simultaneously hated and wanted to be part of; we were rejecting everything around us. Sociology was going to be our ideology, our religion. People in the sociology department were studying things like how do people ride bicycles and how do they act in zoos and how do they give directions to taxi drivers. And we weren't going to do that kind of stuff; we were going to study social issues. And it was sharing that perspective on our work that really made a bond between us." Rachel picks up the thread and continues. "At the same time, I think that there was a really instinctive womanly sense of what life is all about . . . I've been reading Mary Daly's *Gyn/Ecology,* and she talks about sisterhood, the feeling when a woman meets a woman and feels like she's known her for her whole life – I think there really was that between us. There was the idea stuff, but also there was an appreciation of – the orange kitchen. We would just paint the kitchen orange and go, 'Wow, look at this kitchen, nobody's got a kitchen like this, this is so warm'; and we'd just go on and on about it."

After they had lived in their tiny apartment for nearly a year, Rachel came home one day, excited about a conversation she'd had with a professor in political science who was doing research on housing projects. "I liked him, and I was incredibly excited by what he was doing. I was raised in a housing project; I was used to a lot of people, a lot of families, a lot of nonfamilial aunts and uncles around, that kind of thing. This was my turf."

"So," says June, "one day she came home from school and she looked at me and said, 'I'm going to do the definitive community study' – everything is always 'the definitive' – on housing projects – and I'm moving into a project.' And I said, 'Fine, we'll go.' I couldn't imagine that she'd go anywhere without me, so I just assumed that I was going along."

June had a work study grant for the summer, so they both moved into a project and lived among the women they were studying. "At that time," says Rachel, "we had no specific interest in women. But housing projects are, for the most part, communities of women and children. And so the networks that we became absorbed in were networks of women and children." They became especially

close to two of the women, who were a few years older
than they were — "so close," says Rachel, "that at the
end of the summer we didn't want to leave them." They
went back to school, but kept up their relationships with
the women in the project. "We drank gallons of coffee
sitting in each other's kitchens; we'd stay up late at night
together and see each other in the morning . . . If they
weren't in our kitchen we were in their kitchen. It was
like a marriage, us to that community: at that time it was
just what we needed. All we had to do was *be,* we were
accepted. They liked us because we were 'good kids.'
We weren't hippies; we weren't like typical college kids.
They were very protective of us."

During this time, however, the first break in the relationship between June and Rachel was beginning. June
fell in love. She married her boyfriend, starry-eyed and
certain marriage was going to be heaven on earth. "I made
the grand mistake that all women make — I shut out my
best friend. I shut out everybody. It was me and him.
Needless to say, that put an incredible amount of pressure
on my relationship with him, as well as hurting Rachel."

"It was terrible for me," says Rachel. "I felt abandoned,
I felt angry. Also, I had at that time no longing for a man,
and I didn't understand why she wanted to get married.
I didn't understand what she had with him that she didn't
have with me. We weren't lovers — we've never been lovers
— but even with that, I still didn't know what she had
with him that she didn't have with me. I remember saying
to June, 'When a man meets a woman they have a ceremony, and if there was a ceremony for best friends I'd
be glad to have that ceremony with you, because I don't
want anybody else.' "

Feeling abandoned by June, Rachel moved into a
commune shortly after her friend's marriage. The two
were still in touch, and occasionally June turned to Rachel
during crisis periods in her marriage. But as her marriage

deteriorated, she felt that the tables had turned, and that Rachel had now abandoned her for the commune.

Rachel, meanwhile, was finding that communes are no more made in heaven than marriages are. By the end of three years, June had left her husband, and Rachel was on the verge of leaving the commune. June decided to go to England and study women in a housing project there. Rachel went with her. Once more, they were living together in one small room. "It was a joyful reconciliation," says Rachel. They had weathered a crisis together and were still as close as they had been earlier. They had grown individually; they had become aware of feminism and its importance to them as friends and as individuals.

They also discovered that some things had changed for them. "We were lying in bed one night, and we were having this conversation about love and marriage and men, and the future and desires," says June. "I felt like, 'I've been married, and it's no big deal — there's nothing out there that we don't have and I'm perfectly content with you.' And Rachel very clearly stated that one of her goals in life was to be married and have children, to have a committed relationship with a man."

When they came back from England, June moved into an apartment alone, and Rachel moved back into the commune for a time, then into an apartment by herself. "I think it's very significant that we didn't move in together, that June wanted very much to be alone," says Rachel. They were still very close, but some boundaries had been drawn.

The boundaries grew as their lifestyles changed. June became more and more involved in radical feminism, and had no interest in marrying again or in living with a man. Rachel met and married the man who is now her husband. "I felt abandoned," says June.

Rachel responds, "Yeah, abandoned, and mad. I remember a very intense confrontation where I said something to you about 'I love him,' and you said — which is etched in my memory — 'I understand that you love him; I just can't imagine why.' Which is exactly what I'd felt about *her* husband."

Unlike June's marriage, Rachel's has been successful. Recently, Rachel had a baby daughter. June is happy for Rachel, but the two are having to face the fact that their lives have moved in different directions. They are no longer the two friends sharing a mattress, a frying pan, and the same dream.

Rachel feels somewhat isolated from the women's community that is the focus of June's life. She is a feminist, but one who needs "to be with other married feminists, with other mothers — where I can talk about my feelings about my husband and child with women who are living similar lives.

"When I was first married, I had this thing about how June would marry and she'd live next door to me and we'd raise our kids together — I'd make her husband convert . . . it was a joke, but . . ." But the joke was serious, and she'd lost a part of her dream.

"In the course of these changes — being married, not being married, all that — we had to sort of come to the conclusion that, although we've known each other over ten years, that while there's a lot of sharing and while you share a lot with people, you're also alone."

With that realization, they seem to have reached a new understanding of their relationship. They remain remarkably close. Shortly before Rachel's marriage, she felt an intense need to explore her Jewishness, and she wanted to go to Israel. "I wouldn't have her go to Israel for the first time and see it without me — I had to be there when she saw the homeland," June says — and so the two went together. Later, after Rachel's marriage, her husband was considering moving permanently to Israel. She eventually decided that she'd go with him if he went, but Rachel wasn't sure at first if she would be willing to live that far from June.

Though Rachel and her husband didn't move to Israel, clearly June and Rachel no longer assume, as a given, that they'll live in the same place. But they do assume that they will always be important to each other. "Yes, absolutely, we'll always be in each other's lives," says Rachel, "as other people in our lives come and go. I don't feel that my marriage will break up, and I feel this is just as solid. Absolutely as solid. June will always be my best friend."

There is something delightful in the stories of women who become each other's families in college — something reminiscent of the women in the eighteenth- and nineteenth-century boarding schools. Often it is the first time a woman has lived away from home: there is a heady, exciting sense of beginning life anew, full of dreams and ideals. The sharing of these dreams, of that experience, lends itself to a bonding that can last a lifetime. That happened with June and Rachel, and it happened with Cyndi and her friends.

Cyndi is a career woman in her early thirties — a high-energy, active woman who is single and unsure about whether or not she wants eventually to marry. She has a good relationship with her parents and sister. She also has another family — four friends she met in college: Betty, Sharon, Mary, and Elaine.

"I have no idea if this was something everyone went through at the time, or whether this was just me and my friends," she says. "I went to a hip-radical college in Boston in the late sixties and early seventies. That was a period of time when there was a lot of experimentation, a lot of falling away from one's own nuclear family because there were a lot of us doing things that our families were opposed to — a lack of communication which meant that you didn't really go to them for support without the other things being held over you . . . So a group of us formed; I guess we added to each other one after another after another — but the entire group was intact by junior year. Myself and my roommate, the two women in the room next to us, and eventually one more person was added.

"To this would flit in and out various lovers, a couple of other friends who came closely into the family for a while and then drifted out. But the nucleus was the five of us. Four of us were the bridesmaids of the first one who got married — it was that kind of situation. We weren't necessarily all together as a group all the time, but ultimately we did everything together. I spent so much time with Mary that people referred to us as 'Mindi' and 'Sary.'

"We went in and out of liking each other, being angry at each other; there was a lot of growing, of realigning of 'best friend' — that category would tend to change over time. But there was a general feeling of 'we are a unit no matter what else happens, no matter what we do in our individual lives.' "

The ties didn't end after graduation. "It got a little bizarre. At first we all lived in an apartment together. Sharon broke up with her lover, and Mary started seeing him; eventually they got married. Then Mary and I quarreled over this man, because I hated him with a passion. So Mary and Sharon and this man moved in together. I moved into an apartment with Betty. Elaine was in law school in Pennsylvania, but she'd come to Boston to visit, and we were still all communicating.

"The triangle of Sharon and Mary and Phil wasn't working out; Mary and he were fighting all the time. Sharon couldn't take it and she moved out."

There were various other shifts in living arrangements over the next few years, and finally, in 1976, Cyndi, who'd found her life moving in different directions from the lives of her old friends, moved into an apartment by herself. Others began moving to different parts of the country. "But there's never been a time when we haven't been communicating with each other, at least secondhand. People will call each other, and get news of the others — somehow, between us we always know what's happening to everyone. For a while I went to Sharon's home every year for Christmas — her family kind of adopted me when my parents weren't speaking to me. We've always assumed that if there's anything major going on — births, deaths, weddings, crises — there'll be a reunion. And we'll all either be there or check in to see what's happening if we can't be there. And every time, there's some kind of realigning or redefining the interrelationships between each of the individuals in the group.

"Out of the last reunion, which was an extremely chaotic crisis situation, I reestablished communication with Mary — she's still married and has two kids — and with Elaine. Elaine and I, who never went through a strong 'best friend' period, seem to be going through that now because we have more in common. Mary and I, who *don't* have a lot in common now, have established a different kind of friendship. There's the same kind of caring among ourselves that there was before, under what seem to be totally different terms.

"I'm the only one in the group who keeps in close touch with Betty, who's married now and lives out on the West Coast. But it's a standard thing that when people call me up they ask if I've heard from Betty, what's she doing. Even if they don't perceive themselves as close to her, it's important for them to know how she's doing, how things are with her and Mike, do they have kids — the basic catalogue of important things.

"Yes, I think it's safe to anticipate that this will last for quite some time, given how long it's already lasted. There's just too much shared experience, from a formative time in our lives. In some ways it's a perfect example of what happens in regular families — the kids grow up and move away, they get together at reunions, they write letters, and when there's a crisis the support is there. And every once in a while something will happen, someone will move closer. You've always got to catch up on the *basic facts,* but not on who you are. And in a way, that's ultimately what the family has.

"When we were in college, we really had a sense of future history. I recall actually starting to write a novel based on our relationship with each other — I'd been influenced by reading Mary McCarthy's *The Group* — and projecting it into the future, because we all had a sense that this wasn't a transitory 'Well, we're living together this year and then we'll all go on and do what we do' — it wasn't a frivolous concept. We had this sense that we had chosen each other as a family, and that concept was actually discussed, though it wasn't made a big thing of.

"Since that time, people have married, people have divorced, people have developed networks of friends that have nothing to do with the five people we're discussing here. But anyone who's ever been important to any of us, it's almost as if the rest of us have known them by proxy. It's sort of nice knowing that you're intertwined with other people that you don't even know.

"The difference between friends who are family and friends who aren't — it's not in how much you see them. It's a question of, if I was really desperately in need, if I really needed support, these are the people I would go to. And if any one of those people reached out to me and needed me for something I could do something about, I'd do it. If Betty called me from California and told me something cataclysmic was happening in her life, I'd scrape up the money and go out there.

"There are people that are friends that I don't think of in those terms — there hasn't been enough shared experience. They're people I would trust, people I would take to; they're people whom the depth of friendship might over a period of time turn into family. I guess what it is is that a close friend is the embryo of an extended family."

5.

Families Whose Members Don't Know Each Other

The concept of "friend as family" came late to me, though in a way it had been part of both my fantasy and my reality for a long time. Growing up with Ti, John Paul, Clair, Gene, and the others, I lived in a world of both biological and nonbiological family. And my chief daydream for years — while other girls were dreaming of marrying and having children — was that I would have an exciting career (which went through various incarnations, from trapeze artist to nurse to lawyer to playwright), and live with a roommate in Manhattan. I had no doubt, in my fantasy, that my roommate and I would live together forever: we would spend our days doing marvelous work and our evenings in our cozy, comfortable, domestic apartment. It never occurred to me, in my childhood, that roommates were ever anything less than devoted and comfortable lifelong companions.

My image came not from real life — real life was parents and kids living in a house in Queens — but from George Bernard Shaw. I had read *Mrs. Warren's Profession,* in which the prostitute's daughter, Vivie, ends up leaving her mother's home, rejecting the proposal of her respectable and attractive suitor, and settling into a business-and-living partnership with her friend, Honoria, determined to remain a spinster and a businesswoman forever. Several years earlier I had read the Alcott books, which had provided, in different ways, images of women living together in busy, active, comradely lives — especially one amazing scene in *An Old-Fashioned Girl* in which a community of artists shared their lives — and these, combined with the more adult vision of Vivie Warren, set my image of the "family" I wanted.

Except, of course, that I didn't see it as "family." Indeed, that was part of its charm. To me, "family" meant stagnation; it meant being a housewife who never read books or discussed ideas; it meant changing endless successions of diapers and getting kids ready for school and raising them to be mothers who would spend *their* lives changing diapers and shunning intellectuality. For the same reason, "love" didn't appeal to me: it sounded very pretty and nice, but its upshot, at least in the movies and on TV, was that you got married and had kids — the romance was transitory, the dreariness eternal.

I was too young, of course, to recognize what was *good* about being part of a family — to recognize that, although my parents might not "understand" me (and I really did believe I was the only kid to have ever come up with that concept) they did give me the kind of security that was essential to emotional survival. Nor had I any inkling that my dream of happy-ever-after with a roommate and job was at least as romantic as my friends' dreams of Mr. Right — that I had constructed for myself a fantasy as unreal as the world of *Father Knows Best,* which my mother so loved and which so terrified me. I refused to believe our friend Clair when she told me that her career as a dancer didn't make her totally happy and that life with a roommate wasn't always wonderful. And it certainly would never have occurred to me that a woman could marry, have children, and have other interests as well. My vision of "family" was bounded by the parameters of 86th Avenue in Queens, New York, and I wanted no part of it.

I had no idea that my desperate dream of "belonging," of being a part of some group of intellectuals, of living with a roommate, had anything to do with a need for family. My narrow definition of family would have gladdened the hearts of the Moral Majority. "Belonging" was something different, something outside of the banal world of family.

Yet when I graduated from high school and joined Queens College CORE, what I longed for with my fellow civil rights workers was *precisely* family – a group of people working together for a common goal, forming a tight, loving, mutually supportive unit. For a while, with a few of them, it almost became that – though we were never as tight as Cyndi's group, and the fragile bonds dissolved quickly enough.

One bond remained, though. In spite of my dedication to spinsterhood, I fell terribly in love with Mark, and it was a grand, soap-opera passion, at least on my part. I managed, in some vague and undefined way, to combine my two great dreams. Mark and I would never marry or have kids, but we'd stay together forever, working for civil rights, being each other's mainstay and support. I substituted lover for roommate in my grand dream. But the great romance went the way of many great romances, and for all my images of tough independence I was as crushed as the silliest heroine of the soaps my mother always watched. Nonetheless, Mark and I kept running into each other on campus, and slowly we became friends, then close friends, then very close friends. At what point did we become family? I don't know, but I do know that when Mark moved to Boston two years after I did, part of his reason was because I was here. He's lived in the same building I live in for nearly a decade now; we know each other probably better than anyone else knows either of us, because we've been through fifteen years of each other's crises, and joys, and ambivalences. What's the name for what Mark is to me? Ex-lover? Dear friend? In the limited familial terminology that exists, I suppose he's "just like a brother to me." But none of those are really accurate; he's more than an ex-lover, more even than a dear friend, and my feelings for him are different, though no less deep, than those I have for my brothers. I think of the little girl, Caryn, with her litany of the people in her life: my mommy, my daddy, my Helen. Mark is my Mark, he's a piece of my life: he's family.

In 1977, I went through what is popularly called a nervous breakdown: I was at times suicidal, at times simply self-destructive, carving into my arms with pins and razor blades. I knew I needed help, and I knew I didn't want to be institutionalized. I started making phone calls to friends, and the outcome was astounding. A flexible, flowing group of people, some close friends, some near strangers whom I had met through the women's movement, networked to take care of me. Almost every day, for three months, at least one caretaker was with me. I wrote an article about the experience for *Ms.* magazine, and they used it as part of their "family" series.

I hadn't thought of my caretaking network as family until then, and as a whole, I still don't — it seems in a way more of the equally important, but less intimate and less emotionally committed, concept of community. Some of the people I've rarely seen since those days, others I see occasionally as friends. A few have become my closest friends.

But the *Ms.* idea did start me thinking about friends as family. And when I began to do a book on friends as family I had to ask myself who *my* family was. Kathy had already made her Easter remark, and I knew she was my family, as I knew, the minute the question posed itself to me, that Mark was. Who else? Steve, whom I've known for ten years, who's also a close friend of Mark's. We've been through a lot together, and though our lives have gone in very busy and very different directions, and we see each other only a few times a year, he's certainly family. Lisa is, and Molly and her husband, Christopher, to a lesser extent. And the other Steve, New York Steve.

New York Steve I met in 1970, when I was living with his best friend, Larry. There was an instant warmth between us, a warmth that has lasted and grown for years. When I broke up with Larry in 1971 and told Steve that seeing him reminded me of Larry too painfully and that I needed to be out of touch for a while, he was sad and a little hurt, but totally understanding. Strangely — and for me this is a key to which friends are family and which aren't — we both had a deep confidence that it *was* only for a while, that though we'd both gone through many transient friendships, this wasn't one of them.

I moved to Boston, Steve moved to California; sporadically we wrote, phoned, or sent cassette-letters. Steve married, divorced, moved back to New York, remarried. We see each other three or four times a year, usually when I'm in New York for a few days. Recently, I've begun staying with him and his wife, Lynn, when I go there. Last spring, Steve and Lynn gave me keys to their apartment to keep permanently. There was something about the gesture that seemed very moving, very significant — possibly because I was working on this book, dealing with the question of who my family is. I said something about it to Steve. He looked at me, surprised. "Of course, you're my family," he said. "I've known that for years."

Lynn and I have slowly formed an independent friendship; we're moving from the "in-law" stage into a genuinely familial relationship of our own. Their apartment has become "home" in New York to me — both crash pad and haven.

Kathy was one of my caretakers during my breakdown. Before that I'd hardly known her. She, Lisa, Molly, and I were in a study group together at the time, and they were all among my chief caretakers. A couple of years ago an apartment became available in my building and Kathy moved in. Like Mark, she made the move in large part because I was there. Kathy's twelve years younger than I am, but in some ways much older. We switch family "roles" as the need requires, but her temperament is much steadier and more reserved. More often than not, she's the mommy to my somewhat irrational little girl. With her, I have something close to my old roommate ideal — probably because we don't actually live together. (Roommatehood, alas, turned out to be less blissful than my childhood daydreams led me to believe, and over the years I've acquired a strong predilection for living alone.) We have in some ways the best of both worlds — the solitude we often need, the companionship we often want. We see or talk to each other almost daily, if only for a few minutes. Sometimes when we're both working at home, one of us brings her work to the other's apartment — more often I go upstairs, since Kathy's an art student and usually working on a painting. We feed each other's cats when one of us is out of town, and each other's egos when we're both in town. We drink a lot of tea together.

Other friends I'm not sure of. Is JoAnn, my "best friend," also my family? Bob and Claire? Robert? Maybe. It's not that I question my feelings for these people, or theirs for me. I'm just not sure where I draw the line. Partly it has to do with mutual definition — I'm not sure if they think of *me* as family, if they have the same sense of commitment that I have to the idea of being family. (Yet Larry, my boyfriend of ten years ago, I *do* consider family, even though we don't get along when we're together and I haven't seen him in years, and I doubt that he thinks of me as family. But we share a history, and our closeness to Steve keeps us in some way bonded.) To some extent, I think my own definition has to do with an assurance of continuity, not just in the past but in the future. The people I think of as family are people I'm sure I'll feel bonded to as long as I live, people who, although we may not see each other often, will always be a part of my life, my current frame of reference. And for the most part, they're people with whom that continuity has in one way or another already been tested.

What is in some ways most interesting about my family is that, unlike biological families, they aren't family to each other, except for Mark and Boston Steve, and, of course, New York Steve and Lynn. Mark and Kathy are cordial neighbors, but not friends and certainly not family. Neither they nor Boston Steve have ever even met New York Steve. Neither Mark nor the two Steves are friends with Lisa or Molly. Kathy sees both Lisa and Molly as her family, but she doesn't see Molly's husband, Christopher, as part of her own family; I do see him as part of mine. This seems to happen often in chosen family situations, especially as people grow older, change life situations, and meet new friends in new contexts. Some of those friends become family; others don't. There are thus many intersecting families, in which each person is the radius for her or his own family.

A woman who has had such a family for many, many years — since before I was even born — is my friend Maud. Maud is a reserved, quiet, and gracious woman of about

60 — a private person who rarely discusses her personal life.

On first meeting, Maud seems the stereotypical spinster schoolmarm. In fact, she has lived a rich and varied life, much of it in theater. An actress for many years, she has for the past fifteen years worked in a variety of theater box offices. She is one of the most truly tolerant people I have ever known, in the finest sense of that word, and the make-up of her family is a good indication of her openness to people on their own terms.

"Like most people who didn't have any viable family," she begins slowly, "I found it necessary to make my own family. Certainly I had no father, ever, and my mother was never available. Some aunts and uncles and cousins, but they had their own lives and found it sometimes hard to be openhearted and openhanded to this very difficult child."

For most of her childhood, Maud lived in a series of foster homes. "I think children who live in foster homes — and there seem to be more of them all the time — do make their own families. And not necessarily the foster parents or foster care people. They look for people they can feel comfortable with, they can like and admire . . . For a number of years when I was preteen, early teen, there was no place for me to go in the summertime. I was shipped out to summer camp. And some of the people I met there — now that I think back on it, some of them were probably in the same circumstances I was in. And we'd sort of come together."

These short-term families dissolved after a time, but in her later teens and early adulthood, Maud began to create, unconsciously, a more lasting family.

"There are people who go back more than forty years. Kate, for instance, I've known since just past high school. And Lucilla and Emily, almost since the same time. And Nicholas, whose first wife died tragically a number of years ago, and he married a second time, Georgia – they'd been friends for years.

"Later I made close friends in summer stock. Others I worked with in the box office of a big New York theater. Usually they were kids in the theater, who needed part-time jobs – as theatrical people always do. Agatha worked with me there – she had known Rod in summer stock, and when they got married they were *both* part of my family.

"Some.of these people I may not see for two or three or five years at a time, but the feeling is still there when I do see them. And of course, there's the understanding that you'd be there for each other in emergencies."

How does Maud distinguish between friends who are family and friends who aren't? "I'm afraid that I'm the wrong person to ask that question, because since I never had a family, I don't know what a real family is, and I can't make the comparison. I don't think I've ever, perhaps till now, thought, 'Well, this is a family' – I've never really made that connection before." Yet Maud was the first person I thought of interviewing when I started on this book; her relationships with her friends have always seemed so clearly familial to me.

Like many single people, Maud has made holiday rituals for herself and her family-friends. There has been one ritual that has gone on for years. She smiles. "I always celebrate Christmas with them – it started out as 'Christmas Eve for the irascible bachelors' – all my friends who weren't child-oriented. Somehow it seems that now it's the same people but some of them have children, and it's gotten more child-oriented," she says ruefully.

"Peter and Albert are usually there, and Tom and Amanda, and Alan and the Beresfords – supper and presents, it's a nice Christmas Eve. But I don't know if it will go on much longer. The Beresfords have their son now, and children should be in their own home Christmas

Eve. And the Charleses have now moved to New Jersey, so it's not going to be that easy to get here Christmas Eve. That's something that's sliding past . . . It's something I think — I don't know if anyone you've talked to has said this, but — whether you have a family that's a family, or friends that are a family, when you get to a certain age I think you have to accept the fact that to hold you have to let go — no clutching; the open hand, so that if it isn't the same Christmas Eve it was before, the love is still there, and the remembrance of Christmas Eves past; it isn't anything to be heartbroken about. They're still my friends, they still love me."

I ask her to describe some of her family members. "John is someone who comes from a Southern family, and his whole life has been a reaching out and not finding what he's been looking for. And I feel rather protective of him for that reason. Some of the people he counted on most failed him. And that bothers me a little bit. As you do with families, I suppose, I get impatient with him a lot. He makes mistakes. I'll always try to be there for him when he needs me, as best I can.

"One couple — an artist and a writer — when they were married, people said, 'How in the world are you going to maintain this, how are you going to accomplish this?' " The people she's talking of married when the writer was in her mid-thirties and the artist in his mid-forties — an unusual age for a first marriage, especially between two decidedly independent people. "And it's worked beautifully! And another couple that are both beautiful and elegant and very much the most important thing to each other, and if the whole world dissolved as long as they were together they could cope.

"And another couple, Nicholas and Georgia, they were both friends, and I was friends with his first wife and her first husband. They both had children, and their spouses died and they got married, and they've got a wonderful kind of mixed bag of kids that all became one great family, and they're *their* kids . . . No, *they're* my friends, not their children. I'm not child-oriented; I didn't like children when *I* was a child.

"And Reed, of course, who travels by himself, and who is quite grand and sophisticated and spends all his time with the beautiful theater people of this world, and still needs something to hang onto, telephones every Sunday morning at 11:30 to tell me what's happened this week.

"I have one new little member of my family, and it's a relative, surprisingly enough – the daughter of one of my cousins. She's about thirty-five. She's very busy; she has a grand job. But we get together for dinner every two or three weeks. As a matter of fact, I think she's my godchild – my cousin had three of them done at the same time, and I think she's one of them I was godmother to. Anyhow, I'm very fond of her."

But the most important member of her family is her friend Peter. She has mentioned him so often, so regularly during our friendship that I ask after him whenever I see her; I am always a bit surprised to realize that I've never actually met him. "I think the first time I saw him, there was never any question but that this was the prime friend. I realize it's a rather peculiar relationship, but it's as stable as any relationship that I've ever known – family, wedlock, any other way. He has an enormous family, as only Southern families can be sometimes, with hundreds of cousins and brothers and aunts and uncles and what have you, but they're not the people he relates to in himself. I've read somewhere that everybody has an 'other.' Well, this is one of the cases of two 'others' having encountered one another. It's a very pleasant relationship, a very stable relationship. It's been thirty-one years – since June 7, 1949. He's sixty-three or sixty-four now; I'm fifty-nine. That's something you have to stop and think

about — you have a family, the family gets older. Peter is
the one person I really need. I've really wondered sometimes what I'd do if anything ever happened to him. But
that happens in all kinds of relationships. We talk every
day, several times a day, sometimes. As long as he's here
and I can reach out to him every day, then I'm in a state
of grace."

Like most of the people I interviewed for this book,
Maud is white. Indeed, after I'd done several interviews
I began to see that this would be a problem. The interviews were good, with marvelous people, but I was suddenly having to face the classic problem of the white,
middle-class writer — my interviewees, male and female,
young and old, were white, middle-class people, with a
sprinkling of white, working-class people. The black
friends I knew well enough to ask for help were supportive, but didn't have many leads — they hadn't had
these familial networks themselves and couldn't think of
people they knew who did. I turned to one of my former
students. Feeling pretty awkward — the white writer in
search of the token black? — I called Tijuana. She was
immediately interested, and knew just whom I should
contact. "Call my friend Lydia," she said. "But call
her soon. She's only back here on a visit, and she's going
back to Florida this week. And, Karen," she added,
"have your tape recorder ready to go when you dial
the phone." I hemmed and hawed till Tijuana offered
to call Lydia first. The next night, she called me back.
"Lydia'll be glad to talk to you, but she's going back
tomorrow. Call her now."

And so my meeting with Lydia was over the phone —
a wonderful and slightly dizzying two-hour conversation,
at the end of which we were promising to keep in touch
and I was fantasizing a trip to Florida to meet her. The
first hour of the conversation was interview; the second,
we were sharing information about past lives and psychic

communication. Even over the telephone, if Lydia likes you she takes you into her family.

At first, however, she was a little suspicious. She's faced not so much ridicule as total incomprehension from some of the white, middle-class professionals she's had to deal with. She didn't want me making fun of her family in my book. But once she felt reassured, she talked about her family with warmth and energy. Biological and nonbiological kin wove in and out of her narrative; for her the problem isn't how to turn friends into family but trying to remember that other people don't understand that the two are the same.

"It's an *emotional* involvement," she says, "not a genetic involvement. What I mean is, okay, now I have my immediate family. My parents are dead. I'm dealing with my siblings, three sisters and three brothers. There are months when in my immediate family when people aren't speaking to other people, but that's not important, because if a crisis arises with one of the people you're not speaking to, you take care of the crisis . . . Now, three of my brothers have married women who've had children by previous marriages. And we make no distinctions — they're all our nieces and nephews. My sister married a divorced man who had a child; shortly after they were married his first wife died and my sister adopted that child. So I'm saying, you pull in the people. It's hard to describe to people who don't understand, but it's not a hard unit.

"There are very few black infants floating around; it's very difficult for a black couple to adopt a black child, there are none out there. You don't put children away, you farm them out. And it's all understood without any conversation going on about it.

"I've been very ill several times during the past few years — I work, I make a living in food management services; I've even created some courses and taught some classes along that line. Some years ago I became very ill, to the point where they didn't think I would live. The doctors told me I'd never be able to work again. I was only 41. Now, my sister-in-law has been separated from my brother for nine years — that's a long time. But my sister-in-law and I are friends — she is my sister. And when things got really bad for me and I had no place to go because I couldn't work, she came and moved me into her two-room apartment, and there we lived for three years, until I got my act together to move out. I was pleased that she liked me that much, but I wasn't surprised that she would do that, because years ago when she was having all her hassles with my brother — the fact that he's my brother has nothing to do with it, he's a royal pain. So I could put him off to the side and deal with her. So that although they're still not speaking to each other, it has nothing to do with her relationship to me or my relationship to her. And even he, after bitching for a few minutes — after everyone said, 'Oh, shut up. You know that's not how we play the game' — even he shut up. You know what I'm saying? He understands that she looks out for me and I look out for her. She had some children before she married my brother, and those children are my nieces and nephews. And that's the only way we can deal.

"I feel like this: we who are poor have very little to give each other but love. So that, oh, I'm mad at my sister and we may not speak to each other for three years and all the madness that goes with that, but who cares about that? When the deal came down and I had to go to the hospital, she drove all night to be there with me."

On one of the occasions when Lydia was recuperating from an illness, she got a call from her friend Clara, whom she'd been close with for over fifteen years. "She called me from Ohio; she said, 'I know you're sick, but would you like to inherit a thirteen-year-old daughter?' " The girl, a niece of Clara's husband, was an emotionally disturbed child who'd suffered from a history of physical and sexual abuse. Clara and her husband had taken her in, but found that they couldn't deal with her. "It never occurred to them that they were supposed to put this kid in an institution; somebody out there somewhere was going to fix this kid up, now all we got to do is sit down and figure out who we're going to call. And it never occurred to her that she should be embarrassed to call me. Because if I said to her 'I can't do it' she would have known that I couldn't do it. But on the other hand, if I said I was willing to try . . . okay? So I'm saying that we pass ours around; we don't lose them."

Lydia had spent eight years raising her godchild (see Chapter 2), and she took on Grace with equal energy. She soon discovered that Grace needed some kind of emotional counseling. "I had to put something together for her, some kind of program. So I went to find a social worker for her. It took me two months to get through to this woman. She kept asking why Grace was with me, she wasn't my blood relation, I had no obligation to her — all this stupidness this woman is saying to me. And she wasn't trying to be nasty. She couldn't understand why, when I was sick, I was taking on a kid who wasn't my blood relative."

Grace stayed with Lydia for six years. "God was good to me; I could turn that kid around. She came in here three weeks ago and said, 'Aunt Lydia, let me tell you something. I'm sorry I was a pain, I'm sorry I didn't believe you, I'm sorry that I gave you a hard time. But it's taken me this long to realize that you only gave me the business because you love me. Anything I can do for you it belongs to you.' This kid who everyone had wiped out, who's now a student at college."

Lydia herself has occasionally forgotten her own creed: friends are family, and they take care of each other. She relishes laughing at herself when this happens. "Some years ago my brother's house burned down. I was in New York when I heard about it, so I flew back and went to the old home site. His wife, Alva, and he have five children — three were hers before they got married. So I'm concerned, because they are all part of what I worry about. So the house is all burned down and nobody's there and the neighbors don't know where anybody is. So I get myself together and get back in the cab and I'm shooting across Columbus Avenue, and I look out the window and I see a friend of my sister-in-law's. She comes over to the cab and we're talking and I said, 'Where is Alva?' And she looked at me like I was crazy. She said, 'She's upstairs!' I said, 'Where are the kids?' and she gave me a very nasty look and said, 'In bed.' Now why am I being a pain? I knew she was Alva's friend and she wouldn't let Alva be on the street — what am I doing? And that's just where it was.

"I have a sister who has just recently decided to separate from her husband, okay? And she has two children. So I expected that sooner or later she was going to call me up and tell me she was sending the kids to me. And remember, you never say no when people say things like that.

"And it didn't happen. She called me and said she had decided to send the children to her best girlfriend, who lives in the South. When my sister went to school in the first grade, the person she walked up the street with was this girlfriend. They'd been friends for thirty-six years. This woman is the children's godmother, so she's their extended mother. And I couldn't be angry because she didn't ask me.

"And it never occurred to her that she shouldn't send them there, it never occurred to her there'd be a problem. Her friend said, 'Well, put them on a plane, we'll pick them up at the other end.' And they stayed there for a year, while my sister got her act together.

"I think it's terrible that this whole middle-class American dream is so sterile. I don't like it. I'm not moving to the suburbs; I'm not being away from some-body who can come to me if I need them. I'm not going to be so far away I can't go to the people who need me. Because that cuts off your lines of communication, and you don't have anybody.

"I have a friend I've had since I was in high school — Barbara's my sister, okay? — Of Polish Irish stock. I'm Barbara's children's godmother. One of the times I was sick, when I was laying up here dying, having gone from 130 pounds down to 97, and could not deal, who came down here and got me and took me to her house and fixed it up so I could at least keep something in my stomach? Because any time I ate something it would come right back up.

"I don't see her as frequently as I would if she lived here, but Barbara's my sister. And not only that, her husband's my brother. The past Christmas they sent for me, and they wined me and dined me for fourteen solid days. She said, 'I'm glad you're feeling better so you can eat — you haven't eaten in years! Come with us.' Max gave me for Christmas white gold earrings with raw emeralds — I'm family. And his thing is, 'Any time you can't deal, call me up and I'll send you a ticket and you'll come stay.' The point is, you can decide anyone you *want* to be your relative *is* your relative. As long as you two have a basic understanding.

"I have a theory that all children over six months old should be put in a pool. They should all grow up in a central area away from their parents, and when you get to be about sixteen or seventeen and you know where you're coming from halfway, then you pick your family or your sister or whoever you want to be with. I have a couple of brothers, and one of them I abhor. I don't like him at all. I can't find anything redeeming about him.

And someone said to me not so long ago, 'But he's your brother.' My response to that was, 'I can't help that.' All I know is he was here when I got here, and somebody said to me, 'That's your brother.' But dear God in heaven, if it were up to me I would never see him. We can't stand each other: five minutes in the same room and we're both at each other. But somebody out there must like that kind of person; why can't he go find his other sisters that might like him? There's got to be somebody in this world who can relate to this man. So maybe if he hit this central pool, he could have found that mad person who could have dealt with him. On the other hand, you can't hassle him but so much, because I'll hurt you.

"I think that Western civilization has limited itself so much by not dealing with things. When I said to you there are very few black children up for adoption, by the same token there are very few black people in old people's homes. Because we don't get rid of ours. If you're ours, you belong to us. And there's no discussion about it, you're here. We do the best for you until we can't deal anymore. You might go to a nursing home two months before you die, but you'll never spend five years there."

What struck me about Lydia's chosen family members is that, unlike mine or Maud's, even when they don't know each other they are connected by assumptions of mutual obligation. Hence when Lydia's friend Clara asked her to take care of the teenage girl Grace, the fact that Lydia had no previous history with the girl made no difference: she was Clara's family, hence Lydia's. Like the people interviewed by Carol Stack in *All Our Kin*, Lydia and her friends have learned through poverty and oppression that their survival depends on honoring a network of intricate interpersonal obligation.

Another striking resemblance between Lydia and the people Stack interviewed is that their distrust of white people is not an absolute. When a situation occurs in which the white person has proven herself or himself a genuine friend, acceptance into the family network has followed. Stack tells a lovely story of her friendship with Ruby, one of the women from the black ghetto. They became so close that Ruby's friends told them they looked alike. Ruby's biological family treated Stack like kin, and Ruby publicly asserted their sisterhood. When Ruby's daughter was in the hospital and the two women went to visit her, the nurse on duty attempted to stop Stack from going in, since only the child's family could visit. Ruby snapped, "Caroline here is my sister, and nothing's stopping her from visiting this baby." The nurse gave in. "Ruby's claim went unchallenged," writes Stack, "and we were able to visit the baby every day."[1]

6.

Moving to a New Place

Often people don't realize that they have a need to create family until they find themselves alone in a new city or town, far away from the family and friends they have been used to. Alone, without their familiar support networks, they are forced to deal with the need to re-create what they had with their parents or, perhaps less consciously, with their friends.

One of the most delightful stories I've come across is that of my friend Pam and Lorraine, better known as "Mama Blue." Pam is a feminist in her mid-thirties, who grew up in Cambridge, Massachusetts, the only daughter of middle-aged parents, comfortable in the intellectual cocoon that college towns like Cambridge can provide. Then she moved to Chicago for a few years.

Pam recalls, "I was, I suppose, feeling particularly vulnerable about not having members of my family nearby. In Chicago I was living with another woman, and my friends and even job associates were all through her, so I was very isolated, very dependent on this one person.

I wasn't even aware of what I was missing until one day my roommate said, 'I want you to come with me and meet Mama Blue.' I said, 'Yeah, Mama Blue. Sure.' So we bebopped over to this part of town that's in a changing neighborhood – Chicago is filled with ethnic neighborhoods; it's a wonderful city for all kinds of cultures trying to exist side by side. And hers was on the border between Appalachians, Native Americans, and Puerto Ricans, so it was a strange street. At the end of the street was Walt Disney School – Walt Disney *magnet* school – it was very bizarre. There are a lot of triple-deckers, six-apartment buildings. Lorraine – Mama Blue – lived on the top floor of one of these. So we huffed and puffed up to the top floor, and I get to the top of the stairs, and there's this woman, who must weigh 250 pounds, with her arms stretched out, wearing a huge pair of Farmer Gene overalls, saying, 'Pam, Pam, Pam, Pam, Pam, I've heard so much about you – come to Mama Blue!' So I walk up the stairs and I get hugged by her, and just at this moment I think, 'I've finally come home . . . I didn't even know what I was missing, but I've found it. " That was in 1975, and Mama Blue has been Pam's second mother ever since.

As Pam was quick to discover, she was not Mama Blue's only child. "I went into her apartment with her – and there were probably about fifteen people in their twenties or their teens, who'd just dropped in. And this was typical. She always made huge amounts of food – she was a wonderful cook – and expected lots of people to show up, and a lot of people always did. As I got to know her better, I realized that this was her whole life – to be Mama to as many people as she could be.

"The reason she'd cultivated this, apart from her own need for being maternal, was that during the sixties, a lot of young people were running away from home. She was running a nightclub, Mama Blue's, at the time, in the old town section of Chicago, and she'd see the kids. She was famous throughout the city for being the proprietress. She had a different hat on every night, and she had liquor there although she never drank herself. She loved all the musicians that came and played there, and she always put them up at her house. She and her husband, Red Blue (yeah, Red Blue — he had red hair) owned this big house and all these people, people like Dave van Ronk and Spanky and Our Gang, Kris Kristofferson, came there. Finally Red disappeared from the scene and they got divorced.

"She ran her club with runaways who came to the city — even though they were underage she gave them jobs as dishwashers and waiters and that kind of stuff, and she put them up at her house, too.

"It changed as the needs changed. In the late sixties the underdogs were the runaways — suburban kids, rural kids, kids from farming towns. They'd come to Chicago and be lost and then they'd hear about Mama Blue through the grapevine.

"Later on it was druggies and junkies, people heavy into heavy stuff. Nobody ever stole a penny from Blue, anything. She left her house completely open all the time, with somebody always there, all different kinds of people. She's one of those people who is totally accepting, unconditionally, of the way you are. If you come into her life then you are loved — that's it. It doesn't matter how messed up you are, dope or anything, how messed up you are emotionally. Even how together you are — if you're not in bad shape, she still loves you.

"Well, my God, I'd never met anybody like that before, who was so willing to put herself out, who had all these qualities.

"In the seventies, when Chicago, like many big cities, started accumulating this influx of openly gay people, she started collecting gay folks in her house. Whoever was oppressed, she'd go to bat for them. Because she was in touch with all these people, she was very political — very anarchistic, really. Very anti–Mayor Daly, very pro–civil rights, antiwar, pro–free abortions . . . so she was getting a political education too.

"I found myself going there for Sunday dinner regularly, calling her up all the time. Then I found myself needing a place to live. I felt vulnerable, I didn't know how to handle it. So I called Lorraine and said, 'Oh, Mama, I need a place.' So she said, 'Come on over here,' and the next day I was living in her house. There wasn't enough room in all the bedrooms — they were all filled up with other people, indigents, people with no money. I had a job — I was teaching at a community college and doing substitute teaching in the city schools — so I had a sort of income, and I was a welcome member of the house.

"But there wasn't room for me. So she put a cot in her own room and set me up there. And this was a big thing — she kept her room apart to maintain some privacy. But she set up a place for me anyway. She sleeps with all the windows open all the time, 'cause she's so well insulated. The wind and the snow would blow in and I'd be under twenty blankets and my nose would stick out and I'd have to wear stuff on my head at night to stay warm enough, but I still felt totally protected. It was a wonderful experience."

Mama Blue's children don't vanish from her life when they leave Chicago, as Pam found out. "One of the great benefits for Lorraine as a result of having all these children is that she's able to travel anywhere and have a place to stay. She used to come to Boston before I knew her and stay at the Sufi House, because some of her kids had become Sufis. She'd go out and do Sufi dancing with them and she'd just 'cook 'em up a nice big meal.' That was one of her favorite things, to cook 'em up a nice big meal. One time I was over her house for Thanksgiving and she had all six apartment stoves going — three of the stoves had turkeys. There must have been about sixty people there."

Pam also discovered that, when you become one of Mama Blue's kids, you acquire dozens of siblings. Lorraine has three of her own children, one a daughter, Boobaday, named after the Harry Belafonte song ("I guess he was in town when she was born, something like that"). Pam sees them as her family. "I haven't been to Chicago for a while, but I write to several of Blue's kids. And many of my women musician friends when they go to Chicago look up Blue and stay with her, and now they're her friends, her kids, too.

"For someone like me, who's an only child and not used to having a lot of people my own age around me, it's remarkable that I could go into this setting where there are lots of people and just accept them, and be accepted . . . When I first knew Blue, I was — I don't know if you'd call me exactly separatist, but very conscious of my feminism and trying to direct my energies toward women, all that stuff. And I'd try to ignore the men, but Blue would say, 'These are my kids!' and I'd have to agree: you don't turn on your brother. It was a very important stage in my development. So while I was helping Blue's consciousness in some areas, especially about lesbians, she was helping me relax and be at ease among all kinds of people I'd built up defenses around. And it's carried through into my life now. I take more care to give people a chance without prejudging them."

When Lorraine gets to the East Coast, daughter Pam often chauffeurs her around. A few years ago, Lorraine came into New York for the wedding of two of her kids. Pam drove from Boston to New York to spend the weekend with her. She drove Lorraine to the wedding and told her she'd pick her up at the reception later. "So I drove down to this very nice restaurant in Greenwich Village, where this reception was, and they said, 'Come on in,'

so I went inside and there were about ten or twelve of
Mama's kids. 'Hi, babe,' she says, 'come over and sit
down.' I come over and sit down, and I suddenly realize
that she's in the seat that's reserved for the groom's
mother, at the head of the table. And his *actual* mother,
his biological mother, is way the hell back in the back of
the reception room. Lorraine plops me right down next to
her in the middle of this reception. Everybody's all dressed
up; I'm in dungarees and a T-shirt with 'It's better in the
Bahamas' on it. And they say, 'It's time to dance!' and
I'm swept up in it. Not only am I part of *her* family,
I'm part of this whole extended family. I hardly knew
who any of these people were, but I was absolutely accepted — if I was one of Lorraine's kids, well, then, of
course bring her in!"

If Mama Blue takes care of her kids, they also take care
of her. Her club went bankrupt several years ago, and she
was forced to get a low-paying job as a clerk in an insurance company, which barely supports her. But she
gets things from her kids, especially the ones still in
Chicago. "It's the kind of thing where someone will say,
'Oh, you're getting a new stereo? Good — you can take the
old one over to Mama Blue's.' And her household is a kind
of hodgepodge of these things."

It was a long distance that Pam traveled from Cambridge
to Chicago and in the beginning she felt lonely and isolated. But Pam, at least, was in her native culture, and had
no language barrier to deal with. The loneliness and
feeling of alienation multiply when one is coming not
only to a new town but to a new culture — a culture
in which a foreign language is spoken. Such was the case
with Maria, now a young woman in her early twenties.
In the mid-1970s, she moved from her homeland of
Puerto Rico to study at Emerson College in Boston. She
was a student of mine several years ago; I ran into her
while I was writing this book, and asked about her ex-

periences. Yes, she told me, she had been very isolated when she first moved here, and had found a group of people who became her new family. Most of these people are, like herself, Puerto Rican-born Hispanic students.

"I have like, four, five, a lot of friends who function as family here," Maria beams. "They're a kind of support, anywhere from going through a nervous breakdown to finding job contacts, or 'leave your stuff here while you go back to Puerto Rico' . . . It's sort of developed over time.

"It took me a while to adjust to living here — basically because of my accent. I just had to adjust to the fact that people would laugh at it. I had trouble understanding the language. Sometimes somebody would say an expression or whatnot, and I would not know what it means. And I had support for that — for adjusting to the American culture.

"There's also an American woman, a black woman . . . I've always found that these people kind of substitute for family. Because — see, when I go back to Puerto Rico, my family will still relate to me the way I was. It's very hard for them to understand that, Maria has changed, she's grown up. The support I need to keep on going, I can't get it from them. So I just have to reach out to other human resources." She and her friends exchange advice, sympathy, support for each other in adjusting to the Anglo-American culture they find themselves living in. "I'm very lucky that I have this.

"I have separate relationships with them, but they have at times related to each other. I'm considered like the link.

"This one American woman — every time there's been a holiday, she would say, 'Come to my family at the Cape,' and they would treat me in a family situation.

"It's just really happened with these people — I've satisfied their needs, and they've satisfied mine. We'll always be in touch with each other. I know that at any point I can always call on them and they'll be there.

"I find that this takes a big commitment. It just doesn't function one way. I don't like to be labeled things—it's 'like my sister,' or 'this is my family' — but this is my relationship. This is what I need to develop. Especially being single. Especially since I'm not actively pursuing a mate, or whatever. I just want to settle into a career. My priorities are those."

Like many of the people I interviewed, Maria had a precedent for creating family in her own upbringing. "I had a woman that was a friend of my mother's, and she was my aunt. And another woman—they're my mother's friends from way, way back. And that's comfortable to me.

"I think I'd always have bonds with my friends here — even if we grew in totally different directions. Because those bonds are based on mutual personal choices. And because of that, and because of what we've shared, it'll still be there. It's a part of you.

"As a matter of fact, a group of friends back in Puerto Rico—we have decided that in 1985, *no matter* where we are, we have to meet together for Christmas. Because one's in Spain, one is in California, I'm in Boston . . . But we've agreed, in 1985. We knew things were going to change, and we just, one night, we said, 'Wait a minute, we're all together.' So we wrote up this agreement and signed it, and everybody has a copy of it . . . We talk about it when we write to each other."

Maria also had a very good experience with what she considers to have been a short-term family relationship. In 1978, she took an EST therapy seminar. "It really created that sense of family, in a way that—it's incredible. There's 300 people in a room, and for that time it created a family. It satisfied a big need for me; I was very moved by it. It made me aware of my responsibility of communicating to other people. It made me communicate my needs very well. It helped open me to relationships with people." The process helped her to see what she had with her biological family, to accept what they could give her and also to understand what they *couldn't* give her, and to look for others to satisfy some of the needs her original family didn't meet. She feels that, without it, she would have been far less able to create new family friendships.

Maria's sense of isolation when she first moved to the States was eased by the creation of a family of similarly isolated people from her own culture. Eva's story makes a fascinating contrast. For this young Chinese woman, the feeling of displacement was eased by the friendship of people *outside* her own culture—members of the culture in which she now found herself. Unlike Maria, she had come to the United States with her parents, and so the tie to her own background was still with her. What she needed, and found, was a new family of people native to her new environment.

"I was born in Hong Kong, and was a child when my parents brought me over," she recalls. "We moved into a small town in Florida, where my grandfather already lived. There was a family living next door to us, and they were ranchers. And I was interested in horses, in horseback riding. So my grandfather arranged a trade—they could use our pastures if they'd let me ride one of their horses, something like that. And since I really didn't know how to ride, Linda, the rancher's granddaughter, supervised me. So you're riding, and you start talking . . . So we got to be friends. And even after the deal was over, we were horseback riding nonstop. And then it turned out that I was over there all the time; I just went home to sleep—sometimes. I was around 11, 12, like that. And she also went to church with me. For three years we were always together. I worked with her, ate meals at their

house; sometimes I spent the night. It wasn't just a friendship: I learned what they ate, how they lived—I learned
Southern lifestyles and values.

"When we went to meet their friends—they know a
lot of ranchers and they'd have these big barbecues—
they'd say, 'Oh, this is the Chinaman's daughter; this is
my adopted daughter' . . . No, that wasn't racist; they
just meant it as a distinction, because we were the only
Chinese in the town . . . Anyway, they always gave me
birthday presents and Christmas presents. One Christmas
they gave me a calf; it was born on Christmas day."

The father died a few years ago. Eva still misses him.
Linda got married when she was 17 and Eva was 13.
"I was the bridesmaid at the wedding. But a year later
she got a divorce; they never told me why and I never
understood. I kind of lost touch with her. But a few years
later, when I was in Canada, I hitchhiked from Toronto
to where she was, about 200 miles away, to see her, to
find out what had happened.

"The man she married—I was really close to her husband's uncle and aunt. I spent time with them; I called
them 'Aunt' and 'Uncle.' But then when they broke up,
it was kind of weird. She was sort of my older sister,
and to go visit 'Uncle' without her was awkward.

"Linda's into very different things than I am now, and
we haven't really kept in touch. She had a very traditional
upbringing, and she really didn't do anything till she got
married: that's where we differ.

"But I think about the times we had: through her I
met a lot of people; I learned how to act. I learned how to
order ice cream. She and her father were there at a time
that was very important to me. They helped me a lot—
how do you get accustomed to a new country? Some of
my Chinese friends have been here six or seven years,
and they still speak with very heavy accents. They don't
even know what American beliefs are. I got to see both.

I could see the American lifestyle and values, while whenever I was home — once in a while — my parents would tell me about the old ways. Linda and her father were there at the time when I needed them."

Sometimes people *aren't* there when you need them. When neighbors don't function as family — or at least as community — the results can be tragic. Irene is a cheerful, plump, middle-aged Englishwoman who has lived in the United States for many years. She is divorced and has one child, a son now in his late teens. She has recently moved into a large house in Cambridge, Massachusetts, and we sit, drinking tea, surrounded by boxes and boxes of unpacked books, as her son wanders in and out. At one point he brings in his pet skunk to show me. "It's not a cat," Irene sighs, "but it's a pretty little thing."

A college professor, she took a job at a university in Kentucky five years ago. She took her son and settled in, "leaving all the people who could help me or who I could help." She was used to helpful friends, and had never before felt a lack of community. People were very friendly, at first, and she was asked to a number of dinner parties. Then she fell ill, and had to have an operation. When she got out of the hospital, she was too weak to lift pots to cook for herself or her son. Some of the parents of Jonathan's schoolmates were willing to take care of the boy for a while, but Irene was still left alone, weak and a little frightened. "So I phoned the people who had asked me to dinner parties the month before and said, 'That was very kind of you, but I need something more now. Would you be able to bring me a meal on Sunday or Monday? I can't lift a pot or a pan to cook for myself.' A few of them did, but very reluctantly. It was clear that I was making terrible demands on people, asking them to do things they'd only do for their own families. They said, 'Well, why don't you go to a commercial homemaker service?' I don't know, maybe people in the nuclear family suffer so much that they have nothing to spare for people outside."

Back in the more hospitable environment of Cambridge, she has evolved a concept for middle-aged and elderly women taking care of one another. She calls it "Demeter" because, as her leaflet says, the goddess Demeter in her "third and most powerful manifestation . . . is free to roam the earth," but still retains her nurturant capacities. The organization as she envisions it would consist of women 40 and over now living outside nuclear family structures who would support one another emotionally and pragmatically. "When I was sick," Irene says, "I had to deal with insurance. It's complicated and difficult, especially when you're ill. So one Demeter would always go with another Demeter to insurance companies, doctors, lawyers. We'd provide each other with postoperative home care." Childless women could, if they chose, become involved with the children of other Demeters, "taking the place of aunts, really—all the Victorian aunts."

Surprisingly, all the friends she approached with the idea were put off by it. "They feared it, they thought it sounded as if they were going to be alone. And it's just the opposite, really. The truth is there are so many women who are widowed or divorced, there's a need for alternatives. So I approached the Women's Center in Cambridge about starting an older women's group, using the Demeter idea as a basis, and they're thrilled.

"Preparing for old age, that was always considered a thing to do, and it's a thing we need to do . . . as a matter of fact, girls were told not so long ago that one got married not for the here-and-now but to be taken care of in old age. Therefore, one *has* to have a substitute."

In a culture of mobility, such substitutes might well need to incorporate national and even international networks—enclaves of Demeters to whom people can turn when they are strangers in a new environment. The need for family—for nurturance, stability, sharing—does not stay behind when one leaves one's home. Perhaps the Demeter concept is the beginning of a new and important form of family—or at least of community—from which one can slowly draw those individuals who might eventually become family to each other.

7.

Nuclear Families Expanding Outward

O ften people create their own families out of a
sense of isolation—they do not have families of
their "own." One would assume, given the marriage
mythology we have all been raised with, that those who
had spouses and children would find little need to create
other kinds of family.

Yet there have been many happily married parents who
have found it natural to create families beyond the parameters of their nuclear families, without in any sense
abandoning those nuclear families. Eileen, the suburban
housewife that I interviewed in Chapter 4, found that
sharing the raising of children with neighbors created a
familial bond that has lasted long after the children have
grown and left home. Sally, interviewed in the same
chapter, found it comfortable and natural to absorb her
business partner Claudia into her family, Claudia becoming
a sister-in-law to Sally's husband and an aunt to their
daughter.

For such people, marriage has been partially true to

its myth—it has been a means through which they have chosen their family. But they have not limited their choice of family to the marriage alone. As they have chosen mates, so they have chosen friends to become part of their family. Often, as it happened with Eileen, the friends chosen are other couples of similar age and lifestyles.

Leah and Howard are middle-aged people, married twenty-five years and with two grown daughters. Leah is a writer and feminist activist; Howard is a businessman. Leah and I are lunching at a deli near her apartment in New York's Upper East Side. She is a short, plump woman, well-spoken and energetic.

"When I told my daughter, Monica, I was going to do this interview about us and Paul and Anne, she said, 'But that's just friendship.' And then she said, 'If friends don't behave like family, then they're really not friends.' Which I thought was an interesting comment." She laughs, and stops to light a cigarette.

"I met Paul when we were colleagues working on a sixties underground publication, and we became good friends there. Then, about twelve years ago, because of the lousy educational system in New York, and the danger of their three sons in regard to drugs—but also because they'd always wanted to do it and they suddenly had an opportunity—he and his wife moved the family to the Southwest with several other people, families and individuals. I only knew Paul at this time, not his family. I think he and I felt a kinship very early, because we had a similar sense of humor. So when he was moving away, I said jokingly to him that I'd send my kids down to visit him because they could use the country experience."

As often happens, however, what started off as a joke soon became serious. Paul was delighted at the idea of Leah's kids visiting their community, and he urged Leah to bring herself and Howard as well.

"The next summer, my daughter was eleven—really

at the obnoxious age—and I had the kids on my hands all summer, and it was getting to me. I'd always hated summer camps, because my own experiences had been miserable—I'd been a terrible athlete and I was forced to go to camp from the time I was five till I was in my teens, so I wasn't about to ship her off to one of them." She decided it was the perfect time to take Paul up on his offer, and send Monica out to visit them. "It wasn't really a commune—more of a community, really, because while they all owned the land together there was enough land so that individuals lived in separate houses, or two people might live together, or four people in a family might live together. They were very cooperative in helping each other till the land, and were constantly with each other, but there was an element of privacy and separateness.

"So Monica went out there and met Paul and Anne and their three sons, who are all close to her age. They taught her to ride bareback on horses, build houses out of adobe, carry water from a well and from an arroyo . . . and within two weeks she was a member of the family. So the following year she went back for the whole summer. Then my younger daughter followed. Then the next year I went too. The tie became extraordinarily close. The kids related to Anne and Paul as if they actually were other parents. Anne and I started a correspondence, which is still going on, in which we referred to each other as the city cousin and the country cousin. It wasn't completely facetious—we really felt that way.

"My girls and their boys developed crushes on each other, and since it wasn't really blood family it wasn't incestuous, so it was comfortable enough. Paul and Anne and the kids have stayed at our house when they've been in New York, sometimes with other members of their community. One year Anne stayed for three or four months. I have a strong feeling that their place is just as much a place to hang my hat as my own home is, and that my house is just as much theirs as it is mine. And I suppose that's the traditional definition of family." Anne and Paul have since divorced, but they remain family both with one another and with Leah's family. They both live on the communal property, though in different houses, and share much of their lives with each other.

"There's kind of an innocence on the part of all of us, in a way, which precludes the possibility of 'one hand washes the other,' or anything like that. None of us feels comfortable with that sort of mentality. If there were difficulties of income, it might mean that one person might help another in need with the understanding that the other will be helping other people in other ways, and that no direct payment or recompense is expected— a sense that we're all part of a network, which can certainly be called a family, of people who genuinely care about each other and without asking questions go to each other's aid. And you know that these people have the same attitude not just toward you but toward a whole lot of other people as well.

"One of the conditions for a friendship turning into this sort of relationship is that people involved are a lot more considerate of each other than is really necessary— that everybody goes out of the way to help out, that part of the fun of the relationship is how much you can anticipate the needs of other people. You love these people, so you try to guess what it is that might turn out to be helpful to them and you try to do it before you've even been asked. We sort of know we'd die for each other if it came to that."

For Leah and Howard, the idea of extending their family beyond the confines dictated by the social ideology of marriage and blood was a natural evolution of their radical political beliefs. But the extension of nuclear families to embrace other familial friends is hardly limited to leftists. Nat and Dabney are around the same ages as

Leah and Howard, and also have older children. Apart from that, they are as different as politics and lifestyles could make two couples. They live in a magnificent house in an "affluent suburb" in Massachusetts, and Nat has been politically active in "moderate Republican" politics. Yet Nat and his wife also have a couple that have become both family to them and second parents to their children.

Nat and Dabney's friendship with Frank and Jean Crocker goes back many years — in fact, Dabney and Frank had known each other as children. "Both families spent their summers in Southampton, Massachusetts," Nat tells me in his slow, very precise New England speech. "Then for a while the youngsters grew up and began taking a male-female interest in one another: Frank was a suitor of Dabney's." When Nat met Frank and Dabney, he had already known Jean through his college roommate. Nat and Dabney began to date, as did Frank and Jean. By the time Nat and Dabney were married, the couples were firm friends, and they have remained so for over twenty-five years.

Like Dabney's and Frank's parents, the two couples have homes in Southampton where they spend their summers, and it has been largely through these summers that their children have come to know each other. For the rest of the year, Nat and his family live in Amherst, while their friends live in New York City. But there are frequent visits. Both families spend their Christmases in Southampton. "And then we developed — I don't remember how many years ago — a tradition of the Crockers coming to visit us in Amherst for the weekend following Thanksgiving. We've been doing that for ten years anyway," explains Nat. Fairly often, Nat and Dabney go to New York and stay with the Crockers.

Nat sees his intimacy with the Crockers as a direct outgrowth of his relationship with his own family. "I'm a great believer in family," he says, "and hence I've always enjoyed my family—we have very involved, sometimes volatile relationships. I've always felt that family was something special; just being together with them has always meant an awful lot to me. And in some way, my feelings for my family and for the Crockers go together. I'm not entirely sure why and how they go together, but they just seem to—they're all part of the same thing."

Nat's youngest child, Timothy, is still in his teens, and they have arranged that, if anything happens to them, the Crockers will be his guardians. "We see the Crockers as the couple we'd turn to if there's a case of dire circumstances. If I needed money, I would turn first of all to my own blood family. That may be influenced more by cultural tradition, that you don't ask your friends for money except in extreme situations. But I think if Dabney and I were suddenly in an auto accident and wanted to have someone around to buoy us up, they'd be the first we'd call."

Nat and Dabney's friendship with the Crockers has been passed down in a very special way to their two daughters, Wrenn and Priscilla, both in their early twenties: "Frank and Jean are in effect a second set of parents. Our two kids love them as parents, they always look forward to seeing them, and they have the kind of conversations with them that one associates with parents and children. I think in fact they feel freer to talk about certain things with Jean and Frank than they do with us, simply because they're close to them but they're not their actual parents. Dabney and I feel very good about that. It gives the two girls close people to talk to, parentlike people, older people with a great bond of love between them and the girls. I think it's a very valued and valuable relationship, on both sides. They refer to Frank and Jean as 'Uncle' and 'Aunt,' and it is that kind of extended family relationship, but it goes beyond that. I think the causes of it would be hard to explain. Some of it is just a kind of chemical

magic. Some of it obviously springs from that close relationship between Dabney and myself and Jean and Frank.
I've never talked to the girls about it, and I should add
here that Timmy does not have that kind of relationship
with the Crockers, nor do their children have that relationship with us—partly because the same chemistry doesn't
exist." Still, the Crocker children do think of Nat and
Dabney as their aunt and uncle, and there is a sense of
family, without any special intimacy. And the Crocker's
daughter—who was born the same week Priscilla was
born—is Priscilla's best friend.

Much younger than Nat and Dabney or Leah and
Howard are Molly and Christopher. It's too soon to tell
what kinds of relationships will develop between Molly
and Christopher's offspring and the children of their
friends. But Christopher and Molly too have nonbiological
family—in fact, two sets of nonbiological family.

Molly and Christopher have been married almost twelve
years. They lived in California for a time (Molly
comes from California; her husband was transplanted from
his native England), and while there met Gordon and
Hilary. They moved to Boston, where Christopher teaches
at a major university and Molly works as a consultant for
nonprofit organizations. Her chief interest, however,
is the women's movement, and she has been active for
years in a shelter for battered women.

Gordon and Hilary moved to Boston two years after
Molly and Christopher did, and they stayed with their
friends until they found their own apartment. With luck,
they were able to find a place right next door, where they
lived until recently. "We'd look across, or they'd look
across to see if we were in," says Christopher in his quiet
and very British voice. "We saw a lot of each other. They'd
invite us over for dinner."

"That was wonderful," interrupts Molly. Her own voice,
after years of living with Christopher, has an occasional

British inflection. The two interrupt each other often, completing a sentence for each other, or correcting a statement, or asking for confirmation of what has just been said. "Gordon and Hilary like to cook—we really don't. They'd call us up and they'd say, 'We just did an overrun of spaghetti; come join us for dinner.' We didn't do that nearly as much—we'd take them for a nice meal out or something."

The fact of living next door helped the couples' intimacy grow; so did the fact that all four could empathize over family problems. "We've probably confided more family things to them than to anyone," says Christopher. They've also shared positive family experiences. When Christopher's mother came to Boston after their son, Timothy, was born, she stayed at Gordon and Hilary's apartment. And they share other familial functions. "It was Hilary who went down to pick up the midwife when Molly went into labor," Christopher says, "and we're naturally mutually very supportive of one another in the different things that come up."

Recently, because of problems with the landlord, Gordon and Hilary moved to an apartment several blocks away. Although it hasn't affected the friendship, it's made a difference in the day-to-day quality of their association, and Christopher and Molly feel the loss acutely. "It's the various spur-of-the-moment things we miss," Molly says wistfully, and Christopher adds, "We did lean on them a lot."

Unlike many married couples, Christopher and Molly tend to have a number of separate friends, and mutual friends are rarely other couples. "They're really about the only 'couple' friends we have, where we actually do things as couples," says Molly.

Molly and Christopher are somewhat private people, but they talk about the possibility of one day buying a two-family house with Gordon and Hilary, "especially if they ever decide to have children," says Molly. "Even if they don't," Christopher emphasizes. "I could still see doing that one day. They're the only people we could ever imagine doing that with."

Their other nonbiological family consists of a group of several people with whom they were involved in the Catholic left in the early and mid-seventies. (Christopher is a practicing Catholic; Molly was a Catholic convert for a while, but is now wholly disillusioned with the Church.) When three of the group members who were doing ministry work at Harvard were fired by the archbishop in the fall of 1974, several of them did various protest actions. They didn't get their friends reinstated, but they did create a bond among themselves which they consciously decided to maintain. "A few people got together and said, 'Let's experiment and have dinner together once a week or so.'" At first, there was some idea of focusing the group on some kind of ministry work, but people's feelings about the Church were changing. Two members had left the priesthood, though not the Church; several members were beginning to feel disaffected from religion; others remained religious. It soon became apparent that religion was no longer what bonded them to each other and that it was the group itself that mattered. "The religious connection was simply the initial thing—we gradually evolved away from it," says Christopher. He feels that the decision to meet for dinner at people's homes rather than at restaurants helped solidify the familial feelings among the group. "One of the key things," said Molly, "is that it wasn't going to be potluck or anything like that—one person had to do all the cooking and all the cleanup. And if you were married or living together, you counted as two people. Christopher had to do his work and I had to do my work." Since both dislike cooking, they felt that making the commitment to cook meals was, and is, a gesture of bonding of the familylike relationship.

When did they begin thinking of the group as a family? According to Christopher, "We'd known Richard, one of the former priests, earlier. In fact, he would have married us if he had been in the country at the time. Before the group came together, he was a father figure, in both senses of the word, before the group. I suppose we first started to feel that the group itself had family characteristics when the first baby was born to someone in the group. And we were the only people, aside from the wife's father and two sisters and the godparents, who were at the christening. We all stood around in the circle and passed the baby around and wished things for it. It was so much a rite of passage which is so associated with the family, and that was the first time the group had done something more than just having supper together."

Three other babies followed, and one member married. In the rituals surrounding these events, the group members were always participants. One of the members began dating, then living with, a Jewish man, who slowly became part of the group, pulling it still further from its original Christian focus. To the various Christmas and Thanksgiving celebrations was added a Seder—"a very wonderful, very family-style Seder," says Molly.

There have been occasional conflicts within the group. One member lived in a distant suburb, and began coming to the dinners less frequently. Some people felt confusion, as it became evident that he wasn't going to be able to host his share of the dinners. Molly shrugs. "I think we should have just left it and said, 'He's like the cousin from out of town who drops in every couple of months.'" In any event, that seems to have happened, and the man still comes to occasional dinners.

Another problem arose when one of the couples in the group began bringing along a couple that had moved into town for a year. "Some people in the group resented it— they didn't feel right about these people, assuming they were just going to become part of our group," says Molly. That problem has remained unresolved.

"One interesting thing that's begun happening," Molly says, "is that more often recently either Christopher will go or I'll go. We both have so many other things to do, we often can't both make the same Wednesday. And that's happened with the other parent-couple— because they spend so much time away from the children, they prefer to have one of them with the kids when they can."

One thing that makes Molly and Christopher's experience different from that of most of the people I've spoken with is that they see a real distinction between these "familial" friends and their other friends in terms of personal closeness. While there are differing combinations of one-to-one friendships among group members, both feel that the primary relationship is with the group itself. "I probably wouldn't call on one of them first in an emotional crisis," says Molly. "I think that's one of the things that sort of makes them like a family—the fact that I don't always have as much in common with them as I do with my friends. If I were to list who my good friends were, I might say, 'Well, I have this group that's a good thing.' But I might not necessarily list those same people individually. The distinction I make between friends and these familylike people is that with friends I have more basically in common, like values and who we are and what we may be doing. I could drift away from these friends if somebody radically changed in that respect—and I have. I feel really close to my friends. But with family people, I sometimes don't have as many things in common—I might not know people like them if I weren't sort of related to them."

Christopher concurs. "I think the thing with families is that you have your periods of alienation, but you can't be shaken loose from them, even if there's no legal bond. Shared experiences you have with people over a long time, doing kindnesses for each other without any expectation of quid pro quo—that sort of thing builds something over a period. And I do think it's partly the way we define each of the people in the group as a member of the group first and perhaps as an individual second." They feel similarly about their friendship with Gordon and Hilary. "It's interesting," says Christopher. "It's not based on a best-friend type of thing. But there's a very strong bond between us. They're very like cousins in that way."

8.

Choosing To Be Family

As the previous chapters indicate, people's needs for bonding are deep enough that, even in the face of a society that tells us friends are friends and family is family and never the twain shall meet, many of us unconsciously choose friends to be part of, or even all of, our family. But others have gone further. They have consciously recognized the inauthenticity of the dichotomy between friends and family, or they have simply never acknowledged it, and they have deliberately set out to create a family out of friends. Such people reclaim for themselves the power of naming: they declare the familial nature of their friendship—or of the particular friendships they wish to be familial—and they name the kinds of demands, commitments, expectations that they feel go with familial friendship.

There is a tremendous risk in such a course, the same emotional risk that goes into choosing a spouse, with the added dimension that there is no social support for the kind of commitment they are asking for and giving. There are also enormous rewards.

Like the unconsciously chosen family, the consciously chosen family lives in a variety of settings—sometimes living together, sometimes scattered across the world. On one end of the spectrum is the commune, although not all communes have made the emotional and practical commitments of family-style relationships. For the most part, I've chosen not to include communes as a category in this book, since, as I noted earlier, they are the one form of chosen family already widely documented. One type of commune, however, is both more rare and less documented than others—the commune of the elderly. Rochelle Jones, in her book *The Other Generation,* discusses one such commune—a group of people who defined themselves as a family, and who went to court to defend that definition. This is the group known as the Share-A-Home Association, a family of twelve elderly women and men who, in 1977 when the book was written, had lived for eight years in a 27-room mansion in Orange County, Florida. One 85-year-old member said of the group, "This is a real family. We share everything—our newspapers, our books, all our goodies. Sometimes we even fight like a family, but the arguments don't last long."

Apparently this unconventional view of family was threatening to the elderly people's neighbors, some of whom sued on the grounds that the group's living arrangement violated the area's single-family zoning. The circuit court judge, in a ruling that, as Jones notes, "substantiates a new definition of a family," found favor with the Share-A-Home group, stating that a group of people pooling their resources "with the intention of sharing the joys and sorrows of a family life is a family."[1]

Admirable as that ruling is, it is still too narrow to encompass all familial relationships. People often share the joys and sorrows of family life without living together—adult siblings rarely live together or with their parents in our culture, and usually they have never lived

with aunts, uncles, and cousins with whom they nonetheless may share familial bondings. Similarly, nonbiological families do not always live together. People such
as Barb, an old friend of mine from the Boston feminist
movement who now lives in California, create families
as real as the Share-A-Home's family.

Barb is in her early thirties—a blond woman with a
dazzling and infectious energy. She is an interesting
combination: a radical feminist lesbian who is also successful in a very "respectable" career. Her chosen family
is large and scatttered around the country. She thinks
a great deal about what it means to choose family, about
how created families can become legitimized in the eyes
of society. Some of her chosen family members are friends
with each other; many have never met each other.

"I'd say there's maybe about seven adults that aren't
blood related to me that I see as my main family," Barb
tells me. "One of the people I used to live with is like
a sister, Danielle. We didn't select each other intentionally;
we ended up living together because we left our husbands.
And we got so close, as really good friends, that we verbalized a commitment to each other that we do want to
be long-term friends and that we can rely on each other
for a long time.

"Another one is my lover, Fiona, who lives several
blocks away. And another, Baba, who is 30 years older
than me, lives up north in California, so there's three
women who live in California. And then there's my ex-
husband, out in rural California, who's also family. One
of the elements that I think is important about family
is that I would rely on people—if I'm very sick, if I were in
a car accident, if I ran out of money, if I needed a place
to stay and be nurtured—and I could go there being really
upset and know that it was okay.

"I was sick out of town once with a friend, and I felt
a little embarrassed being there, a little bit like I was

putting her out, even though she was nice. And that made me feel that she's really not quite family yet.

"One of the elements has to do with borrowing and lending money. There would never be a question. I would take my entire savings out for people that I consider family; I would just give it to them and trust that they'd pay it back, they wouldn't rip me off economically or emotionally. People could come and stay at my house and I'd take care of them for an extended period of time; I'd support them. Like, I paid Fiona's rent once, and I know she'd do it for me. I feel that in terms of money with my ex-husband: I could lend him money and he wouldn't rip me off. And I would borrow money from him.

"Another element is that I want to know what's happening with these people. I like getting updates on Richard, my ex-husband; I like knowing how his job is, who he's relating to. There are degrees of family, and he's maybe like a cousin."

Barb is concerned about the lack of vocabulary for chosen family. "I can't say to Richard, 'Oh, now you've become my cousin,' and I can't say to Danielle, 'Now you're my sister.' It's so important to have names for this kind of intentional family — particularly since parts of the family are not related to one another. So I can say I have *my* family, but it's not necessarily like the Smith family; it's people connected to *me*. That in some way makes it weaker than the traditional family.

"Another element: most of my family are lesbians, and one of the things that unites us is not only a common oppression in society but a common *risk*, a common decision to live in such a way that we know we're not going to be allied to men sexually. We know that we're never going to have a nuclear family in the way that the society accepts; we know that in these ways we're outcasts. Many of us have been rejected by the regular hetero-blood family because of being lesbians. Some of us don't have grandmothers and grandfathers and mothers and fathers anymore, because they have rejected us. So we're left sort of floating. We're left without the economic security, without the emotional security, without some needs being met. Now some others of us *have* all that, but we don't see it as very valuable; we don't see it as satisfying anything because we don't see real love in that family; we see more obligation than love. And the roles are so predetermined that it doesn't give people very much flexibility. But we're operating without a script.

"One of my family saw her mother today, and she said to me, 'Once I'm a lesbian to my mother I'm not a daughter anymore in some ways; she doesn't know how to relate to me—and what do we talk about? She doesn't want to talk about things in the old way and it's like she doesn't know what to say to me 'cause I'm not gonna have a husband and kids.' Once you leave one definition, you may not realize it but you may be leaving a whole lot of other definitions. I didn't know I was going to get this whole big lifestyle when I made this decision. I just fell in love.

"A lesbian's not always rejected by her family. Fiona's mother and father know that she's gay; her sister is gay; her other sister isn't. She's very close to her mother and father, so she still has her original family. So there's a real variety in this group.

"But one thing that's similar is that none of us is satisfied with the regular family setup. We're not happy with the mother/father roles. But we see those roles as having filled certain functions of nurturance, of continuation, of security, of something to fall back on economically, of recognition in the larger society that you are part of an intimate network.

"So we've been talking about this among ourselves. One of the things that families do for you or you do for families that's very important is that they bury you when

you die. And they visit you when you're in the hospital:
they take you to the airport and pick you up, and you can
always stay at their house when you're traveling. You
know they'll feed you.

"When I go to my parents' I know that I can always
stay with them, I know that they're always glad to see
me; I know that they won't charge me; we try to keep
in touch. And those things feel good to me. All those
things that make me feel good I still want to be ful-
filled . . . But they don't know I'm a lesbian.

"My friendship family and I, we've identified functions—like economic security and picking up at the airport. But there's, say, Row A, and Row A has functions
1, 2, and 3 in it. Row B has functions 4, 5, and 6 in it.
That's in the regular family. But when you do it with
an intentional family, functions 1 and 5 may go together
and functions 4 and 2 may go together—there's no *roles*
that carry all those functions . . . Also, we've learned we
can do without some of the 'security.'

"I've got this friend, Joanne, who's in charge of burying
me. I'm in charge of burying her—it's a deal we've made.
So that's taken care of, I don't have to think about it.
In terms of money, Richard's probably who I'd borrow
money from because he's got the most money. Who I'd
call when I'm upset, it's either Fiona or Danielle—sometimes it's both. Sometimes it's Rochelle. So these roles
don't all go in a package. And there's also this role of,
who do you take to the office party? Now I'd take
Danielle or Fiona."

Much of her concern is about creating official recognition of a nonbiological family. "Danielle's cousin was in
a car accident recently, and she could leave work because
it was someone who was part of her family. Now what if
I was in a car accident, and the hospital called her at work?
She's my 'roommate,' because that's the name that's put
onto my function. 'My roommate is in a car accident;

I have to go to the hospital.' Chances are there's not a clause in her work contract that says she can leave because of her roommate: that's not recognized. We're fighting the fact that we don't have names for the relationships; we haven't a systematic way to put relationships with names or with roles. So we're looking into the legalities."

Barb is also concerned about continuity. "One thing that happens in a blood family is that you know there's going to be some kind of continuity. The chosen family just isn't as secure. Because we're not recognized by society we can do whatever we damn well please and nobody's going to guilt-trip us, because the expectations aren't all that clarified and they don't have names. If you're a traditional family member and you don't show up for Christmas, somebody's going to talk about you and what a shit you are for not showing up for Christmas. In the traditional family, the kids may move away, but still there's some kind of commitment to check things out before you make a decision. You don't just move away from your husband or wife. But with this family no one checks things out. It's just assumed that your freedom is yours; there's no commitment of staying in one place. Danielle and I aren't sure where our commitment is: even with a lover you're not always sure. Danielle is going to Alaska for a while this summer, and she's wondering whether or not she'll stay there. I'm thinking of going to graduate school in the East again. It makes me feel shaky, but we don't know how much of a commitment we want to make to one another. But at least we do try to explore the expectations."

She talks about a mutual friend of ours, Rochelle, with whom she had been friends in Boston. "When I moved from Boston Rochelle was very angry and hurt by my leaving. But at that time I didn't feel as connected to her as she did to me. Now she's part of my family. And I'm not sure how that came up. It's easier for me to feel family with lesbians than with straight women. Part of it is because she was really persistent—she kept writing, she came to visit twice, and she acted like a family person. And she started calling long distance, and sending little CARE packages on my birthday. And then I started thinking of Rochelle as family. I talk about her to people out here—that's another aspect of family. She talks about *her* other friends too. So Fiona knows Joanne, even though Joanne now lives in Spain and we live in San Francisco. Baba knows Danielle and now they're getting to be friends. I'm slowly bringing my family members together. Some of them have other families too—it's interesting.

"This past Thanksgiving I was with my parents and I gave them a typed-out list of the people they should know that are friends of mine. I said, 'If anything happens to me while I'm with you, or that you know about, these people should know.' And the people on the list were my close family. I've never done that before, and it was a heavy thing. It's important that my family know about one another, what my history is with each person. So for instance Fiona will say, 'How's Joanne? Have you heard from her?' They're conscious of how they're connected with you."

The theme of continuity keeps cropping up in Barb's conversation; it explains at least in part her relationship with her ex-husband. "One thing that Richard and I have discussed is that we really don't want to be in one another's life very much. But we serve several functions for each other. And one is continuity. Besides the fact that we really love each other, he's the only person that I know that knew me in certain stages, sequentially. He knew me in college when I was a little coed type; he knew me in Female Liberation, he knew me when I was a teacher. He knew me through all kinds of different phases. And I knew him through a lot of *his* phases.

"And there's my friend John who lives in Australia, who's coming to visit soon. I feel sort of family with him—we used to live together. He could always stay at my house and I always want to know what he's doing, and I think I'll know him forever, even though I may just write to him three times a year."

She talks several times about the importance of holding oneself responsible for the welfare of one's family. "Rochelle in Boston hit her head once and had a concussion. She called and told me she needed to be awakened every few hours. She said, 'Would you call me midnight your time to wake me up?' And I felt good; I was at a party at midnight that night and I said, 'I've got to call my friend in Boston and make sure she's okay.' If she wasn't okay or didn't answer I was supposed to call her friend Margaret. There are certain responsibilities, little jobs for family members that you have, and it makes you feel good to have them.

"Baba, who's sixty, came down here when she thought she had cancer, for some nurturance. I thought that was a heavy responsibility and I wasn't sure how I felt about it, but in some ways I relished the fact that I *had* a responsibility, that I was expected to do something . . . and Danielle and I felt good nurturing her.

"I feel this incredible need for recognition of this kind of family. I would like to write contracts with each person. And I am researching the legal implications of it. Danielle wants to write a will and to put me in it as her executor. I put Fiona and Danielle on my life insurance policy. These are important things. What if you go insane, who's responsible for you? Who's responsible for your debts? What if you become a junkie and you've got debts all of a sudden? A husband and wife have that. But when you're a lesbian and you're not going to have a husband or wife who does all those things, who ultimately has the responsibility? Or even if you're a straight single woman.

I think that's a heavy issue, because in this society there are legal realities.

"And if there's not societal recognition of what we're doing, sometimes we forget that we're doing it, or we feel like we're not real. I don't know what other family groups are doing, how someone else runs their intentional family. Maybe if some of us who are doing this deliberate family development, if we could talk to one another . . . Maybe we should have a conference on deliberate families. We could get together and have representatives to different workshops and exchange ways of working out different things, like how you go about talking about it on the outside, what some of the contracts are, some of the understandings. What are the elements that make up a family? What are some of the desirable things that you got out of a regular blood family? What are some of the things that you don't want repeated?"

The questions Barb asks are complex and disturbing ones, yet they are necessary for some of us. They also suggest other questions. Do we *want* to create firm structures for nonbiological families? If we do, do we risk institutionalizing them, as the biological family is institutionalized? Can we strengthen, without rigidifying, the nonbiological family? The questions are numerous, confusing, yet very exciting.

9.

Creating Neighborhoods

For some people, having friends who are family living in various parts of the country isn't enough. They miss, and need, the intimacy of daily connection, of frequent and regular sharing. And so they, and members of their chosen families, begin to seek out houses in the same neighborhood, slowly building a community of family members who live within a small radius and are available to each other on a regular basis.

One such woman is Kay, a widow in her mid-forties who has for many years lived in California. She grew up in a large Irish family in which biological and nonbiological family intermingled all the time, and she takes such intermingling for granted. (Kay's honorary aunts and uncles were discussed in chapter 3.) Kay's "extended family," as she calls it, is a mixture of old friends and a group that began coming together in a familylike structure over a decade ago. One of the most fascinating things about talking with Kay is realizing that she takes quite extraordinary things for granted — she certainly doesn't perceive herself as a revolutionary. Yet some of the myths she and her friends have broken down are startling.

For one thing, in Kay's framework, it isn't only spouses and lovers who change residences to be with a person they love. "Years ago when my husband and I lived in Florida, friends came from as far away as California and Portland, Oregon, to live near us and work together. When we moved back to Oregon there was a young fellow of about nineteen or twenty, and he moved out to the West Coast, and two other families moved to Portland, Oregon, so we could all be close." More recently, another friend moved from Pasadena, California, to Venice, California, "because she felt she wanted to be closer to me, and felt that we ought to be near enough to see each other frequently and do things with each other and for each other."

A number of her family people date from these earlier times in Kay's life, but her more formal family is a group of about a dozen people who knew each other in MENSA, a group called Family Synergy (see chapter 12) and the Unitarian Church. "It isn't necessarily that I chose my friends from these organizations, though," she says. "We happen to gravitate to them because of similar interests. Very often it happens that these friends were not part of the organizations but joined later, because we happened to be associated.

"I have a very close friend who's like a sister. I had an automobile accident several years ago; I stayed at her home and she took care of me during that time. Then there's another couple who live seven blocks away. And then my roommate, of course—I live with another woman who's very close. There's one other woman from Boston. These are the closest ones.

"When my husband died a few years ago, the couple did most of the things families do—they came and stayed with me; they made the funeral arrangements. Another friend came and stayed with me, too. And there's a man who was my husband's best friend—I call him my brother. They're the closest friends, they're the people I would call for any of the things that family do—if I were in the hospital, for example.

"Then I have two very close friends who are just about like sisters that I've known since college, for thirty years. They are the ones, if you're in the hospital they come to see you, if you're moving or doing anything, they're the ones who pitch in and help. They live in the same city, but not as close to me as the others.

"I found that geography is very important—the number of times you see each other and have potlucks together . . . I seem to interact more, and gradually have more closeness with, the people who live only six or seven blocks away.

"In our family, we *talk* about being a family. We say, 'This person is like a sister to me' and 'I feel like it's a family,' so we sort of expect our biological brothers and sisters to accept our chosen relatives as *their* chosen relatives—in other words, to treat this person as a sister, or at least as a cousin. So there's sort of an unconscious scanning when you meet someone about whether this person will become one of those people like a family.

"I have a close biological family. My two sisters don't get along very well; they just don't have similar interests at all and they clash. But they actually feel if there's anything important, good or bad, in the other one's life that they will stand by her. My brother lives very near my sister in northern California and they don't even talk on the telephone from one year's end to the other, and yet you just sort of know you have relatives there.

"I don't live very close to my [biological] family, and the interesting part of it may be that that may be another motivation—that you learn a certain pattern of living in a family with these various connections, and you miss it if you're away from it, so you try to reconstruct it. So I feel that having people interacting in a close geographical area is awfully important. When you're used to having family relationships you want to continue them . . . I have the feeling with such people that we're always part of each other's lives."

Some of Kay's chosen family members, however, don't live nearby. "I have a number of people in Portland, Oregon. I hadn't been there in seven years. But we'd talk on the phone and I'd see some of them when they were down here. And when I visited them recently, it was actually a physical shock to me to realize that seven years had passed. Here were all these people and when I visited them it was just as though I'd been with them the day before. And they all called each other up and I went from one house to the next to stay. It was just amazing to me to realize how much closeness there was with these people I hadn't seen in seven years.

"I've lived in various places in my life. I lived in Florida for years, and then in Spain and Mexico and then in Oregon. And when I moved back here to the Los Angeles area there were my friends and we continued just as though the time and the space between hadn't existed at all. It's amazing how people select people who will continue to be close and warm, just like the biological family."

Kay and her husband had no children, and she's never regretted that decision. But she does have relationships with some of the children of her extended family. "My girlfriends' kids who are in their twenties now, they were in their teens when I got to know them, and my husband and I and the others started interacting in raising the kids—they would act toward us like relatives. One of them recently had a baby. When she was born we all felt there was a new baby in the family.

"The mother is one of three sisters in the family. One of the sisters is married, and they have a child and they moved to Hawaii. Then they wanted to move back here, and her husband came up looking for a house. He came over to see me. It happened that my house was up for sale. There was no idea that they'd buy my house, but it worked out; we made an arrangement and I did sell to them. And I think it's definitely because they were in the family. I think it was a matter of a few thousand dollars' difference, and they probably wouldn't have qualified for a loan on the open market. Everybody outside our group was horrified and said, 'You gave them a better deal than in the market,' and I said, 'Well, they're family.' People thought that was a little peculiar—I mean people who don't have this concept. But we felt—the mother and I and all the friends—that this was just a natural thing to do."

The youngest of the three sisters recently graduated from college. As a graduation gift, Kay gave her a trip to Egypt because "the one sister just had a new baby and the other just got a new house, and we couldn't leave this one out."

Sometimes the children in the family are the ones who do the good deeds. "The woman who moved from Pasadena has two daughters. At this point they live in New York, but of course they stay with any one of us when they come out here. At one point before they moved to New York, my father was living with me. He was in his high eighties—eighty-six or eighty-eight. And one of the daughters took him as a grandfather. She'd come over and play guitar and sing with him, and when I would go away she'd come stay in the house and take care of him and cook for him—that's definitely something family does. It was very nice; her girlfriends would come and visit him, and they'd say, 'We don't know any old people like this.' My father was a very, very darling man. He had a beard and a beret, a very rakish-looking man."

The family members spend a lot of time together, one to one and as a group. Often they have potluck dinners together. And, like many Californians, they get together frequently in one friend's hot tub. "Very often we fool around and see how many people we can get in the hot tub. And it's a pretty close activity. The general thing is to wear bathing suits, but when we're just the close group together we go in nude, at night especially. There's quite a lot of intimacy that way — you don't just get undressed and take a bath with anybody. It's very relaxing, sometimes combined with head or foot massages. That's the place where we usually have great talks, great chats.

"We're also on the phone fairly frequently. We have an almost automatic interaction where if somebody needs something, we'll call. There's a single man, and he's sixty, an aerospace engineer, and he lives — oh, about a mile from the rest of us. He's a fountain of knowledge about various things. He can also fix things and repair things. Two other men are engineers and they can fix cars and door latches, and they are always willing to help out with that kind of activity. The man who was my husband's best friend, he's the one who always moves any of us if we have to move. He doesn't have a truck, but he seems to be the one we always call if we're moving.

"We have potluck dinner together at least once or twice a month, and go sit in the hot tub and visit at least once a week. Then we have a bike path here on the ocean and go bike riding together. We go to cultural or sports events together. And anything around illness or death or problem solving. Someone's going through a change and selling their house or getting a divorce or buying a car; that's when we all interact — who knows about this and who can find out about that — finding information for one another. Matchmaking within the group and outside the group: We do some he-ing and she-ing, finding mates and dates for others in the group — we do that through parties or just introducing people.

Hospitality—the people or their friends and relatives can stay over, or we'll pick them up at the airport and show them around town. Or little things like helping fix up the house or hang pictures.

"The way the family people are, let's say my girlfriend Rhoda wants something. She calls me and I say, 'Gee, I can't do anything about that,' or maybe I'm not home, she'll just proceed down the list and call the next one or the next one, and go right on until she finds someone. The women in the group call the men for everything from escorting them somewhere, transportation, fixing something—or if they're just lonely and want company they'll call someone from the group and say, 'Why don't you come over and have dinner with me?'

"A sister of one of the men was visiting from Philadelphia, so I called up this other friend and we all just went out, slipping around nightclubs together—it's that kind of thing. You have a relative from out of town and anyone knows they can call me to pick someone up at the airport or ask me to have the person come stay with me.

"The engineer who fixes things for everybody has a daughter who's going to be married soon, and several of us will go back to her wedding. And if she comes out here she'll come to visit us. Even though she's not really close, she considers that we're her family here.

"The two friends who've been my friends for thirty years and who, wherever I've lived, in Oregon or Florida, have always come and visited me, don't interact very much with the others. They live a little farther away and we see each other at different times. They're the people I'd call first if I needed really to have a long discussion on something I was planning, something I was thinking about. They're the closest to me.

"It's interesting, too . . . with this housing market we've all talked about different ways of living together.

When I sold my house, other people were saying, 'How can you sell your house?' and when I thought about it I realized I really had any number of places to live, because so many of my friends had houses. Then two of them sold *their* houses, and that way I lost two of my other houses to live in." She laughs—it's clear that she knows that no one in the family would let anyone else go homeless.

I ask her about the composition of the group. "There's one man who never married, that's the one who was my husband's best friend. Incidentally, he has biological family here but he feels closer to us than to them. Then this other man is divorced. There's a married couple— they have children who don't interact with us. The three other women are divorced, and the two sisters are divorced. About a dozen of us."

They also have the kind of people one finds in the traditional family—the ones who are troublesome and irritating but are still loved because they're family. "There's one woman who's consciously called one of the family, and she's a very dear person—she does all the things, runs errands for you if you're sick—but she's rather abrasive, which everybody verbalizes. We'll say, 'Well, you know how she is.' And there's another lady and her son; everybody says about them, 'Well, you know they're part of the family.' He's in his twenties and has been part of this since he was about ten. But both these women are very aggressive, very abrasive, and they really are the kind of relatives that you tolerate because 'they're Aunt so-and-so and they're good-hearted and you can always call them up to ask them to make something or sew something,' but you really don't share with them the close things that go on in your life, because they're rather cantankerous and judgmental."

Does she see a difference between friends who are family and friends who aren't; "I have a number of friends I don't consider family. There's a different feeling

with the people you feel are family. You think about them
when you're doing things and you want to include them
and you share all kinds of things with them. I have a very
good friend who could never, never, never be family.
First of all she's rather aloof and distant, a do-it-yourselfer
to the extent that she would think it rather undignified
to be part of a family or to disclose yourself. So she
couldn't even be one of the remote, distant relatives.
Most of the others know her and sometimes we do things
with her, but we know that she isn't really part of the
family. And what differentiates us is that there are things
you tell in the family, and things you do with people
who are part of the family, and you *talk* about being
part of a family."

Interestingly, Kay's biological family members also have
chosen family. Her sister runs a displaced homemaker
center, and helps bring people together as "grannies"
and "sisters." Among this sister's own family network
is a widow whose elderly friends have chosen her as their
"intentional heir" and are helping her to put her son
through college.

Kay and her friends' decision to live close to one
another seems to have evolved slowly, almost organically.
Barbara, a middle-aged artist and former nun, made the
decision a little more consciously. For her, the concept
of neighborhood was very important. Her network of
family started in the mid-1970s. "I lived on just a
one-block street in an old Victorian neighborhood in
Atlanta that's been renovated. I got a friend and her
husband to buy a house down the street from me, and
then there was a house across the street that friends
rented. There were then four or five friends living on
that street.

"We started having Sunday-night dinners. And it also
included people we were seeing at that time, who did not
live on the block. At first it was a block dinner, and then

it became more than that. People would move from this place to other places and get involved with other people. There's a core group.

"There have been some changes. But people still eat together. There's an ex-lover of mine in the group who is my very good friend now. He's done all the work on my house — he's a sculptor and builder. He's built all my furniture.

"There are three or four kids in the network — three, really, until a couple of months ago when someone had a baby. Suzanne and Pat have three children and Betsy has one. It's like a niece-and-nephew situation. It's good because those of us who've chosen not to have children enjoy them; they're real darling. You can do all kinds of stuff with them and then you can go home.

"The other thing that's real interesting and that lots of people like is that we're all living in houses. I bought a house — we all bought old houses because they were cheap. We're always renovating, so we have these big shitty jobs that you don't want to do yourself. We usually meet about an hour ahead of time, about 5:30 or 6:00, and do an hour's work. You do a big job — ten people in one hour so you're getting ten people hours.

"We all have wood heaters; we have these big piles of wood in our houses; so we take our chain saws and we cut it all up so it can fit into the wood heaters. We all move huge mounds of earth when we want to do some landscaping. Generally it's a crappy job, but it's real fun with nine or ten people.

"We see each other a lot individually, or else in couples, aside from the Sunday dinners. Betsy and I are close, and she lives on the block. She and I see each other every day. Scott, who I'm involved with, lives down the block. I see him two or three times a week. Scott and I do things with Max and Marsha as a couple."

As usually happens in families, there are a lot of

problems and quarrels in Barbara's group. "I've been having a difficult time lately. There are protectors and rescuers in the group—there are women who emotionally protect the men. I've been talking with a few people who have been anxious about the situation in our neighborhood because it's been real unsafe and there have been a few rapes. We've tried to talk about it in the group. The men get real uptight and then these women come to their rescue.

"Last Sunday night it was at my house—we go over to each other's houses. I wanted to talk about where we're going and how we feel about the group. I brought it up, and a few of the men attacked me." This led to a discussion about the group's dynamics. "What we are going to do now is go around the circle and talk about where we're at so we can get rid of paranoid fantasies. The evening was good. I think what's happening is that we're getting closer and that's real scary."

There is a lot of support and caring within Barbara's group. "When I had an abortion and needed cash for the next day, I asked everyone—and one man, even though I knew he probably didn't approve of abortions, he gave me the money. There's a real sense of commitment. One woman got a divorce several months ago, and her husband withdrew from the group—we were real angry that he wasn't going to be our friend any longer." Yet she's not certain whether, if the group stopped meeting regularly or if people moved out of town, the members would stay in touch. "Some would. Five of them. The others I'm not sure of—I'm not sure it means that much to them." The idea of impermanence with her family group doesn't seem to upset Barbara.

Barbara's concept of family is very tied up with that of community, of neighborhood. "We live in the oldest part of the inner city. About eight years ago people started buying the houses real cheaply and fixing them up.

Most of it's really elegant; some of it's high-priced property . . . The neighborhood system in Atlanta is real strong; it's real organized, and very active. We stopped a freeway that was going to cut through our neighborhoods; it took us ten years. They had taken down an enormous stretch of houses by the time we could finally stop them. We also have our old neighborhood credit union. It lends money, second mortgages, only to people in the neighborhood . . . It's important for me to live in a neighborhood that's a real mixture of people age-wise and economically. We get two or three hundred people out for a protest in our neighborhood."

Barbara does not miss her life in the convent, and has little sense that the "sisterhood" of nuns formed any kind of family. Interestingly, she was in her order both at a time when it was a strict, traditional order and when it was affected by the ecumenical changes of the mid-sixties. "I was a nun for fifteen years, 1953 to whatever. It was a pretty wealthy order so we all got educated and traveled a lot. I went to Europe for nine months. I went into the convent when it was real traditional. It really has changed. People are out in ordinary clothes, living in apartments, supporting themselves, and sometimes with a couple of other women. Five of us were sent down here to do that in 1967.

"In the order when it was traditional, there was very little personal talk to each other—everything was very formal. When we came down here, the five of us tried to make a family, but it was almost impossible. It cannot be so artificially made. It grows organically.

"In the convent, we were warned not to have 'particular friendships.' They said not to have friendships that would be taking you out of the community—you could only have friendships in terms of the community." Now she has found a different kind of community—one that truly gives her the support she needs.

Like Barbara, George and his friends have consciously chosen to create a family by buying property in the same neighborhood and to integrate the sense of community with a commitment to the already existing neighborhood. The commitment that his friends feel toward functioning as family was dramatically illustrated a few years ago, when George learned he had cancer.

I came across George's story early in 1980 — some friends sent me an article he had written about his recovery in *New Age* magazine. It was an important article for me: I had only recently learned of my younger brother's cancer.

George's doctors described his recovery as "a miracle." He had used a combination of surgery, chemotherapy, vitamins, spiritual healing, and visualization. Perhaps most important, he had used his friends. The people closest to him had networked, making sure that at least one of them was always with him — talking with him, singing, holding his hand, sometimes just being there silently by his side. They stayed by his hospital bed all night, so that whenever he awakened someone was there to reassure him.

It was, of course, a tremendously heartening story, and I sent a copy off to my brother right away. I also kept a copy for myself. George's experience with cancer had been very much like my own experience with severe depression, except that in his case the stakes had been higher. He lived in Philadelphia, not too far from New York, and I wrote to him, asking if I could interview him for this book. I was anxious to meet this man who had recovered from cancer, and whose friends played such a large part in his recovery.

George lives in Trollheim, a big, rambling communal house, with his wife, their children, another couple and their children, and several other people. Four of them sat around in one of the air-conditioned bedrooms talking with me on one of the hottest days of the summer's heat wave: George; his housemate, John, who was one of the people who had formed the network; Ross, an old friend and former housemate who had come back to Philadelphia from New York to nurse George during his recuperation; and Barb, a housemate who had moved into Trollheim recently, long after George's hospitalization and recovery, and who has a benign tumor, which she is dealing with through holistic healing methods. Except for John, they are all members of the Movement for a New Society, a leftist group committed to effecting both personal and political change (see Chapter 13). They are also all involved in reevaluation counseling, a somewhat controversial peer-counseling technique that has been popular in parts of the left in recent years.

Members of Movement for a New Society, including George and Ross, started the Life Center in Philadelphia in the early seventies. The Life Center is a large building located a block from where George lives: its goal was to create a close-knit community in which people who were working together for political change could live near each other and share their daily lives. "We were feeling stretched out in our different communities," says Ross, a soft-spoken, amiable man, who, for all his radicalism and informality has an air of almost old-fashioned gentlemanliness.

They bought houses and rented apartments in the neighborhood—where possible, on the same block. "We began to realize that we had to set up living support mechanisms, things that weren't just occasional routines but that really made us feel that a sense of the continuity of support was there. And so we began learning, largely by trial and error, how to have house meetings, how to be supportive to people on a daily basis when they were going through personal crises, how to handle the question of child care when they were single-parent families, that even regularly parented families need help a lot," Ross continues. Communal living served a double purpose; it brought those who were living in the same household more closely together, and it cut down on the cost of living, so that the members of the Life Center could afford to work part time and put the greater part of their energy into the political and personal work they felt was so vital. There are about twenty households now, most of which are communal but a few of which are composed of individual couples. They share their personal lives, and they get together regularly for political meetings and social activities.

"We've got quite a range among these various houses," says George thoughtfully. He is a tall, wiry, and utterly healthy-looking man of about 40. "It's one of the advantages of having a variety of houses—people's needs are different. For example, in our house: eight years ago when John and Marcy moved in, and Berit and I, and another couple, this third couple was into very intense community right away. They really wanted to work very hard establishing a whole lot of closeness. And the other four of us didn't want that; we wanted it to grow organically over time. And that was the major split. So they moved out because they thought we were terribly slow-poky and cold. So there are these differences among the houses. And the houses tend to get characterized by that—people find other people who want either more 'family' or less 'family.' "

House meetings, struggles around child care, and the effort to live as a community strengthened the relationships of the various friends, and created a strong support network. Child care was shared, though, says John, "it's very clear to everybody whose children are whose and whose parents are whose, so that we're not a nuclear family; we're more like an extended family." '

"Yes, but every once in a while while Ingrid [George's daughter] calls you 'Daddy.' " George laughs.

John is short, blond, and bearded — friendly, but less expansive-seeming than George. He is also several years younger. "A lot of the way we grew," says John, "was a sort of bouncing off the way we grew up. We knew what we didn't like about that, and we were trying other things. George and Berit had been married for twelve years in a fairly traditional kind of relationship, and Marcy and I were just starting to live together, and some women's issues were coming up in those relationships, and there were lots of different changes happening at the same time. So lots of things have come up for us about what commitment means in each of our marriages — particularly in the context where we're getting a lot of outside support, unlike most marriages where the expectation or the hope is that most of your support is going to come from your spouse. So that each couple had gone through a lot of changes internally. And we're all going through a lot of changes about how close we are at any given time and how much commitment we hope for."

Ross, though he left the community and now lives as a "househusband" with his wife and her two children in New Jersey, still feels bonded with the people in the community — especially with George, whom he has been close to for eighteen years. "We all need home-based persons, and I feel that especially in this culture at this time it's just a waste of human energy investment when you break with another person you've lived with for a number of years, to not try and figure out ways of sustaining that relationship. There's so much bombardment that we're going to find people holding on for longer to each other, because there's so much insecurity. And we all need to have some kinds of familiars."

With their sense of personal commitment and connection, it seemed natural that when disaster fell on one of the community, the others would be there to help. George's cancer was seen as everyone's problem. "They were like concentric circles of people," says George. "The most immediate circle was what we called my support group. That consisted of John and Mary in this house, and three people from other houses. Ross wasn't in the Living Center at the time—he was in Albany—but he took off for a month and came down and nursed me after I got out of the hospital.

"The support group was Berit's idea—she didn't feel she would be able to handle it alone. She asked me who I wanted, and I named those people. They got together very frequently in the beginning—twice a week—when there were heavy decisions to be made, like whether to do chemotherapy. Then it got to be once a week, then every other week." Sometimes George himself was part of these meetings, sometimes not. Members of the support group also got together in groups of two or three, dealing with their own feelings about death, about cancer, about their fears for George. They made sure that he was never alone, except when he wanted to be. He had a private room in the hospital, and for the first six days after surgery people were with him around the clock. They talked to him, held his hand, played musical instruments. Once he awoke in the middle of the afternoon to find his hand being held by a friend sitting beside him in the chair, sound asleep. They also took over his household chores and child-care responsibilities. After he left the hospital, they made certain he never had to go alone to the doctor, or to face alone the nausea that followed chemotherapy treatments. They discussed various treatment alternatives with him; they prayed with him.

He had trouble at first accepting all the caring. "I get uneasy if I cannot 'pay back' someone for the attention I get," he wrote in his article. "I have an emotional block to the experience of grace. Lying in the hospital bed, with a variety of tubes coming in and out of me, there was no way I could reciprocate, and the result was teary feelings of unworthiness surfacing in the presence of 'unearned love.' "[1]

Another problem he had to deal with was that people outside of his community didn't understand what was going on. "There was a head nurse on my floor who stopped one of the people coming to visit me in the middle of the night, and said, 'Don't you realize that you folks are going to kill George off? We all know that you can't have so many visitors and survive. Why don't you give him a chance to heal?' And my friend had to try to interpret to the nurse that the people with me knew what they were doing. One of the things through living together and working together as part of this community is that the skill level has become very high."

George was able to use his experience later, when another member of the community was hospitalized for a serious illness. "When Gary got sick, my first thought was, 'Who's coordinating his visits?' I called around to find out who the coordinator was. That's a very important function—keeping the overview of who's visiting when. In his case, he didn't want a whole lot of visitors, which was a really different choice from mine. So instead the arrangement was that we used the chapel, and he was 'at home' at certain hours each evening in the chapel. And we'd be there, telling him funny stories, helping him to open up. Because one of the problems in this whole support thing, of course, is how much support can you stand? And you have to respect different needs."

"I really think George's experience was a model for how people got together to handle my problem this year," says Barb, who has said little throughout the interview but has listened intensely. "But even when there's not a large problem happening, people have learned to be okay with asking a friend to grow with them through anything that's difficult, to not face anything alone when you're really likely to get wiped out by the result. And just that recognition—not toughing it out or playing a macho or take-on-the-whole-world attitude toward stuff— is a big shift for a lot of people, especially a lot of political people."

None of the people I spoke with feel a commitment to live in the same house, or even in the same city, with each other, though George does see himself staying permanently with Berit, whom he calls his "life partner—I don't like the institution of marriage." But George and Ross, at least, see a permanency in their relationship. "I think if I moved to the other end of the world," says Ross, "I'd want to be in a space to say, 'Gee, I'm going to be in touch with this guy at least once or twice a year.' But I don't think we've ever said that to each other. It's just been, by the grace of whatever, that we've been close enough in time of need. We just presumed on each other; we said, 'Help, I need you now.' We've both done that. It's nurtured a very important bonding. We're trying to define that middle space, where you don't get locked in and you don't feel like a complete butterfly."

That "middle space" is a crucial one to nonbiological family—and I suspect that if we would only admit it, to biological family as well. It is the space whose exis- tence is denied by writers like Novak and Lasch, who insist that there is only complete self-negating absorption into marriage and parenthood, or total selfishness. In each relationship, people can and must define the bound- aries of commitment. If the relationship is sexual, is it monogamous? Will the members of the relationship live together? If not, will they commit themselves to living in the same town, the same geographical area? In what ways will their needs for either solitude or companionship mesh; in what ways will they clash? When we abandon the notion that there is one set of rules applicable to all relationships—and when we choose family, we implicitly abandon this notion—there is the complex but rewarding work of creating appropriate rules for each individual relationship. Whether this is worked out verbally or subliminally, it is there in all relationships. The more conscious people are of creating friendship families, the more clearly they will attempt to seek out, and define, that middle space.

10.

How Professionals Make
Families for Themselves and
Others

S ome of the people I spoke with were conscious not only of their own need to create family from friends, but also of the need to extend what they had experienced in their own lives into the larger world. For a lucky few, the nature of their work created a means of doing this. Among those I spoke with were two therapists, a sociology teacher, and a community organizer. All have created, or are in the process of creating, their own nonbiological families, and all have taken their concept of creating family and brought it to their work.

One of the therapists I spoke with was Jane, a totally delightful woman in her early forties, who has a laugh that is both frequent and infectious. Her talk flows in a comfortable stream-of-consciousness, and we find

ourselves digressing often: I'm surprised, listening to the
tape of our conversation, that we've spent nearly ten
minutes discussing our favorite soap opera. She's one of
those people whom I instantly feel I've known for months.

Jane brings her concept of "family" to her therapy.
Sometimes she counsels friends who are having problems
in their relationships — a kind of platonic couples counseling. More often she sees her clients in groups and
introduces them to the concept of the therapy group
as a temporary family. As we talk, she connects this
concept to her personal experience. "When I look for
recognizing a friend who's family in my own life, there's
something very primitive about that attraction, and I
guess it has something to do with the quality in my family
of origin which I call 'enmeshed,' to use a sort of clinical
term. That having come from an enmeshed family as
opposed to a disengaged family, the 'kid' in me who's
still looking for family responds to people with whom I
can become very enmeshed. And when I do therapy, one
of the first things I try to find out in a group situation is
what kind of family of origin people have, to see who's
likely to match up with one another. For instance, if somebody came from a very distant, sort of disengaged family,
when they're in trouble they're probably going to seek out
the harsh familiarity of somebody who's going to give
them advice, maybe, rather than a lot of support, love, and
affection — someone who will almost parent them in the
old, authoritarian sense of parent. So when we're talking
about a therapy group becoming a chosen family, we're
talking very overtly about the kind of matching that
people are probably going to find most useful. And it
seems to work out that someone from a very disengaged
family will feel really crazy if they're matched up with a
warm, sticky sort of intrusive cohort from the group,
whereas someone from that sort of family will go for that

when they're in trouble — and they'll think of the person they turn to as a sister, a cousin.

"In a therapy group, if you say in the first session that one of the functions that we're going to serve is to be a family for one another, the connotations of the word 'family' make some people very nervous. They think in terms of intimacy — that they don't know these people, they get very scared; and others think in terms of arguments, bad vibes, and they get very scared too . . . But about three to four weeks into things, people start to talk about 'the family.' It's still artificial because it hasn't had time to mature, but the thing is that they get used to the idea and they start smiling to themselves at the idea of being able to do this in a deliberate way.

"One of the problems for me in this is that it's more than likely that, as the therapist, I will be cast in the parental role. I have to watch the 'children,' if you will, make friends with one another and know that in order to be effective I have to stay out of that. They can go off to a bar after sessions and have drinks together and do stuff like that, or they can call one another during the week and go to the movies."

An important part of her work is counseling couples — whether romantically or platonically linked couples. "When people say 'couples counseling,' they almost always mean heterosexual couples, and they certainly mean people who feel a commitment to each other that society will recognize — a sexual or romantic kind of thing. I've worked with women and encouraged them to work with their friends who are family in that way . . . I don't know exactly what the distinction is, where people decide they won't be lovers but will be this kind of family to one another. There's some sort of mutual decision . . . It sounds awfully Freudian, but if you feel that you're with a real sister, then it depends on how you feel about having sex with your sister . . . They've chosen, and it probably hasn't been too hard a decision, not to be lovers but to be family in this other way. They may call themselves a family, but more often they'll say that they're close, close friends . . . They'll say, 'We have a commitment to one another, so that we want to work through this problem we're having; this is part of a long continuum of time.' "

In her own life, Jane is in the midst of redefining some of her familial relationships. She has just left her marriage of over twenty years, but still feels strongly bonded to her husband: he's no longer her spouse, but he's still her family. "We may or may not get a divorce — we probably will — but he'll always be family, though not husband. These terms — I don't know how you're ever going to make head or tail of them. To me it's very clear that Michael's family. We touch one another in a certain way. I don't want to be a wife anymore, but that has nothing to do with our connectedness."

For Jane, it's been important to clearly choose to be family: she hasn't found that friendships have evolved into family relationships. "I've wanted that to happen, but it hasn't worked: it hasn't lasted."

Some of her chosen family have been couples with whom she and Michael were close. "There's one kind of family in which a marriage will adopt couples and their children as family, and there's more compromise than you'd have made with individual friends. This one couple that we know, there's a couple sense of family — spending holidays together and so forth, and the kids are definitely like cousins. They feel like my sisters' and brothers' children, except my sister and brother don't have children. There's a real incestuous quality there in some ways. Now that I think of it, the breakdown is really that the guy and I are the two people that really have the family sense, between the two of us — we fuzz it with this couple thing, for sexual reasons. It's an erotic bond as well as a family bond, but of course there's a big taboo on it . . . I don't know what's going to happen with this couple now, which is one of the questions on my mind — are they still going to let me be a member of their family if I'm not married?"

The people in Jane's chosen family aren't a family unit — some know each other; some don't. "I have to go back to this transference notion that I just keep repeating over and over — that in my family of origin, people talked to one another as a group but the really meaningful inter-actions were not done in groups but it would be two people getting together, and that would be when the sense of family was highest. So I repeat that fantasy in my adult life. I have a fantasy about, wouldn't it be nice if all seven of these people in my family were talking on the same wavelength? But we don't; that's really not how it works. So I tend not to go seeking that with the other family.

"One of Michael's brothers is a member of my family. He was married and his wife was like family to me too, but that was an entirely separate operation. But Ken's not really family to Mike — he's more like my brother than Mike's.

"When Ken and Sue got divorced — it was before the day of no-faults — they had to have grounds for divorce. So both of them, because I was part of their family, asked me to testify in court that he'd been cruel and abusive to her so that they could get the divorce. Everybody in the extended family thought it was outrageous, because they didn't think it was appropriate that I should play this role. But to these two people and to me, it was a facilitative role to take. If the court is making jackass distinctions then we have to go through jackass rituals. So, okay, because we're family we do this for one another.

"One family member who comes to mind is a guy who lives in Arizona whom I haven't seen in a long time.

We get in touch with one another around birthdays and like that, but if he were to come to Boston or I were to go to Arizona, there's absolutely no doubt that we'd revivify our old language, our way of being with one another. Of course he's my family and he knows that too. You know Vonnegut's notion of a 'kurass'? That's what I keep thinking of as we have this conversation — almost like a sense of destiny with some of these people. There are in some aspects either a shared set of experiences or history — it could be a past lifetime, or you've done things in distant cities but in similar ways. In a couple of important ways, you're twins. So there's an element of narcissism in all this, too. One of the people I feel very close to in this way, we discovered with no surprise that we'd been very depressed at the same exact time before we knew one another, for a very limited period of time and for very similar reasons. Now, I could meet another person I didn't have the same kind of bonding with, and we could say, yeah, we were depressed from September to November in 1978, and it would just be a coincidence."

Are any of her friends also family to her children? Oh yes, she tells me. "Ronnie is an aunt to Hilary and Leslie, but not to Paul and Jeff so much. Ken is uncle to . . ." She stops, confused, and bursts out laughing. "Oh, I forget — he's a *real* uncle. Let me say this right: Ken, my brother-in-law, is Jeffrey's real uncle, and also his actual uncle — more so than any others in the family."

This brings up the whole area of biological family who are also chosen family. "One of my biological sisters is also a member of my family — we're very close — that's not true of my relationship with my other biological sister.

"Now in my family — the one in which I am the mother of children — I have trouble with boundaries around my role as a parent and wanting to be, not a peer, because if you remember when you gave birth and what it was like, there will never be a completely peerlike feeling . . . But for instance, one of my daughters does a lot of writing, I really do feel like I'm talking to somebody who is more like a sister than a daughter, in the sense that I don't feel particularly that I'm way up here talking on one level of expertise . . . Some people have not understood that lack of boundary in the relationship between myself as a mother and those kids as my daughters or sons. And they've said it's not fair to children to have blurry roles like that; it should be sharp and clear and distinct. I'm not sure I agree about that, but I don't know. We may find out later, as they lie on a couch ten years from now and say, 'She never acted like my mother,' that it wasn't a great thing. But for now I really don't know that: can your children be members of your family of friends? At what age? Is it fair to them for you to want that from them? It's almost as if you have two relationships with them. One they could tap into if they needed to, like 'I need you to be my mother and I need to be the kid right now.' But then there might be the relationship on a level of intensity which is quite separate from the fact that one of you gave birth to the other and that one has a certain obligation to take care of that other, and that other has the right to ask for unlimited services up to a certain age.

"The one thing I would like to leave out of my family as an adult is the same thing I would have liked to leave out of my family as a child, which is people who tell you what to do and give you a lot of advice and in general have all the power. Critics and blamers I try not to have in my adult family at all. It's funny, though: these people have certain kinds of qualities, a certain kind of objectivity, that I've been looking for in my life. They won't become my family, but I might want them in there at some time. I might not call them and say, 'I think I'm going to get a divorce,' because I know what they think

about divorce. But I might call them after I'm safely
settled for a while, to get some kind of balance in my life
— like theirs is a reality too and now I'm strong enough
to hear what they have to say. It's a sort of dress rehearsal
for the real world, whereas the family people are a sanc-
tuary for when you're going through a hard time. And
I want them out there. If they're going to be considered
family in any way, shape, or form, then they're kind of
like stepfamily. There's something illegitimate about that
group. They're needed, but there's something about them
that's not quite right.

"To paraphrase Marge Piercy's 'the writer is one who
writes': The family is one who families — whether that
consists of having tea together and not emoting, or whether
it consists of three a.m., and you're crying and saying,
'I have to be irrational now,' and the person doesn't
say, 'Well, why don't you call a crisis hotline?' And it's
recognition . . . I try to get my friends when I am feeling
sane, and say, 'Sometimes when I go crazy here's what
I do; would you kindly monitor me?' I usually try to
monitor myself, but sometimes I do a rotten job of it.
And so they do. And I expect them to tell me their signs
of craziness too, so we can heal. So that, if you say that
your jaw aches, I'll know that means you are very uptight.
I won't just say, 'Oh, that's too bad.' I'll know that means
you've been crying for three days, or whatever it means."

Another therapist, Francis, also tries to build the
concept of family into both his personal life and his practice. He is a homosexual whose therapy clients are pre-
dominantly gay. He is in his early forties — pleasant,
soft-spoken, relaxed. "When I have gay groups," he tells
me, "I try to cement networks among them. You're
here together, you should be here for each other. It's
beginning to work that way in one of the groups."

In his own life, his chosen family consists of about ten
people, male and female, gay and straight. Some of the

people are those he was living with at the time I spoke with him (he now lives alone, but hopes to find a communal situation again in the future). Interestingly, he feels that because his commune wasn't a consciously planned family, it had unresolvable problems. "Since 1969 I've been living in what I've always called an alternative family, and it happened without any kind of conscious choice. Suddenly I found myself in a communal situation, and it was my family. The deepest things that went on in my life they all shared. But I've found in the past few years that it isn't working out. The reason is that we never sat down to say what we are about, what we are to each other, what are our responsibilities. We have a child living with us: we never discussed are we going to participate in her upbringing, are we going to be responsible for child care?

"It's three men, one woman, and a female child. And I think that's one of the big problems. I've discussed this with the woman in the house, and it's too hard for her. When there was another woman living in the house it was much more balanced, and it was working out much better. So I've seen that for me, I need the balance of children, adults, male, and female . . . Most of my extended family are women, not men — although that's changing; there are more and more men that I'm finding now that I can relate to in ways like I have with women, in terms of being more intimate, being there in a supportive way.

"Extended family isn't just the people I'm living with, but friends that I've met since I lived here. Most of the people I've lived with at some point.

"The difference between friends who are family and those who aren't? There are those I feel a real deep connection with, the same kind of connection that it's assumed you're supposed to feel toward your biological family. There's love there, real deep love, and a lot of trust and a lot of caring. There's that quality versus a kind of casual friendship, people you see a few times a month, you go out to a movie together — it sort of has a lighter quality to it. They're not the people I would call if I was really freaking out or needing support.

"There are places I know I could go, like some people say, 'I could visit my aunt and she'd always feed me and let me in,' and there are certain places in the country where I know that's true. It's family, and they're going to be there for me and vice versa. It's people that I've gone through a lot of changes with. One of them is my ex-wife, actually, which is really nice. There's still a deep connection.

"The more and more I get in touch with this, the more conscious I am not only of the excitement, but of the level of commitment that it involves — you can't be casual about it anymore. In the past, because I was so mobile for a while — I was out of the country for several years — there wasn't this level of commitment. It would never have occurred to me, 'Well, I can't leave so and so,' whereas I might have done that if it was a lover. Suddenly I'm seeing that I have to look at that. It's scary, because I like having the mobility.

"In almost every house I've lived in there have been children, and I've always felt real close relationships with them. And I've always been involved in the child care. I love it; I like kids and I really like being around them. I'm hoping that the next living situation I get into will have more balance, will have more kids.

"I'm thinking of moving out and living alone for a few years, just to get a little focused — I haven't lived alone since 1969. Just to kind of look at things and look at the issue of children. I've been putting out the word — 'if you hear of anyone that's having an abortion, let me know.' It's come real close. In fact, a close friend was having an abortion, and she and the man she was with decided they couldn't give it to me because it was too heavy in terms of knowing me so well, how they'd feel knowing I had the child, so they went and had the abortion. But that caused me to do a lot of thinking, because I had to decide. I had told them I was interested and we had to sit down and talk about the implications, and it forced me to really look at where I was in terms of a child. And I realized that after all the agony I went through and all the doubt, that I wanted it, even though it was going to be difficult to do alone, being a gay male and all the things I'd run into. So I've been thinking of foster parenting. I don't know, it's hard to find situations where you can parent as a single male."

His therapy work in the past has involved creating familial situations with children; he'd like that to happen again.

"I have a fantasy about spending my old age around a lot of kids — I haven't figured it out yet. I used to do day care, and then house parenting with emotionally disturbed kids in Oregon. I loved that, and I also think when I get much older of getting back into that. I really think the concept of grandparents, or just older people, being around emotionally disturbed kids can be very powerful. Most older people tend to care for kids with a kind of mellowness and a kind of stability that a lot of younger people who are working with them don't have . . . So my fantasy is: let's have the house parents take care of all the nurturing and the discipline, and I see myself as being more free to take care of the nurturing, not having to be so concerned about all the house rules, so to speak. Anyway, that's one of the things I've often thought of. But however it happens, I do envision children being in my life."

Unlike Francis, Anita, also a therapist, doesn't especially see children as being part of her life. But in other ways, she is much like him. A lesbian who is very concerned with creating familial friendship networks, she brings her theory into her work both as a counselor and as a college teacher. She is an impressive-looking woman: tall, large-boned, with steel gray hair and a firm clear voice.

For many years Anita has been concerned with the concept of strengthening recognition of friendship ties, and for two consecutive years taught a group of graduate students who were doing their masters' theses on friendship. "Both times, we surveyed about one hundred people. The first time we interviewed second-year students about what their friendship networks were, and the second time we interviewed counselors about *their* friendship networks. I was amazed that the majority of counselors said they discussed with their friends the kinds of friends they wanted to have, so that it was a conscious thing."

Anita's method of conceptualizing friendship networks is far more methodical and complex than anyone else's I spoke with. "Essentially what I do in the surveys is first have people list their friends. I then ask them to look at the different ages of their friends: that tells you something about your own agism, as well as your historical perspective. Another variable that's important is history — how long have you known your friends?

"But the most important thing is your relationship to them. I have them draw a bull's eye. I usually do a three-level bull's eye. Say you were doing this. You'd place yourself in the middle. You'd place your friends in the inner circle, second circle, third circle, in terms of both closeness and involvement. By closeness I mean sentiment, emotional stuff — how you *feel* about the person. By involvement I mean how integral are they to your life? Those two factors are key: you need both of them to be meeting your needs in a broad perspective. You can feel very close to a friend who lives in California — and they meet emotional needs, support needs, just knowing that they love you. But they can't meet the needs of talking over an issue so much. I've never done it in figures, but the 'closeness' rating for that person may be eight on a scale of ten, and the 'involvement' only three. So you probably wouldn't put them in the inner circle because of your lack of involvement with each other — involvement in time, in different aspects of your life, your work, your family, your history, your social life. The broader the involvement the more close they will be to you, and the more they will be there for you.

"If you consider your lover or your spouse your friend, they're often in the inner circle. People have asked me about children, and I usually answer, 'If you consider your child your friend, then include them.' But I somehow have an uneasy feeling about that, because a child is usually a drain, rather than a give-and-take relationship.

"There's a conference coming up, and I want to do a presentation on reconceptualization of family — about the friendship network as a reconceptualization of the family.

"I also *do* counseling. Just as we work with families, I'd like to do counseling for people and their friends. For the straight world, essentially what I've done is conceptualize the network as your nuclear family *plus* your friendship network."

As a lesbian feminist, does she differentiate between men and women in friendship networks? "I have men friends in my own network. I have some sense — there's a little documentation for this, some of the developmental stuff that's come out — that woman have a different kind of friendship with each other than they have with men and than men have with each other. Women have a closer, more intimate, more involved network; women have it fairly close with men, and men with men have it less. But when I bring it up with my students it's hard to get anything substantive; people rebel against that idea. This year somebody said to me that they felt that men were just as intimate with their friends as women were, but that the character and nature in which that is shown is very different. I can't say no to that, nor can I say yes.

"Part of my whole agenda is trying to get people to be more conscious of their friendships. Our attitudes have really been that friends just come and go and that's cool, that's the value, the worth they have. So I've been advocating more consciousness, advocating that people build their friendships, build the kind of friendships they want with each other. I do that with the people I make friends with. We don't necessarily talk about all the details but more about how we'd be there for each other or how much of a commitment we have — like if I got seriously ill, would someone take total care of me — a working through the friendship. How much we might see each other, be in each other's life, that sort of thing.

"Mostly when I think of friends and friendship networks I'm thinking in terms of gratification, need meeting. That's what a family is about — meeting each other's social, psychological, emotional needs. And I'd go so far as to say that the majority of those needs are really met by friends. So for me, being with each other is the most important thing — though I have one friend who's like family that I've known since grade school and our lifestyles are so much in conflict that we haven't had much contact in recent years. But it's very clear to me that in time we'll be back together again.

"The reason I call it a 'network' is that I feel it's essentially a social system that we're the center of — that I'm the center of. The people in it aren't necessarily connected with each other at all, but they're all connected to me. This system is pretty open in that people can come in and out of it — the boundaries are not tight. But the function of the system is to meet my needs, and for me to meet other people's needs.

"What that means is that there needs to be a certain number of people in my network, so that if I have *A* to

N needs, then I need to have enough friends to cover those, as well as the kinds of friends who are going to give me different viewpoints, and so forth. But I also need in many instances more than one friend per need. So that, for example, if I have a need to be held and cry with somebody, I need more than one friend in my network that I can do that with, because the person may not be there at the time, or have their own problems to deal with at that time. In terms of the fluidity, mobility of that network, the network and its need-gratifying capability need to remain stable, ideally, but the people in the system constantly change and shift. They shift in being closer to me, and they shift in that as my needs change my relationships to the people in it change. One of the things I feel is really important is to periodically look at your network and see what's cooking there, because it's a very human thing — it's like a live organism, and as it changes it may really be causing stress for you, or you may really be feeling down in the dumps, depressed, frustrated because of it.

"When I was working on my network in the past day or two, I put in my inner circle Toni, my lover, and Debbie, a friend who used to live with me — we were very tight and she was obviously and clearly an inner-circle friend. Then a year ago she moved to an hour away from here and is in town once or twice a week, but there are also periods when she isn't in town at all. And I realized as I described what my inner-circle friends looked like (and this is what *mine* looks like; it isn't necessarily what other people's looks like), that over this year I'd continued to see Debbie as an inner-circle friend. But according to my own definition, for a friend to be inner circle I really want them to be in touch with my daily life — not that we necessarily see each other every day, but that the frequency· of contact is enough so that we're familiar with what's happening every day. Which also means that we're

there for each other on much smaller issues than we would
if we were on a weekly or monthly level. So I realized
when I was writing this thing that Debbie wasn't really
an inner-circle friend now, that she really is much more
of a second-circle friend. And then I thought, 'My God,
that's why we're still having hassles with each other.'
So during the year that change has happened in our
relationship, but I've still thought of her as an inner-circle
friend; I've had those expectations.

"I'm aware that I haven't been very satisfied with my
friendship network. I'm putting too much into Toni and
not enough into other people. A lot of that has to do with
the shift of Debbie out, which has led me to depend more
and more on Toni. And finding another inner-circle friend
isn't a simple matter — particularly when I wasn't really
looking for one, or even open to one. I don't mean that
now I'm on the prowl for another inner-circle friend, but
I'm open to it. While Debbie and Toni were my inner
circle, I didn't need anyone else there; I didn't have any
more energy for it. So that's an example of how mobility
affects it.

"Part of what I'm trying to do is build a structure, a
way of thinking, of seeing your friendship network so that
you can look at it, you can talk about it. To me the
network is my family. The nuclear family, the way we
generally think of family, is the inner circle, and extended
kin might be the second circle. What I'm saying is that
that's too limited for what's really happening, for what's
real for me and some other people. I really need more
people than that in my life. Sometimes I include a fourth
circle — which is kind of a community, like the women's
community. If you have a sense of a portion of that community being your community, that's really a piece of
your network."

If regularly seeing each other is a major component of
her definition of familial friendships, how does she relate

to my feelings for Larry, my ex-boyfriend, whom I never see anymore but who still feels like part of my family? "A lover I had, we've seen each other once or twice in the last two years and we keep trying to rebuild that friendship and keep clashing. I think we'll probably come together again in the future, because we really have a strong commitment to the friendship. I feel very close to her. When I heard she was sick, I really wanted to come, but she didn't want me to. So I know some of what you're feeling, and I don't know what to do with it either. The thing that comes to my mind is, this concept in the Huna religion in Hawaii — they talk about *aka,* which is like a psychic tendril that emanates, that runs between us. And once two people have been sexual, there's an incredible psychic power between them, and they're tied to each other for the rest of their lives. I don't believe it in terms of just the sexual. I interpret it in terms of when you've been *lovers,* and both the emotional and sexual tie exist, then you're tied for life. So in some ways I'd put your relationship with Larry in that category. That's part of why I include both involvement and closeness when I talk about friends. Because I think you can feel very close to people and not be very involved with them. Then you have the kind of situation where there's a tie, but there really isn't much more than that."

One of the questions I asked Anita — and for some reason didn't ask anyone else — is whether she feels that the dead we've loved and been connected to remain part of our family networks. Maybe it's simply timing that made me ask Anita: it was only a few days since I'd interviewed John Paul in New York, talking about Ti and Gene and my sense of them as ongoing parts of my own life fifteen years after their deaths. She answers, "I've been doing these lectures on friendship networks, and fairly consistently over the two years I've been doing this, someone asks me, 'What about people who have died?' And I really feel that's on target — that people who have died are not dissimilar to people who've moved far away, in terms of the value they have for you, they continue to have for you; in terms of the needs they meet; in terms of the tie . . . I believe that our spirits continue on after death. I don't believe that we continue on in this form, but I believe that people who have died still know me and know my history. Part of that is that when we get into the psychic realm there is no future, there's no time as we know it. Death is just that somebody's in a different time zone, in a way."

Since the concept of lesbianism weaves in and out of her conversation frequently, I ask if she thinks it has a special relevance to the concept of friends as family. "Yeah, I do. When I was heterosexual, a few years ago, the friends that I had then — what kept happening was that I wanted to get closer and they kept saying to me, 'You want things that I don't think are relevant to a friendship.' And these weren't people that I was in love with, or anything like that. And then when I moved into lesbian feminist circles — and you have to remember this was also *feminist,* because I did the two together — it was so clear to me that the ties of friendship could be so much stronger, and that in fact there was an expectation that they should be, that I felt like, 'Hey, I want to be part of this!' In fact, that's part of what pulled me into being a lesbian — that the kind of relationships I had been wanting to have seemed to be what people in the women's movement were trying to achieve.

"Also, I feel really strongly that our patriarchal system, our system of marriage, really reinforces the notion that you have one person who is your intimate — you have a private, exclusive relationship with that person and you don't talk outside about personal matters or get needs met by other people. Except for some of the subcultures, like Italian groups, intimate friends aren't really acceptable, and you get into a lot of hassles with husbands.

"What's very interesting to me is that I'm aware now that I probably could have had intimate friends other than my husband when I was married, but it was so silently socialized into me that I had a husband now, that that's where my needs were supposed to get met, that I never opened myself to those friendships; I never thought it was possible. I don't know how much of it now has to do with the women's community as a feminist community and how much of it has to do with lesbianism. But," she adds, echoing all the other gay people I spoke with, "as soon as you get into friends as family it becomes more important in the lesbian community. Because that's your family, those lesbians. Many lesbians don't have connections to their family of origin, and there isn't usually the dream of building some type of nuclear family."

Unlike Gail, Francis, and Anita, Mel King is not a sociologist or a therapist. He is a state representative and a community organizer — a black activist who is one of the most dynamic figures in Boston, a city increasingly known for its racism. He is brilliant, charismatic — a strongly outspoken advocate of civil rights for blacks, for women, for gay men and lesbians. Yet he too uses his concept of family in his work. He explains why in a turn-of-the-decade article in the January 1, 1980, Boston *Phoenix:* "this culture has created a situation where we need a redefinition of family. We have to articulate it and shape it and form it. The reason I know this is I've probably got the biggest family around. A lot of people around here play very important roles in my life, not just my brothers and sisters and children, but others."[1] As soon as I read the article, I knew I wanted to talk with King. I also knew that he was a very busy and in some ways very intimidating man. We'd spoken at the same rallies a couple of times, but we'd never met. I wrote him a note; a few weeks later he called and left a message with my answering machine. I called his secretary, he called my answering machine, I called his secretary. Eventually we managed to touch base, and I interviewed him at his office at MIT, where he works on a community action project. As we talked, it became clear that his concept of "kinfolk" involves as much the idea of community as of family — that, in a sense, he doesn't believe that there are boundary lines between the two.

"The reality is that the nuclear family isn't the only family. I got a little disturbed by the whole White House Conference on the family. It's an attempt to recapture what's not possible to recapture. It's as if people don't understand that the culture as we know it is on its way out. You just listen to the radio and hear a person comment that more industry is now developing on-site day-care centers. The White House Conference and that approach is thinking about a situation that existed one hundred years ago, fifty years ago. There was an economic payoff to a certain kind of structure and relationship then, and somehow these people believe that that still exists and can be effective, when in fact we're so far away from it . . . People's definition of self gets tied up in it. But now most women are working, and women aren't accepting roles, repression — you've got different relationships. But it seems like those folks are hell-bent on returning to that kind of relationship.

"See, I'm blessed with having my kinfolk. And what that means is that there are a lot of people who look out for me, and I look out for a lot of people. Some time ago, I accepted the reality of use of human resources. I would not allow myself to be cut off from access to the human family and the resources that the human family represented. So that's allowed me to explore different kinds of relationships with different kinds of people . . . I think it's being open to share and listen and take risks with people about what you're thinking, what you're feeling. Maybe you can't do that with everybody, but there are some bodies you *can* do it with. More often than not I run into people where there are different things in me that I can share and get feedback and some joy in working with. I try two things. One is to put my ideas out, and two is to get other people to put their ideas out. I'm an elitist — there's no doubt about that. I like people who are smart; I like people who are creative; I have a thing about people who play music, write poetry, sing; I have a thing about some athletes and the way they do certain things.

"Like you're here now, right? And we might start talking about something and find that we have something in common, some idea, and we just maybe pursue it . . . My concept of kin comes from . . . let me go back; I'll tell you where. There are two things that really arrived in my head about it. One thing had to do with the election, when I was running for mayor, and a piece of — I don't want to call it hypocrisy, but . . . if, for example, you're supporting my candidacy, or anyone's candidacy, and you go to knock on the doors of people on your street, but you've lived there five years or two years or whatever and you haven't knocked on those doors ever, I think you ought to feel kind of hypocritical. Because you haven't had any contact with the people who live on your own block, in your own community, and now all of a sudden you're going to ask them to give you something. And I looked at the people who were organizers, and found that very few of them — of us — knew many people on their street. Folks don't even know the people in their apartment buildings. They get in their car or go to the bus station, and go to some *meeting* to deal with issues on a very global level, and nothing's done on their streets —

except at those particular points when they want the people on the streets to do something. And I've always been uncomfortable about being in an electoral political situation where that's the behavior, the pattern.

"The second thing came out of a series of meetings that a group of us pulled together — Representative Doris Bunty, Saundra Graham, and some other folks — around what was going on in the black community relative to male-female relationships. In one of the first sessions, one of the things that got talked about was that because of mobility the support networks weren't around, that there were a lot of people who had moved here from someplace else and they didn't have the baby-sitting support. If they were married or had a child, they didn't have the person from the family like the aunt or sister or uncle or cousin that was nearby that you could just go and talk to. And at the same time, those folks weren't around to say something about your behavior when they knew that you and some friend were having some difficulty. So one of the things people were saying was that one of the breakdowns in the black community was the kinfolk network support system we had historically relied on didn't exist now.

"I also thought about a behavioral pattern that exists in the islands — Jamaica, Barbados — where they don't have the concept of 'illegitimate children.' If a child is born out of marriage, people take care of it. It's identified as somebody's child; they use a term like 'yard child' or whatever. So as we talked, we began to feel the importance of developing support mechanisms for people. It's a question of the woman in particular having a child with nobody to give any relief; that has an effect in terms of relating both to the child and to other adults, and to a man. So we got into a lot of that.

"Another piece is the Wednesday-morning breakfast club, a group of people I've been working with. Some of the people work in community agencies, some work in state and city agencies. And after a while, coming together to deal with a particular problem — whether it was stopping [ex-Massachusetts Governor] Dukakis's workfare problem or trying to get technical assistance for community-based groups — to a lot of folks the particular problems seemed almost incidental. Because what they were really needing was a place as professionals to talk to other people who were struggling. So a lot of different kinds of relationships were developing, and in many instances instead of paying attention to the speaker or the issues, they were off in these little groups talking to each other . . . So in subsequent years we began to make the issue of family and support systems and significant others a big thing. We were developing a family that was made up of all of us, people supporting each other . . .

"We think it's important to get people to talk and address key issues in their relationships that political organizing groups don't get into. What they do is extremely valuable and important, but they don't have discussions on their block about racism and sexism, or about being gay or lesbian, or what it means to be handicapped, or what anti-Semitism does to people. They don't have those discussions, and as a matter of fact they avoid them. And when they avoid them I think they're very unreal, because you're never really building those kinds of roots. Too many organizers just take a look at people and say, 'I know you need more money, and therefore I'll deal with your auto insurance; you're upset about that and you're upset about the MBTA' [Boston's public transportation system]. And that's true. But some of that has to do with how I'm relating to you, as a friend, as a neighbor; how I accept you; whether or not there's a sense of you as a person that I understand.

"So we're now trying to get those pieces. People talk to each other, try to get to know each other. In one meeting one of the things that we did was to list different kinds of roles that people play — caseworker, for example — and what that means. So we came up with a list of resources and skills that were in the room. And we got to talking about bartering, exchanging. My father worked on a sugar boat, and he participated in the organizing of the union. So people used to come out to the house. He was good at a lot of things. He used to make trusses. So he'd do that and they'd do something else. They had this exchange of skills, services. And I think that's a kind of thing we need to get to, especially in these times. So we looked at the different skills people had. We had a potluck, and people started asking each other for recipes. And people started seeing each other in terms of their resourcefulness to each other."

King's sense of building community out of people working together, and building family out of community, comes out of his own life, both in the present and in the past. Like many of the people I spoke with, he has rarely lived within the traditional boundaries of family, neighbor, friend, acquaintance. "I have this kind of kin, probably more than most people. I have people who call me Uncle Mel — I used to do community work, working on the street corners, and a lot of the young people I worked with still identify me in that way . . . Whenever anyone in our group has a birthday, they usually come have the cake at my house; and my wife, Joyce, will bake the cake, or my daughter — one of them will do that. And they're there for holiday dinners, or any time.

"We have these Sunday brunches. People come to the brunches from all around the world, but there are core people who always come. George comes. Sometimes George will bring mussels, clams, lobsters, shrimp — and really cook. The other day Gloria, who comes somewhat regularly, just brought her stuff over and cooked it there. Joan and Beverly always come.

"When I was young I lived on Sanders Street. We had two things going. First of all, I lived at number 32, and my aunt and her cousin lived at 26. And my other aunt and uncle lived maybe a seven-minute walk away. The family was so close that my cousins who were older were always at my house. They called my mother 'Aunt,' and as we grew up, I did what they did — I called my mother 'Aunt' for the longest while . . . so that was one thing. And the second level was the people who lived on the street. I was weaned on pizza, lasagna, matzo, Chinese food, Greek food, Arabic food. 'Cause those were the folks who lived on the street, and we were all in each other's houses. And any of the older folks would chastise you. Everybody on the street knew everybody on the street, and looked out for everybody on the street — and these folks were all of different races and cultures. So that was it."

Out of his own eclectic upbringing, then, Mel King has been able to create new kinds of familial networks that challenge the rigid boundaries set up between family member and neighbor, neighbor and friend. For him, family is a flowing and changeable, adaptable concept. And he isn't content to keep his creation of family a personal choice: he brings it out into the community in which he works. Like the women's movement he admires and supports, his credo seems to be that the personal and political are interwoven, and that creating "kinfolk" is as important politically as fighting to keep abortion rights or restore Medicaid cuts.

What King and the other people in this chapter demonstrate is that the creation of family, individual though it is, can also have a public dimension. They are demanding through their work an acknowledgment of, and commitment to, the building of nontraditional forms of family. They are helping other people create the structures that they, the professionals, find so important in their own personal lives.

11.

Organizations as Families

S ometimes it isn't individuals on their own who make their families. Often people will turn to organizations that have created structures for bringing together people who want to become part of new families. The form these groups take, the degree of structure, the amount of involvement of the organization itself in the families they catalyze all vary extremely. The families are formed by church groups, by alternative political groups — even, sometimes, by government agencies.

For example, ACTION, a federal agency, sponsors a Foster Grandparent Program in which nearly 17,000 low-income elderly people become paid "grandparents" to children with special needs. They work at least twenty hours a week with their "grandchildren," some of whom are mentally retarded, emotionally disturbed, or physically handicapped. The services they provide vary with the needs of the children, and include tutoring, playing with hospitalized children, taking the children on shopping excursions, or giving "failure-to-thrive" babies the lengthy feedings they require to stay alive. "In homes with a history of child neglect or abuse," writes *Ms.* staffer Phyllis Rosser, "grandparents strengthen the family by serving as loving role models, helping the parents with their daily tasks and offering encouragement."[1] A Chicago grade school uses this concept in reverse: an "Adopted Grandmother" program, started as a one-shot Mother's Day event in which students "adopted" elderly women in a Chicago housing project, fosters continuing relationships in which the youngsters regularly visit with their "grandmothers" and go shopping or to the movies with them.[2]

The Unitarian Church has set up several alternative family programs in different parts of the country. Its program was started in 1971 by Marya Weinstock, a psychologist who was also an active church member in Santa Barbara, California. In a telephone interview she told me about the origins of the extended family program. The church board had had a meeting in which "we talked about how awful it was that family members were moving away from each other. It was a lot of down talk — kind of sad and depressed talk. So I said, 'Why don't we put families back together again and make them?' The room took off, all of a sudden a lot of energy. I went to the bathroom, and when I came back I was chairperson of a committee."

At first they began to look around to find "a model somewhere, an expert to tell us what to do." They found that there was no expert anywhere around — that they would have to become their own experts and create what they wanted themselves. They did.

"We spent about three months talking — that was the original planning group. We selected some people from the church we thought were good, warm people — comfortable people who might help other people get comfortable. We were very clear that these weren't encounter groups, that we weren't looking for leaders but for facilitators. We

invited about twelve people who knew a lot of people
in the church to become a training group. I worked with
these people all summer, one night a week.

"What we would do is try out some simple, get-
acquainted kinds of things. Sharing parts of our own life
stories with one another. We were practicing it as it would
be in the families — each person took turns being a facil-
itator. That group hated to break up when it was time to.

"We began to call it the 'extended families program.'
Some people didn't like the word 'family'; some thought
extended families meant living together — all kinds of
definitional things. Sometimes we tried to figure out what
the hell else to call it, but we kept coming back to that
name. Much as some people hated it, some people loved it.
And I think it says what we're trying to aim at."

They began by asking people to make at least a
three-month commitment. "We really didn't want people
bopping in and out, looking for dates. At the end of
three months we asked that each family assess where they
were at — which ended up being foolish, because they
didn't need to assess."

A few of the families disbanded after three months;
most stayed together for a longer period. The families
averaged twelve people each, with "as much diversity as
possible — different ages, married, single, with and without
kids, the whole show." They would meet weekly or
biweekly, at different members' homes. Sometimes they
would picnic, or go to movies or plays together; sometimes
they would potluck; sometimes they would simply discuss
what was happening in each other's lives. In a 1974 church
newsletter, the pastor, Dr. John A. Crane, described some
of the needs the families served for each other. "One
family helped a member redecorate a somewhat shaggy
house that he had bought . . . Another family helped
a member pick avocadoes that needed picking. And one
family helped two of their members, a couple, face the

rather early death of one of them . . . Some welcomed a
newborn infant into the family . . . Many gave going
away parties for members before they left for Europe
or the Pacific, or welcomed members back from their
journeys."[3]

Their program attracted attention from other Unitarian
churches, and they put out a handbook explaining their
program and how it grew. Seven years later, Marya put
together another booklet, based on a questionnaire they
had sent out to five hundred other churches that had
requested copies of the original booklet. What she learned
was fascinating: Their idea had mushroomed, and there
were programs throughout the country, even in Hawaii
and Canada. Over 350 families had been created, com-
prising about 5000 individuals. Some lasted for only
short periods; some continued indefinitely.[4]

It's interesting to note that the definitions of a family
"lasting" are somewhat different from the definitions
used by most of the informally organized people I spoke
with: the Unitarian families "end" when they cease to
meet on a regular basis, though many maintain individual
relationships with family members and many groups have
reunions several times a year.

All the groups responding to the questionnaire agreed
that it was a need for community, warmth, intimacy that
brought them together. One reported that their group,
which originally began as a "singles" group, found that it
didn't work; when they changed it to "extended family,"
the pressure implicit in "singles group" vanished, and they
stayed together, involving themselves in "a wide diversity
of activities."[5] Some families have made it a point to
include elderly people or shut-ins in their families.[6]

Weinstock herself was in one of the 14 families the
church launched at the end of 1971. Her family stayed
together for seven and a half years of weekly dinners.
"We used to laugh and reflect on the fact that we weren't

sure what we were to each other," she tells me. "We weren't friends in the usual way; we were just tossed together. I think it was a cross between distant relatives and a close support group, which is really a mixture. For me, the support element came through the strongest. It was a place to tell our stories and to listen and be heard. And occasionally to do something really fun with. And occasionally to handle some really heavy stuff.

"The family that I was with lived through three deaths during the life span of that family. And we got very good at playing hospital. The first was a very young girl, who was lovely and very courageous, really quite an experience to be around. Real kind of an up-spirit person. That was within the first year and one half of that family's existence. Then there was an incredible amount of support mobilized around a man who was dying of cancer. He was a man we had already grown very fond of, and his wife knew how to ask for help and let people be helpful. We would sleep over her house in platoons so she didn't have to face the hospital alone in the morning. The kinds of things we didn't know we had in us, except there it was.

"We celebrated some things together, too, but mostly it was meeting and talking, sharing. Whoever is the host person would toss out a topic, and we would all respond to it. I've read some descriptions of Quaker things that sounded very much like that. We used to gather, chitchat, and drink wine. When everybody was there we would form a circle and the person in charge would frame some kind of topic — a time when you were most frightened in your life, for example. Little by little, we were sharing chunks of ourselves."

If a group works, I asked her, why does it break up?

"Well, in our family there were a couple of people who made suggestions — maybe we should meet less often. We talked about it and rejected the idea. But that was one signal that something was changing. I looked in the mirror one day and said to myself, 'Do you want to meet with these people every Friday night for the rest of your life?' I decided no — I wanted different things. Having that group so regularly in my life was almost taking the place of a social life. So I decided I would not be part of that group on a regular basis.

"I knew people had trouble resigning from families. Others would say they wished the families would dissolve because they didn't want to go anymore. They would melt away and just stop coming." Marya didn't want to do it that way. She went to a meeting and told her family of her decision. Several members felt the same way, while others wanted to continue as a family.

The smaller family didn't work, however, and the group dissolved. "But what has happened is that somebody calls every two or three months for a reunion, and those are wonderful. It's a time to catch up, and there's a lot of laughter and warmth. Without anybody planning it exactly, it *is* ongoing."

A very different alternative family structure is provided by Family Synergy, a California-based organization whose purpose is to "facilitate the exchange of ideas and the dissemination of information about all types of expanded families and to provide ways for people interested in these ideas to meet, to get to know one another, and to keep in touch. It is . . . based on the premise that people can live fuller, more rewarding lives, achieving more of their potential, by living in committed (but 'open') families larger than the nuclear family."[7] They have frequent meetings of small groups within the organization as well as with the entire membership, and the meetings listed in their newsletter cover a broad spectrum of activities — from a book review group, to a "work party" to help two members move their garden shed, to support groups on open .relationships. There are also "massage parties" and "clothing optional swim parties,"[8] but the group is clear that it isn't simply a "swingers" organization. The newsletter is full of letters from members discussing their difficulties with different expectations about commitment and sexuality. As one member writes: "How do we deal with the hurt of a person whose partner has outgrown the relationship . . . in a group that is committed to community and caring? . . . It becomes obvious that each person, couple, or relating group needs to design a relationship based on values that are comfortable for them . . . while benefiting from the support gained from knowing that we are all working on common problems."[9] Judging from the newsletter, its members seem to have a wide variety of personal and familial lifestyles, supported and encouraged by each other. Kay, interviewed in Chapter 10, is a member, and, though her own "extended family" isn't only made up of Family Synergy people, she is enthusiastic about the organization and the support it offers individuals in finding or creating nontraditional families.

Another organization that provides a setting for the creation of nontraditional families is the Movement for a New Society (MNS). George Lakey, the man whose friends helped him through cancer (in Chapter 10), belongs to, and helped found, MNS. Less lifestyle-oriented and more political than Family Synergy, "it's an outgrowth of a group called Quaker Action Group, which had been an organization from the 1960s, mainly against the war but also on liberation issues," George explains. "What we found by the end of the 1960s was that a lot of people were getting burned out, and also we found that our own analysis was shifting toward the left. So we decided to get rid of that organization and free up our own energies, to start a new one — particularly with the lessons we'd learned from the 1960s. Those lessons had to do with avoiding burnout, with providing support — a way of organizing that would be giving support to people. And that could be in one house under the same roof, like a communal house, or through other means by which people would be opening up to each other's lives." Out of this, the Movement for a New Society was formed. Its organizational booklet describes MNS as "a network of small groups working to bring about fundamental social change through nonviolent action," based on collections of people working closely together. "Most of us have grown up with the conventional structure of family, school, neighborhood, work and government. Most of these institutions hurt people, break the trust placed in them, and cannot respond well to real needs."[10] Hence the collectives MNS forms are expected to be both politically active units and personal support mechanisms for the people involved in them.

The concept of "community" is key to MNS, though it allows for a flexible definition of community: "It is a household, a neighborhood, a circle of friends, a group that shares common goals and values . . . The artificial barriers of our social systems keep us from knowing each other as whole human beings. By living close to people whom we would only have known in a limited way, our relationships are more complete — both challenging and supportive." Though they never use the word "family" to describe their communities, their descriptions of how they function make it clear that family is really what they're talking about: "Some of us live together. Others study together, share the tasks of child care, buy food cooperatively or borrow each other's cars. We move into the same neighborhood. We make commitments to each other and form networks to make common decisions about our work and our lives. When enough people come together for personal and social change, we call it a 'life center.' "[11]

In one of their newsletters, a Chicago MNS member, David Finke, describes it in more personal terms: "There was more a sense of joining/discovering an extended family than of a mass political movement . . . The attention to *personal* relations, intimacy, and growth has been for me a distinctive MNS contribution to social change work . . . Although when I found MNS, I was already moving toward a more radical analysis and personal/familiar practice, MNS provided the ready-made congenial group in which I've found support to continue this growth." He notes rather ruefully one drawback that is a pitfall for many alternative organizations. Though there has been much support for his efforts to break down his male role and share parenting and housework with his wife, "there has been less support . . . for being in a nuclear family (not a commune) of husband, wife, and child."[12]

Another member of MNS, George Lakey's nine-year-old daughter, Ingrid, writes in the same newsletter about what she likes about living in a community: "People come all over and play with me; they take care of me . . . I just made a list of grown-ups outside my house I especially think are wonderful — eight women and four men — Grown-ups in the MNS care about children. They play with children a lot and they take care of them. They tell you that they like you."[13]

Some of the members aren't happy with the high turnover. Barb, a woman who lives in George Lakey's household in Philadelphia, says, "I don't know if I want to stay here, it's too transient. I really want to put roots down and stay, make a long investment. I want to have children, to raise them in the community, and it's hard to do that here because of the transiency. I'd like to look into other MNS communities . . . Here, we bring people in to train them — the Philadelphia Life Center is a training center — and they don't necessarily expect to stay, though a fair number of them do. I would say that probably seventy percent of the people who come here for training are pretty young, so they're trying this out, and it's not necessarily where they're going to put their own roots. None of that fits for me. It's why I wanted to be in this particular house – a household of people who'd already lived together for seven years, two separate families but with some kind of interaction, some kind of merging. It's the way I'd like to live – not limited to father, mother, children. You sense a high level of turnover in some of the houses – you see it physically evident in a house if you haven't felt that it was home long enough to put anything into it. And I have very strong needs for a home."

She's optimistic, however, that she'll find what she wants in a different MNS community, and feels that MNS itself has already provided some of the community she needs: "The underlying principal of MNS is that you hang in there through the hard times and grow together and come out of it closer for the work that you've put into it together. I was consistently unable to find that before MNS. I was making commitments in the traditional sense to working in cooperatives and collectives and things with a certain political context, out of my understanding that we were struggling to make ourselves and the group grow and improve – and then I'd find that when the going got rough, people would leave. And we'd be left wondering, 'How could we have salvaged this with this person?' So the whole idea of intentionality is important: I'm chosing to do this because this is the kind of life I want to live; I'm in it for the long haul; this isn't just a game I want to play. It's meant a whole lot to find other people who are willing to say that, who *have* been saying it for ten years or more. I know wherever I live I'll be connected in some way with the people who are in MNS: that in itself is a kind of long-term friendship . . . At the last training session, talking about networking, I was saying, 'Make a part of what it is for you as a political person be that you stay in touch with these people you put these two weeks in with, because you've really grown together in some way; make an issue of trying to visit them, send them a tape of an important lecture you really liked that made you think and grow. Plan your schedules when you travel so you can stop in this place and that, and you can bring not just what you yourself bring but, as you go to each stop, you carry these messages with you'. . . Yeah, that makes a real kind of family."

12.

The Ugly Side — Negative Chosen Families

A ll the nonbiological families I've discussed so far have been essentially positive ones, whatever problems they've faced. And, indeed, the premise of this book is that the creation of alternative families isn't only a historical necessity, but a healthy manifestation of human variety. People need more than the traditional family provides, and they have, even within its constraints, managed to find what it is they have needed.

But human needs aren't always healthy, and the patriarchal structures under which we live exacerbate existing negative needs and create new ones. Needs unmet become perversions of themselves, and the values of a dominating society can corrupt the relationships of both the oppressors and the oppressed. The relationship *between* oppressor and oppressed are to some extent inevitably corrupt to begin with.

Traditionally, men are trained to need power and control — to protect, perhaps, but not to nurture: men in patriarchal society need to be conquerors. The needs bred into women are different: we need admiration for our looks and, secondarily, for our ability to nurture. We need to be submissive and sought out; we need to manipulate others rather than to go directly after what we want. When women are strong and direct, they are accused of being narcissistic on the one hand, "unfeminine" on the other. (It is interesting to note that the whole myth of the new narcissism sprang up in the wake of a widespread women's liberation movement.) Traditional familial roles perpetuate these needs in both women and men; existing as functions of patriarchy, this is what they were created for. Occasionally, strong and determined people can transcend the nature of the family and, within its confines, create relationships in which men are nurturing and women strong, in which power divisions set into the family are challenged and even overcome. More often, though, this happens in the nonbiological family.

But sometimes nonbiological families come into existence that mirror the worst aspect of the biological family — the unequal power structure in which the family as we know it has always been rooted. Dominant members can prey on the needs of the weaker members (whether that weakness is economic, physical, or emotional) for nurturance, companionship, or security, and thus destroy the people who turn to them.

The negative nonbiological family has as many forms as the positive one does, and the damage it can do ranges from mild psychological harm to murder. The former often occurs in the workplace family, which encompasses a built-in power structure. Years ago, in the days of micro-miniskirts, I worked briefly as a proofreader at a small advertising firm. I worked next to the typists — four late-middle-aged women, three widowed and one single

— who had acquired a limited amount of clout over the years because they were good at their jobs and, I suspect, undemanding in terms of salary and benefits. They were a tight little family, much involved in one another's lives, and it was clear that they were one another's major emotional support. It was also clear that they had absorbed the definitions that patriarchal culture assigns to aging and unmarried women, and that they were bitterly aware of the powerlessness that their age, sex, and dead-end job left them with. They were hostile to me from the start — I was young, sexily dressed, and obviously attractive to the men in the firm. They saw me as a threat (as in a way, of course, I was), and did what they could to make things difficult for me. Eventually, they got me fired. The family they created was useful and nurturing to them, but it also gave them an ability to attack an "outsider," to utilize the pathetically small amount of power they had in a destructive way.

They, at least, were directing their destructiveness outward. The "office family" structure can lend itself to a kind of self-destructiveness as well — a self-destructiveness carefully fostered by management. A friend of mine who was active in her company's union told me that one secretary, though sympathetic to all the union demands, refused to join the union because she saw her boss as "family" and didn't want to hurt him. The concept of the secretary as "office wife" lends an air of warmth and domesticity to oppressive expectations that the secretary will do her boss's gift shopping, make his coffee, or even, in some cases, perform sexual services for him.[1] The notion that a workplace and its personnel are just "one big happy family" might create a superficial comfortableness within the workplace, and it might even provide an illusion of warm and important relationships, but it masks the fact that "Daddy" has all the power and few of the obligations that the biological family assigns him.

He can demand obedience, but he has no obligation to care for his "children" and he can "disown" them at any time. "In a real family," notes Jean Tepperman, ". . . supposedly parents love their children, and exercise power to benefit them."[2] For whatever aura of camaraderie exists in an office, the boss rarely loves her or his "children" — and in any event, an adult in a childlike relationship to another adult is inevitably demeaned.

A sales manager for Dunkin' Donuts describes the company as having "a sense of belongingness now — like the company and franchise owner being part of a Dunkin' Donuts family."[3] This particular manager's job was to decide whether or not one franchise owner should lose his franchise; one of the mechanisms for deciding was an unannounced inspection visit to the franchise.[4] Whatever the legitimacy of the company's complaints against the franchise owner, it's clear that the Dunkin' Donuts "family" takes the form of Big Brother, and that the naughty child runs the risk of being disowned.

Anita, the counselor and college teacher in Chapter 12, has seen this sort of misuse of family constructs in her college. There had been various issues that faculty members were angry about and which they had discussed with people outside the college. "I almost puked in a faculty meeting the other day when people on the faculty were saying, 'How come we didn't know about this before it was said to the whole world? How come this wasn't kept within the family?' " In such a situation, the use of "family" simply instills a misplaced sense of loyalty to those in power over people. It's a power similar in spirit, if not in intensity, to the emotional hold slaveowners were able to maintain over those slaves they could convince owed them "family" loyalty.

The workplace is one area in which the notion of family is used to preserve a fundamental inequity. Equally insidious is the use of family to preserve forms of male supremacy.

Sometimes this takes the form of "male bonding," which has been so glorified by centuries of male writers. Sometimes, as in the case of soldiers, the bonding serves two functions — one a healthy uniting against an oppressor, the other an evil uniting to harm or destroy others.

Nowhere does the dual reality of men's friendships appear more strikingly than in Robert Brain's 1976 study *Friends and Lovers*; the duality is the more striking because Brain himself often doesn't recognize it. He is intelligent enough to recognize and repudiate the shallowness of a Lionel Tiger, and to reject the claim that men's friendships are inherently greater than women's. But he is also invested enough in patriarchal values to ignore the misogynist component in many of the male friendships he documents. Thus he can comfortably note that "by marrying his best friend's sister, a Melanesian is expressing the role of women as a form of cultural communication between men,"[5] that some cultures instead of exchanging Christmas gifts or buying their friends drinks "give cotton mats, armshells, their sisters,"[6] even that in certain African cultures, arrangements are often made between friends for the killings of both men's mothers in time of famine.[7] But even Brain recognizes the danger of male bonding in the institution of "mateship" in his native Australia. Mateship — romanticized by D. H. Lawrence and others, began with the early colonizing of Australia by the British and was "functional friendship between lonely men in the bush: later . . . it provided the theme for countless novels, stories, and songs extolling the companionship of stockriders, tramps, and gold-miners."[8] It "began with the mutual regard and trust between men working together in the lonely bush, men whose isolation and need for cooperation called for mutual helpfulness . . . The chief article of faith was that mates should 'stick together.'" It was, he tells us, usually a kind of pairing; only rarely were three or four men each other's mates. "The intimacy depended to a great extent on the

complete loyalty exacted from each other which was
naturally expected to override loyalty to kin or wife . . .
It was a complete union between two men which was
as close if not closer than marriage, based on complete
understanding and sympathy between two persons living
and working together in daily partnership. It continued,
ideally, until death." The institution of mateship, Brain
says, has lasted until the present day, but without the context of frontier life it has degenerated into a misogynous
and sentimentalized form of "beery" male bonding.[9]

Brain sees the misogyny in contemporary mateship,
but ignores it in his description of traditional mateship.
Nor does he comment on the oppressiveness of its very
origin — the "mates" were profiteering from imperialism;
they were invaders of a land of nonwhites, much as the
American frontiersmen were invaders of a land of Indians.
He quotes, without comment, a description by an Austra-
lian writer, Henry Lawson: "each would take the word
of the other against the world and each believed that
the other is the straightest chap that ever lived, a White
man." Doubtless deep and loving relationships formed
between mates, but they were relationships whose foundation was racism and imperialism, and into which was
built misogyny. Like soldiers in battle, they were a family
of oppression, whose very love for each other functioned
to harm others.

Sometimes the male-supremacist alternative family
does not take the form of men bonding with each other,
but of an individual man controlling a group of women.
In *Female Sexual Slavery,* Kathleen Barry discusses the
use of family imagery by many pimps in order to insure
loyalty and obedience from the prostitutes who work
for them. One pimp actually set up a contract for "his"
women which began: "You are reading this because you
have passed one of the requirements to become a member
of the illustrious family of _____." It goes on to

state that "anyone or anything opposing my will must be and will be destroyed."[10] The image is that of the patriarchal family at its worst: the father/husband figure is in absolute control of the woman's life, and her only virtue is total obedience to his will.

Part of that obedience may entail bringing other prostitutes to the pimp. Barry quotes one pimp telling a hooker: "You get them for like, you know, sisters . . . Just get 'em to come and help you and the . . . more that you get, the more sisters that you can get . . . the better it is for you . . . You bring 'em home, I'll do the rest."[11] Sometimes, the "sisterhood" part actually works: Barry reports one case of a woman helping her "stable sister" flee a pimp who had brutally beaten her.[12] But where the emotional attachment to the pimp as husband/father/ "head of household" is stronger — or where the very practical fear of the man wins out — the "sisters" can serve to reinforce one another's bondage.

The cults which have mushroomed in the United States in the past fifteen or twenty years are another form of negative alternative family. "These groups are usually structured as surrogate families: their members are all 'brothers and sisters,' who act as devoted children of a single parent figure — be it a guru, a self-appointed messianic figure, or the leader of a self-styled religion," writes Leora Zeitlin. Like the pimps described by Barry, the cult leaders demand — and get — renunciation of all other family outside the cult. Zeitlin's paper, exploring the effects of the cults on the siblings of cult members, quotes several of these siblings on the loss of the family member they love. "When I visited [my sister] about two years after she got in," says one woman, "I met her husband. She introduced me and said, 'This is my sister,' and, you know, he looked at me and said, 'Oh, *blood* sister,' and walked away. It's a very powerful thing, to have someone taken away from you in that drastic way. Because there's no relationship at all. It's like she was dead." Parents are equally off limits: Zeitlin quotes a psychiatrist who says that parents are defined as "being infected with Satan's influence, and parenthood is reinvested in the leaders of the cults."[13] New friendships are also not permissible. The "family" created by such cults is an isolated emotional unit and, as a result, becomes more restrictive, more oppressive, than the original family.

Though there are cults led by women — Ed Sanders describes several in his book on Charles Manson, *The Family* — most seem to be led by men who run them as exaggerated forms of the patriarchal family. The followers, male and female, are expected to renounce any independent thought or action, and to follow their leader in blind obedience. Although the news reports about Jonestown in 1978 ignored the obvious parallels to the traditional family, the events showed a horrified world the extent to which this blind obedience to the father-figure could injure people.

A decade before Jonestown, a little band of men and women who followed Charles Manson committed hideous murders at his command and reveled both in the killings and in their own self-degradation.

Manson and his followers actually called themselves "the family." According to Ed Sanders, when the "family" members "are together they seem bound by iron bands as if connected to the same body and will."[14] Aside from the ones who actually lived with Manson, there were several outsiders dubbed "sympathetic cousins" by the group.[15] One "family" member, Paul Watkins, became known within the family as "daddy's boy."[16] The Manson crew took their family status seriously. They made what they called "home movies" of some of their grisly rituals, which involved the killing of various animals, and sometimes of people.[17] Manson called his followers "my children" and defined them as one another's "sisters and brothers."[18]

The "brothers and sisters" often showed loyalty to one another, as well as to Manson. Stephanie, a teenage family member who had become disillusioned with Manson and, in the face of threats against her life, fled to her parents' home, returned because "In spite of Charlie, I loved everyone so much."[19] When various members were arrested for petty crimes, the others would beg, borrow, steal — and often risk arrest themselves — to get their friends out of jail.[20]

This loyalty, however, did not extend to members who tried to leave the family. Manson sent his people to terrorize, beat, and even kill defecting family members: since they "belonged" to Manson he had every right to kill them.[21] And he controlled every aspect of his "children's" lives. Women were regularly ordered to perform sexual acts with Manson and with various of his friends and cronies; they obeyed him without question. The most minute details of their lives were in Manson's control: one male member wistfully remarked at one point that "Maybe someday Charlie will let us grow beards."[22] They seem to have reveled in obedience as much as they reveled in bloodshed because they were given a community — a sense of literally *belonging* to the family.

It's interesting that Manson, like so many cult leaders, saw himself as a version of Christ. Perverted though the use of Christianity is in such cases, there is one important correlation — the patriarchal power of the father, with its concomitant demand that the adult "children" give themselves wholly, unquestionably, to his control. "Be it done unto me according to thy word," says the Virgin to the Angel Gabriel. "Wives, submit yourselves unto your own husbands, as unto the Lord. For the husband is the head of the wife, even as Christ is head of the church . . . Therefore as the Church is subject unto Christ,

so let the wives be to their own husbands in everything."
The negative nonbiological family, then, is less an alternative to the traditional family than a mechanism for taking
it to its logical extreme. Like the traditional family, its
ideological base is total power on the part of the head,
total submission on the part of his followers.

For those seeking to create true alternatives, there is
an important lesson in these perversions of family. We
carry our early training with us, and it is easy to unwit-
tingly transform "alternatives" into an uglier version of
what we are attempting to escape from. Negative created
families show us that it is possible to escape the forms of
the traditional family but maintain the philosophy behind
it. In this sense it is far more "alternative" to work to
change the roles within the traditional family than to
simply assume that the lack of a legally recognized structure creates a true change. If the power relationship of
the traditional family remains unchallenged, there is no
real "alternative," but simply a variation. For those of
us consciously concerned with creating new forms of
family, a look at the negative family can serve as a guide-
post for what to avoid — and a warning not to be too
smug about what we are doing.

13.

No One Said It Would Be Easy

E ven when the alternative family is essentially decent, there can be problems. Creating alternatives to the traditional family isn't always easy. We are going against concepts we've been raised with, and we're stepping outside of the boundaries society has created for us. Because of this, we lack our own set of rules and roles, and we have to decide for ourselves, individually or together, what rules to make, what guidelines to follow.

Often, our guidelines are in direct conflict with the guidelines of the world outside. Sometimes there are legal prohibitions against living the lives we have defined for ourselves. Homosexuality remains, at least on the books, illegal. Many towns and cities have zoning ordinances limiting the number of unrelated individuals who can share a single household — in Belle Tere, California, only two unrelated individuals can live together in a single-family dwelling. Hence, people who are attempting to form communal or collective families in such areas are out of luck.

Some judges have proven helpful in this regard, however. On the case of the elderly commune in Florida, discussed in Chapter 10, the judge redefined "family" to include the kind of group the elderly residents had formed. And the New Jersey Supreme Court, overruling such an ordinance in that state, recognized that there are some legitimate concerns among people who want to preserve a community atmosphere in their area. But it suggested that communities might require families, whether biologically related or not, to consist of "single, nonprofit housekeeping units," and that zoning provisions could legally restrict the number of occupants, related or not, according to sleeping and bathroom facilities in the house or apartment.[1] Until other courts follow the example set by New Jersey and Florida, however, the law will continue in many areas to discriminate against nonbiological families.

Legal discrimination exists in other areas of the nonbiological family as well. In the summer of 1980, Harold Greene, former patronage secretary of Boston Mayor Kevin White, refused to testify before a government commission investigating charges of corruption in the administration's awarding of building contracts. Greene was sent to the Charles Street Jail for contempt of court, and stayed there eight days. During his stay in jail a family friend who had lived with Greene and his family for four years[2] — a man whom Greene referred to on a television newscast as a member of his family — died suddenly. Because the man wasn't a blood relative, however, the law didn't allow Greene to leave the jail to attend the funeral. He decided to testify, in order to be released and go to his friend's funeral. "I had to weigh the death of a close friend against principle," he told reporters. "I determined that the death of my friend was more important than principle."[3] Had the dead man been a brother or a cousin — whatever Greene's emotional attachment to him might or might not have been — he could have gone to the funeral and then gone back to jail, but there is no legal recognition of the family of friends.

Sometimes it isn't the law that interferes with friendship families, but simply social attitudes. Almost everyone I spoke with had experienced minor hassles from non-familial friends, relatives, and strangers who couldn't deal with their unconventional families. Freelance writer Emily Prager wrote a poignant article in *Ms.* about her relationship with her friend Bill. Never lovers, she and Bill lived together for three years, but the relationship was far deeper than a conventional roommate arrangement. During the first year, both had recently ended their first serious love affairs. "We needed time to recover. Except for the hours we went to work, we mainly stayed home and licked our wounds."

Their friends were hostile to their arrangement. Some refused to believe that they weren't lovers; others who did believe it "felt that in a time when living together and sleeping together had just become acceptable, living together without sleeping together was distinctly perverse." But the two continued to maintain a close, warm bonding, going through their period of "recovery" together. When friends had parties, they went together — "running interference for each other."

In time, when they felt more open to forming new sexual or romantic relationships, their friends again put a damper on it: In spite of their insistence that they weren't a couple, their friends all assumed that they were lovers who weren't monogamous. It became impossible for either to meet potential mates.

It upset both of them. "We had established a home base, a family . . . But what others could not understand was that this attachment did not preclude our having lovers."

When Emily fell in love, the pressures became too strong; her new lover was horrified by her relationship with Bill. The relationship proved awkward, and Emily decided that she couldn't have "an all-encompassing love relationship" and still live with Bill. "We had managed to recreate the perfect adult childhood," she notes. "Security and love without sex, without risk. We were too entrenched to change it. We could only leave it behind." They soon moved into separate apartments, but remain a family: "We still spend Thanksgiving and Christmas together, and probably always will. We grew up together, Bill and I."[4]

In a sense, the saddest thing about Prager's story is her acceptance that such a relationship had to end — or at least to change form. Perhaps it did. But it's hard not to wonder whether she would have felt differently if Bill had been a brother — or a sister. How much did the definitions of their friends, of the world around them, create *their* definitions? Maybe they needed to live apart in order to be emotionally free to create important sexual relationships with other people. But in reading the article it's difficult to be convinced of that. The tone, the emphasis on friends' views of their relationship, suggest that their separation may not have been as much growth as capitulation. At the very least, the hassles that their friends put them through illustrate the difficulties of creating alternative families even in "liberated" circles.

But it's not only outside forces that cause problems when friends become, or try to become, family. The social concept of friendship as transient — a concept Christopher Lasch seizes on in his celebration of the mythical happy family of the past, *Haven in a Heartless World* — has a certain superficial appeal. Friends, we're told, make no demands on each other, have no major expectations of each other, make no major commitments to each other. Thus they can function as a relief from the demands and commitments involved in family or romantic relationships. But — and this Lasch conveniently ignores — when people begin to define friends as family, they usually lose that convenient, casual component of friendship. Depth in a relationship entails a loss of casualness: If someone is important, even necessary, in your life, then the interaction between you and that person becomes fraught with the same problems and uncertainties that characterize a romantic relationship, or a familial one.

But while there are social formulae for commitments to both family and lovers, there aren't any for commitments to friends. Your family — your parents, siblings, children — are yours for life. You may not be able to stand each other, but you belong to each other; there are certain obligations (often reinforced by law) that you have to each other. You don't even have to make a commitment; the commitment is made for you. With your spouse, you *do* make a commitment — but the commitment is clear. To have and to hold, for richer for poorer, till death do you part. However frequently that commitment fails, however obscured and confused it becomes in a supposedly "permissive" society, it retains at least its mythical power. The ideal you are expected to strive for is to love each other, to work through any problems you have, to live together for the rest of your lives.

But friendship commitments need to be defined by each of us for ourselves, and it can be terrifying. We want continuity, but what does continuity mean? Will you still love me tomorrow? Will you turn down a wonderful job because it's five hundred miles from where I live? If you have a new friend, will you get bored with me? Adolescents are allowed to ask these questions, but when they grow up, they are supposed to transfer all that intensity to a lover. What happens when we begin to transfer back — to reclaim the right to take friendship seriously?

Many of the people I interviewed are concerned with this. Pam, who talked about her relationship with Mama

Blue in Chapter 8, is involved in familial relationships with the other feminists in her household. "I think alternative family structures have to figure out about what obligations are, the whole moral question. What is it that we feel we can ask another person to provide for us? How do you set that up? What's appropriate — what's morally appropriate — to ask of someone when they don't readily give it to you? If there's not a Mama Blue around and you need what she gives, you have to ask. And how do you do that without feeling guilty, wrapped up in self-interest, demanding, imposing — or hurt — when people say no?" She worries too about re-creating traditional familial roles. "In our house, there's usually a mother, or in a mixed house a mother and a father — there are those roles. They change, but they exist. I think that's negative, because who wants to be a child all the time? Or who wants to be the nagging bitch? It takes a lot of work to step out of the conventional framework, and a lot of people don't have the time or energy to devote to it."

Another problem is that people's degrees of commitment to creating alternative family, or to the particular relationship itself, are different. Martha, the retired government worker who now works with an elderly people's service (see Chapter 4), befriended another woman several years ago, and the two formed a somewhat familial relationship. Martha recalls, "Her children were grown and seemed not to have much to do with her, since she was having to live on food stamps." Martha invited the woman to Thanksgiving dinner, and the two began to regularly spend holidays together. Then, however, the woman got involved with a man. "Now I don't see her very much. He seems to be there every night, and she's involved with him just about a hundred percent of the time. With him and her full-time job, she doesn't have much time to devote to anybody else. I speak with her occasionally on the phone, but she's just kind of drifted out of my life." Martha takes it pretty philosophically. "It's a shame, although I'm happy for her that she's in a much more stable position. I think that she's a very traditional type who thinks that everybody should have a gentleman friend, so she feels it's much better having this friend around. I think she's allowing him to monopolize her life, and if he ever leaves, she'll be right back where she was."

Traditional roles can become a factor even in non-traditional relationships. Sometimes such roles can cause rifts as painful as any between lovers or between parent and child. Elaine is a college professor in her mid-thirties who is also an activist in the women's movement in California. When she was twenty — a very young, insecure twenty — she became close friends with another feminist organizer, a woman ten years her senior. Their relationship quickly took on a traditional pattern: Francesca would jokingly call Elaine "the daughter I never had." At first, everything went well. Elaine admired Francesca's work and supported all of her decisions in the political groups they were in — first an antiwar organization, then a feminist group. They shared each other's lives and confidences; although they were never lovers, they lived together for three years. But inevitably, as Elaine grew older and more self-assured, she began to evolve ideas and goals of her own. Sometimes at meetings she would disagree with Francesca. And she began to realize the importance of her career in her life, and to put more of her energy into it than into her political work.

Francesca couldn't handle it. She was herself committed to an alternative lifestyle, and found Elaine's emphasis on her career "bourgeois." She was angry at being disagreed with at meetings. She accused Elaine of betraying her politics, and there were bitter quarrels. "She was my mommy, and she couldn't stand that I'd grown up," Elaine says. She eventually left the apartment they shared — "never to darken her doorstep again." She laughs now, but the laughter is bitter. "I feel like I was disowned by my parents," she says. "What do you do with that? In a way I hate her, but I can't just forget about her — she was part of my life, she was my family. Things like this aren't supposed to happen in the women's movement." Francesca and Elaine occasionally run into each other at political rallies; when they do, they don't speak to each other. Their shared past — the friendship, the work they did together and to which both are still committed — remains a part of Elaine's life, but a sad and disillusioned part. And, says Elaine, there's an added irony. Because friendship isn't acknowledged as familial, she has never gotten the support she needed. "If my husband divorced me or my mother disowned me, there'd be concern, understanding. But no one really understood what this did to me — I had to deal with it alone."

People who create family also suffer another kind of loss. In the chosen family, as in the blood family, people sometimes die. "I had that happen to me one time," says Jane, the therapist interviewed in Chapter 10. "A friend who was family to me killed herself a couple of years ago, and that was preceded by a depression in which she wouldn't talk to anybody for six to eight weeks. Before that, there was a period when she'd say really scary things to me like 'everything is nothing' and 'nothing is everything.' She shut me and the other members of her family out. That loss — it might as well have been a member of my family of origin. In some ways my husband had a lot of trouble understanding what I was going through, because he just saw this person as a great friend, so he couldn't understand why six months later I'd hear somebody who sounded like her and get all teary-eyed . . . It's been a year and a half now, and just recently I drove through the town that she lived in, and the tears just started .coming, and I had that feeling once again, 'Oh, yes, you don't get by this.'

"The more you make yourself that open, that vulnerable, that caring, to a large network of people, the greater the number of losses you must suffer in your life. And one of the things that bothers me about the intensity with which I approach these people is the intensity with which I have to deal with anything happening to them. When they are in crisis, in some profound way I have to be too — and if there are a lot of them, I begin to feel a little bit like *As the World Turns* . . . If it isn't Bob, it's Lisa . . . that kind of thing."

Confusion over the extent of a commitment can create nearly as great a problem as loss. When people are clearly committed to their friendships, the question of what that commitment means can be a loaded one. I don't worry that my friend Kathy will forsake me for a lover, but I do wonder what the extent of her commitment is to me — and what the extent of my commitment is to her. I joke about it — "You can't move out of this neighborhood unless I go with you. Of course, *I* can move any time I want." And Kathy laughs. But we know it's serious on some level; we both know that the mechanisms for creating continuity aren't there for us. We want commitment from each other, and we feel commitment to each other, but neither of us knows the parameters of that commitment beyond the present. We've both had bad experiences. One friendship of mine ended because the friend wanted more "family" than I did; with another, still-close friend, I'm constantly aware that I want more than she does, and that this is an ever-present undercurrent in our relationship. Who sees who as family, and what does family mean to each of the people involved?

"It's come up in the stuff I've done," says Anita, the counselor and college teacher interviewed in Chapter 10. "I'm reminded of a woman who, about a year ago, decided that she really wanted to build family in a conscious way, and really let people know that. Toni, my lover, was one

of them. Toni's reaction to it was that she really liked the
woman, but she didn't know her well enough to know if
that's what she wanted. So she told her that she didn't
feel at this point that she could consider herself part
of her family. I'm aware that Toni was also concerned
that a family relationship in that case might mean a
drain rather than an equal sharing. Toni being an older
woman means in some way that younger women in the
women's community see her in that 'older woman' role.
She's a very warm and nurturing person. So she really
sees that if she's going to be family with somebody, it
has to be an equal kind of thing.

"The woman felt hurt, but she could understand it —
and Toni also said she was open to building a relationship
and that at some future time she might be ready to be
family with this friend. About a year later, it did work
out that way."

When the relationships with friends involve children,
there's another element of confusion to deal with. You are
family with the offspring of somebody else, but what
degree of authority, of input into the raising of the children, do you have? Again, there are no social guidelines.
You're not a parent, or a stepparent, or a guardian. You're
"just a friend." The deeper the involvement with the child,
of course, the more difficult the problems. For people
living communally, conflicts can become major. George
and John, who have lived communally with their wives,
the children of both couples, and several childless people
for nine years, talked about some of the problems they've
had. "John and Marcy and Berit and I used to have much
more in common in the way we looked at childrearing, say
two years ago, than we do now," George says. "The diver-
gence has gotten to the point where it's a problem in the
house, and so we're asking somebody from another house
to come and do some conflict resolution to see if we can
'agree to disagree' in ways that are creative and mutually

helpful rather than just being a tension producer." They feel that the reevaluation counseling skills that they and many other Movement for a New Society members have learned and used will help them reconcile the differences.

In other communes, people have had to deal with the problems of being separated from children with whom they feel closely bonded. "I get freaked by Jan wanting to take Sam away," says a man quoted in Nell Dunn's *Different Drummer.* "That's a big disadvantage, this insecurity because Jan is his biological mother. It feels as if she can take my kid away."[5] "This seems to me to be a rock-bottom problem of this collective," says a member of a different commune, quoted in the same book. "The biological parents have power over the kids that the nonparents just don't have, although the nonparents are giving just as much in the way of care . . . The nonbiological parents suffer from insecurity, the acute insecurity of having no legal power over *their* children."[6]

The problem can work the other way around as well: a child growing up in a commune may view *all* its members as parents, and be as devastated as any child of divorced parents when commune members decide to leave. Michael Weiss in *Living Together,* an account of the commune he, his wife, and their child lived in for several years, wrote of the effect on his son's life when two of the members decided to leave. Sobbing, the boy demanded to know if the couple was really leaving. When his mother told him that they were indeed planning to leave, he cried: "It's just like last year with Gil and Wendy . . . Communal living just isn't worth it if everybody keeps going away." "Shouldn't a kid feel that there are people he can depend on absolutely?" Weiss asks.[7]

Weiss didn't come up with an easy answer to this question – and indeed there are no easy answers. The effort to balance freedom with commitment is never an easy one, even among adults. In some relationships, the needs provide their own balance — when both (or all) the people involved need or expect the same degree of commitment and the same *form* of commitment. In others, the balance can be achieved through facing the problem, acknowledging the disparity of need, and working through it with each other as seriously as one would with a spouse or lover. But the confusions, the inequities, remain a given. Sometimes they are unresolvable, and the relationship ends, as Elaine and Francesca's did. Sometimes they're unresolvable and the relationship *doesn't* end — the people "agree to disagree" and accept the pain that accompanies the inequity. But these are problems that are organic to any relationship, not simply to nonbiological families. The difference is that we have fewer mechanisms to disguise them, fewer outside forces to define what we *should* give to each other and want from each other. In attempting to create bondings without bondage, we are forced to acknowledge and confront the conflicts within and among ourselves. Eternal vigilance is the price of personal, as well as political, freedom.

Conclusion

Although I've finished writing this book, it's become obvious that I haven't finished learning about people's nonbiological families. Everyone I've mentioned the book to has had a story about their own or their friends' experience. A woman from a college antidraft group I spoke to told me about her grandmother — "only she's not my grandmother, really; she's been my grandmother's best friend since they were girls, but we've always called her 'grandma,' and she's always been a grandmother to us." A middle-aged, recently divorced Irish American woman tells me about the man she is dating and how her best friend's Sicilian husband went to the man and said, "I'm her brother, and you'd better treat her right."

Recently I was the keynote speaker at a conference on "New Kinds of Family" at La Crosse, Wisconsin. I spoke for an hour to an audience that was one of the most responsive I've ever addressed. Talking about my own workplace family, I was suddenly aware that, in the back, a woman was softly crying. The man next to her

— her husband, I assumed — had a comforting arm around her. Later, the two came to talk to me, to tell me how much the speech had moved them. They were not, as it turned out, either spouses or lovers: they were coworkers, and she was leaving the job because her husband's office had reassigned him to another city. They knew they were a family, and they knew what her departure was costing both of them. Throughout the day, people shared stories of their various families — the commitments they had made to their family-friends, the commitments they regretted not having made. And everywhere, people were excited that I had begun to name what many of them had experienced but never defined.

The varieties of people I've spoken with, the marvelous range of age, lifestyle, and value systems, have meant that in many events I was politically uncomfortable with some of what people said to me. The idea of MENSA, an organization based on its members' high IQ's, strikes me as frighteningly elitist. EST has always seemed like a destructive movement to me. And I'm ambivalent about reevaluation counseling. But each of these groups figured into the family of someone I interviewed. Often people I talked with comfortably accepted traditional sex roles within their nonbiological families. Sometimes they accepted as legitimate behavior what I perceived as unforgivable disloyalty. I've tried to put my own politics aside in recounting these stories; sometimes this has been difficult. But these stories, told on their own terms, *are* the book, and the radicalism of what these people are doing, intentional or not, far outweighs any reservations I might have about the mechanisms through which they've created their families.

What has been so consistently amazing, so consistently thrilling, is that people have created such diverse families in the context of a culture which has told them for centuries that they can't do that — that the only family is the biological family. Few of the people I interviewed were setting out to destroy a myth, or to break down the nuclear family, or even to create alternatives. They've simply done what they needed to do, even while believing at times in the sanctity of "the family." It's an astounding achievement, this creation of nonbiological family in the midst of an all-pervasive ideology of biological family. The Moral Majority may be influencing the country with its worship of the all-encompassing, God-fearing nuclear family. But their vision is not only oppressive — it's also very, very sad. The human capacity to love, to nurture and seek nurturance, to create the conditions under which that love and nurturance can best express itself is large and beautiful, and utterly inspiring.

If people can create so many variations of nonbiological family now — if they could do so even a hundred years ago and more — what does it say of our potential to do so in the future? When we're no longer trapped in legal and cultural propaganda, when we're not given a false choice between the traditional family and the shallow swinger life — there are no limits to the structures we can create for ourselves.

It will take work, of course, and the biggest task is in reeducating ourselves. We need to throw off all the patriarchal propaganda we've absorbed for generations, and start naming our own realities.

The saddest thing I've heard from people when I've spoken on friends as family is that they *don't* have the kind of friendships that are genuinely committed, genuinely familial. For such people, the place to start creating family might well be through the kinds of organizations created by the Unitarian churches, Family Synergy, and others. Coming together with people who share the recognition that the traditional family isn't either available or sufficient to meet their needs is probably the best way to begin the relationships that lead to familial bonding.

For others, the starting point may be closer to home. I was taken with Anita's "bull's eye" idea: drawing a circle with oneself in the middle and different levels of friends in the surrounding circles. It doesn't have to take so structured a form though. Anyone can look around at their friends, see who are the closest, the most committed, the most interwoven. These are the people with whom one might begin verbalizing the concept of family — *naming* the relationships, and going on from there.

Once people see themselves as family, Barb's notion of some sort of conference of chosen families becomes fascinating. The fact that there is no body of common assumptions about chosen family, as there is about biological family, is what gives it its freedom, its potential to be a liberating and not imprisoning form of commitment. But it also leaves people confused, and often unvalidated in their nontraditional families. A conference — or conferences — might help people learn about similar problems, similar joys, different possibilities for defining family, without institutionalizing and hence stifling the nonbiological family.

There is a card in the Tarot that has come to mean a lot to me in recent years. It is the Magician, the first card in the 78-card sequence, and it means the ability to "bring desired things into manifestation through conscious awareness."[1] Lately, I've been connecting the card to the chosen family. We can all be the Magician. We can all translate our ideals of deeper, freer family structures into reality. We can name, and we can create.

Notes

INTRODUCTION

1. Susan Dworkin, "Carter Wants to Save the Family, but He Can't Even Save His Family Conference," *Ms.,* September 1987, pp. 62, 98.
2. Beth B. Hess, *Growing Old in America* (New Brunswick, N.J.: Transaction Books, 1976), p. 26.
3. Terry Davidson, *Conjugal Crime: Understanding and Changing the Wifebeating Pattern* (New York: Hawthorn, 1978), p. 6-7.
4. Naomi Feigelson Chase, *A Child Is Being Beaten* (New York: Holt, Rinehart, & Winston, 1975), p. 185.
5. Lynn Langway, "Unveiling a Family Secret," *Newsweek,* Feb. 18, 1980, pp. 104-106.
6. Christopher Lasch, *The Culture of Narcissism* (New York: Warner Books, 1979), and *Haven in a Heartless World* (New York: Basic Books, 1977).
7. Pierre Grimal, ed., *Larousse World Mythology* (London: The Hamlin Publishing Group, 1965), p. 9.
8. Mary Daly, *Beyond God the Father: Toward a Philosophy of Women's Liberation* (Boston: Beacon Press, 1973), p. 8.
9. Davidson, p. 108.
10. Davidson, p. 110.
11. Chase, p. 17. Infanticide itself seems to have occurred chiefly among the poor — though as always there is reason to suspect its occurrence, discreetly covered up, in more affluent families as well.

12. Judith Papachristou, *Women Together* (New York: Knopf, 1976), p. 19.
13. Davidson, p. 98.
14. Lu Emily Pearson, *Elizabethans at Home* (Stanford, Calif.: Stanford University Press, 1957), p. 248.
15. H. F. M. Prescott, *Mary Tudor* (New York: Macmillan, 1953), p. 26.
16. Alison Plowden, *Tudor Women* (New York: Atheneum, 1979), p. 8.
17. Alison Plowden, *The House of Tudor* (New York: Stein & Day, 1976), p. 47.
18. Lacey Baldwin Smith, *A Tudor Tragedy: The Life and Times of Catherine Howard* (New York: Pantheon, 1961), p. 28.
19. John Bale, *Select Works* (London: Parker Society, 1849), pp. 140–240.
20. Mary M. Luke, *A Crown for Elizabeth* (New York: Coward-McCann, 1970), p. 191.
21. Philip Hughes, *A Popular History of the Reformation* (Garden City, N.Y.: Hanover House, 1957), p. 98.
22. A. G. Dickens, *The English Reformation* (New York: Schocken, p. 27).
23. Simone de Beauvoir, *The Second Sex* (New York: Bantam, 1961), p. 95.
24. Judy Foreman, "9 to 5 grows, so does its clout," *The Boston Globe*, Sept. 28, 1979.
25. The quotes from television shows came from the diligent research of Lisa Leghorn, one of my chosen-family members, who selflessly spent hours watching "M*A*S*H" and "Love Boat" to cull them for me.
26. David S. Reiss, *M*A*S*H: The Exclusive Inside Story of TV's Most Popular Show* (New York: Bobbs-Merrill, 1980), p. 35.
27. Frank Swertlow, "TV Update," *TV Guide*, June 6, 1981, p. A-1.

PART I.   FAMILIES WITHOUT NAMES

1. Margaret Adams, *Single Blessedness* (New York: Basic Books, 1976), p. 180–185.

1. THE WAY WE WERE – NONBIOLOGICAL FAMILIES OF THE PAST

1. John S. Duss, *The Harmonists: A Personal History* (Ambridge, Penn.: The Harmonist Associates, 1970) (1st ed. 1943), pp. 121–122.
2. Duss, p. 28.
3. Duss, p. 144.
4. Duss, p. 170.
5. Duss, pp. 23–24.
6. Duss, p. 74.
7. Duss, p. 91.
8. Constance Noyes Robertson, *Oneida Community: An Autobiography* (Syracuse, N.Y.: Syracuse University Press, 1970), p. 325.
9. Robertson, p. 55.
10. Robertson, p. 321.
11. Robertson, pp. 45–48.
12. Robertson, p. 268.
13. Allan Estlake, *The Oneida Community: A Record of an Attempt to Carry Out the Principles of Christian Unselfishness and Scientific Race-Improvement* (New York: AMS Press, 1973), p. 54.
14. Estlake, p. 69.
15. John Thomas Codman, *Brook Farm: Historic and Personal Memoirs* (New York: AMS Press, 1971), p. 115.
16. Codman, pp. 64–65.
17. Marianne Dwight, *Letters from Brook Farm*, ed. Amy L. Reed (New York: AMS Press, 1974), p. 39.
18. Dwight, p. 50.
19. Dwight, p. 25.
20. Dwight, pp. 83–86.
21. Dwight, p. 88.
22. Benita Eisler, ed., *The Lowell Offering: Writings by New England Women, 1840–1845* (New York: Lippincott, 1977), pp. 110–111.
23. Eisler, pp. 83–95.

24. Herbert C. Gutman, *The Black Family in Slavery and Freedom, 1750–1925* (New York: Vintage, 1977), p. 224.

25. Gutman, p. 217. Quoted from Orlando Patterson, *Sociology of Slavery* (Madison, N.J.: Fairleigh Dickinson University Press, 1970).

26. Gutman, p. 154. From Solomon Northup, *Twelve Years a Slave*, reprinted in Gilbert Osofsky, ed., *Puttin' on Ole Massa: The Slave Narratives of Henry Bibb, William W. Brown, and Solomon Northup* (New York: Harper & Row, 1969), p. 365.

27. Gutman, p. 222, quoted from Charles Alexander, *Battles and Victories of Allen Allensworth*, 1914, p. 27.

28. Gutman, p. 155. Quoted from *American Slave, South Carolina Narratives, II, Part 2,* pp. 6–10, *Part 3*, pp. 33–34.

29. Gutman, *American Slave, South Carolina Narratives*, p. 219.

30. Gutman, *American Slave, South Carolina Narratives,* pp. 226–227.

31. Gutman, p. 223.

32. Gutman, p. 217, p. 223. Barbara Chase-Riboud's novel *Sally Hemings* (New York: Viking, 1979) provides an interesting and disturbing portrait of emotional and psychic ties between slave and master.

33. Elizabeth Jenkins, *Jane Austen* (New York: Macmillan, 1975), p. 2.

34. Jane Aiken Hodge, *Only a Novel: The Double Life of Jane Austen* (New York: Coward, McCann & Geoghegan, 1972), p. 90.

35. Hodge, p. 111.

36. Hodge, p. 201.

37. Douglas Bush, *Jane Austen* (New York: Macmillan, 1975), p. 2.

38. Louise Bernikow, *Among Women* (New York: Harmony Books, 1980), p. 151.

39. Winifred Gérin, *Charlotte Brontë: The Evolution of a Genius* (Oxford: Oxford University Press, 1967), p. 75.

40. Gérin, p. 100.

41. Gérin, p. 126.
42. Gérin, p. 416.
43. Janet Dunbar, *J. M. Barrie: The Man Behind the Image* (Boston: Houghton Mifflin, 1970), pp. 335–336.
44. Andrew Birkin, *J. M. Barrie and The Lost Boys: The Love Story That Gave Birth to Peter Pan* (New York: Clarkson N. Potter, 1979), p. 71.
45. Dunbar, pp. 160–161.
46. Birkin, p. 110.
47. Birkin, p. 186.
48. Dunbar, p. 185.
49. Birkin, p. 149.
50. Dunbar, pp. 217–218.
51. Dunbar, pp. 236–237.
52. Viola Meynel, ed., *The Letters of J. M. Barrie* (New York: Scribner's, 1947), p. 22.
53. Birkin, p. 242.
54. Birkin, p. 244.
55. Meynel, p. 93.
56. Birkin, p. 293.
57. Birkin, p. 130.
58. Dunbar, p. 267. The term "lover," which in our era suggests a sexual relationship, in the nineteenth and early twentieth centuries simply meant "one who is in love with" or "one who is fond of."
59. Birkin, p. 232.
60. Dunbar, p. 301.
61. Meynel, p. 195.
62. Dunbar, p. 373.
63. Alice S. Rossi, ed., *The Feminist Papers: From Adams to Beauvoir* (New York: Bantam, 1974), p. 378.
64. Rossi, p. 383.
65. Miriam Garko, *The Ladies of Seneca Falls: The Birth of the Women's Rights Movement* (New York: Macmillan, 1974), p. 169.

66. Rossi, pp. 384–385.
67. Midge Mackenzie, *Shoulder to Shoulder* (New York: Knopf, 1975), pp. 269–271.
68. Blanche Weisen Cook, "Female Support Networks and Political Activism: Lillian Wald, Crystal Eastman, Emma Goldman," *Chrysalis,* no. 3, Autumn 1977, p. 44.
69. Cook, p. 49.
70. Cook, p. 50.
71. Cook, p. 52.
72. Cook, p. 53. Quoted from R. L. Duffus, *Lillian Wald* (New York: Macmillan, 1938).
73. Cook, p. 53.
74. Nancy F. Cott, *Bonds of Womanhood: "Women's Sphere" in New England, 1780–1835* (New Haven: Yale University Press, 1977), p. 171.
75. Carroll Smith-Rosenberg, "The Female World of Love and Ritual: Relations Between Women in Nineteenth-Century America," *Signs: Journal of Women in Culture and Society,* 1975, vol. I, no. 1, pp. 508.
76. Cott, p. 168.
77. Smith-Rosenberg, pp. 10–11.
78. Smith-Rosenberg, pp. 23–24.
79. Cott, pp. 176–177.
80. Smith-Rosenberg, pp. 18–19.

2. HONORARY KIN

1. Adams, p. 139.
2. Carol B. Stack, *All Our Kin: Strategies for Survival in a Black Community* (New York: Harper & Row, 1974), p. 59.
3. Stack, p. 60.
4. Stack, p. 60.
5. Raymond Firth, Jane Hubert, and Anthony Forge, *Families and Their Relatives* (New York: Humanities Press, 1970), p. 323.
6. Firth, Hubert, and Forge, p. 322.
7. Firth, Hubert, and Forge, p. 116.

3. WORKPLACE FAMILIES

1. Norman Dennis, Fernando Henriques, Clifford Slaughter, *Coal Is Our Lives* (London: Tavistock, 1956), p. 181.
2. Dennis, Henriques, and Slaughter, p. 79.
3. Dennis, Henriques, and Slaughter, p. 182.
4. Dennis, Henriques, and Slaughter, p. 202.
5. Dennis, Henriques, and Slaughter, pp. 203, 205.

PART II.   FRIENDS AS FAMILY

1. Adams, p. 92.
2. Adams, p. 92.
3. Robert Brain, *Friends and Lovers* (New York: Basic Books, 1976), p. 260. The notion of the hopelessly pathetic single may be slowly dying, however. A 1979 study by two psychiatrists, Carin Rubenstein and Phillip Shaver, delivered at the annual meeting of the American Psychological Association, showed that "living alone causes loneliness only for people whose characteristic reactions to solitude are negative" and that often people living in families are less happy than those who live alone and have created the kind of social networks that fill their needs. ("Alone Is Not Necessarily Lonely," by Judy Foreman, *The Boston Globe,* Oct. 11, 1979).
4. Michael Novak, "The Family Out of Favor," *Harper's,* April 1976, p. 39.
5. Adams, pp. 180–183.
6. Ellen Willis, "The Family: Love It or Leave It," *The Village Voice,* Sept. 17, 1979.
7. Jane Howard, *Families* (New York: Simon & Schuster, 1978), p. 262.
8. Howard, p. 265.
9. Barbara Smith and Beverly Smith, " 'I Am Not Meant to be Alone and Without You Who Understand': Letters from Black Feminists, 1972–1978," *Conditions,* no. 4, 1979, pp. 62–63.
10. Howard, p. 269.

11. Stack, pp. 57–58.
12. Howard, pp. 266–267.
13. Adams, pp. 99–100.

CHAPTER 5.   FAMILIES WHOSE MEMBERS DON'T
             KNOW EACH OTHER

1. Stack, p. 21.

CHAPTER 8.   CHOOSING TO BE FAMILY

1. Rochelle Jones, *The Other Generation: The New Power of
   Older People* (Englewood Cliffs, N.J.: Prentice-Hall, 1977),
   p. 58.

CHAPTER 9.   CREATING NEIGHBORHOODS

1. George Lakey, "Getting the Goods on Cancer," *New Age,*
   December 1979, p. 55.

CHAPTER 10.   HOW PROFESSIONALS MAKE FAMILIES
              FOR THEMSELVES AND OTHERS

1. "Ch-ch-ch-changes: Nineteen Survivors Look Back at Trying
   Times," *Boston Phoenix,* Jan. 1, 1980.

CHAPTER 11.   ORGANIZATIONS AS FAMILIES

1. Phyllis Rosser, "Intergenerational Friendships in Everyday
   Life," *Ms.,* August 1980, p. 90.
2. Rosser, p. 91.
3. Marya Weinstock, *Developing an Extended Family Program*
   (booklet) (Unitarian Church, Santa Barbara, Calif.: no
   date), p. 5.
4. Marya Weinstock, *The Extended Family Program Reconsidered:
   Seven Years Later* (booklet)(Unitarian Church, Santa Barbara,
   Calif.: no date), pp. 3–4.
5. Weinstock, *The Extended Family Program Reconsidered,*
   p. 9.

6. Weinstock, *Developing an Extended Family Program,* p. 9; *Helping Extended Families Go . . . A Handbook for Facilitators* (Unitarian Church, Santa Barbara, Calif.: Fall 1980), p. 7.

7. *Synergy,* September 1980.

8. *Synergy,* September 1980.

9. *Synergy* (letter from Nina Indman), August 1980, p. 7.

10. New Society Packet, Movement for a New Society, Philadelphia, Penn., no date.

11. New Society Packet.

12. David Finke, "David," *Dandelion: A Journal of the Movement for a New Society,* no. 1, 1980, pp. 8–9.

13. Ingrid Lakey, "Ingrid," *Dandelion,* p. 4.

CHAPTER 12.   THE UGLY SIDE

1. Jean Tepperman, *Not Servants, Not Machines* (Boston: Beacon Press, 1976), pp. 40–41, 3.

2. Tepperman, p. 61.

3. Hirotaka Takeuchi, "Dunkin' Donuts II," in E. Raymond Corey, Christopher Lovelock, and Scott Ward, *Problems in Marketing,* 6th ed. (New York: McGraw-Hill, 1981), p. 273.

4. Takeuchi, p. 278.

5. Brain, p. 11.

6. Brain, p. 21.

7. Brain, p. 37.

8. Brain, p. 68.

9. Brain, pp. 68–71.

10. Kathleen Barry, *Female Sexual Slavery* (Englewood Cliffs, N.J.: Prentice-Hall, 1979), p. 75.

11. Barry, pp. 81–82.

12. Barry, p. 98.

13. Leora Zeitlin, unpublished paper, 1980.

14. Ed Sanders, *The Family* (New York: Avon, 1971), p. 19.

15. Sanders, pp. 55, 59.

16. Sanders, p. 96.
17. Sanders, p. 220.
18. Sanders, pp. 291, 333.
19. Sanders, p. 351.
20. Sanders, pp. 254, 335.
21. Sanders, pp. 359, 373, 377.
22. Sanders, p. 195.

CHAPTER 13.   NO ONE SAID IT WOULD BE EASY

1. Jones, *The Other Generation.* Rochelle Jones, "Resolving a 'Family' Affair," *Boston Globe,* Aug. 1, 1979.
2. Timothy Dwyer, "'Ready to Go Home?' And Greene Sure Was," *Boston Globe,* June 25, 1980.
3. Dwyer.
4. Emily Prager, "Roommates, but not Lovers," *Ms.,* April 1979, pp. 16–19.
5. Nell Dunn, *Different Drummer* (New York: Harcourt Brace Jovanovich, 1977), p. 33.
6. Dunn, pp. 50–51.
7. Michael Weiss, *Living Together* (New York: McGraw-Hill, 1974), pp. 133–134.

CONCLUSION

1. Eden Gray, *A Complete Guide to the Tarot* (New York: Crown, 1970), p. 23.

Karen Lindsey is a poet, free-lance writer, feminist, and leftist activist whose articles have appeared in *Family Weekly*, *Ms*, the *Boston Phoenix*, the *Boston Globe*, and the *Boston Herald American*. She teaches feature writing at Emerson College and is the recipient of two journalism awards from the New England Women's Press Association. A member of the board of the Massachusetts Foundation for the Humanities and Public Policy, Lindsey is also the author of two books of poetry — *Falling Off the Roof* and *A Company of Queens*. She is a spinster and lives with her two cats in Somerville, Massachusetts.